EU–Turkey Relations

This book focuses on the hidden but ever-present civil society dimension of the EU's policies towards Turkey and uncovers the pitfall of EU–Turkey relations.

It establishes the growing depoliticization of Turkish civil society (in contrast to what the EU's policies aimed for) and engages with the questions of why and how Turkish civil society depoliticized. It discusses how Turkey's retreating democracy, and the intense polarization in Turkish political and social life make rights-based activism more difficult. Finally, this book investigates what implications Turkish civil society's depoliticization bears for EU–Turkey relations, reveals the diminishing leverage of the EU's policies and discusses how this reflects on Turkey's already closing civic space. It explains why and how EU–Turkey relations deteriorated over the last decade, examines the current stalemate, and discusses why civil society matters.

This text will be of key interest to scholars and students in the field of EU–Turkey relations, Turkish studies and civil society studies as well as more broadly to NGOs, European studies and politics, and International Relations.

Özge Zihnioğlu is an Associate Professor in the Department of Political Science and International Relations at Bahçeşehir University, Turkey.

Routledge Studies in European Foreign Policy
Series Editors: Richard Whitman
University of Kent, UK
and
Richard Youngs
University of Warwick, UK.

This series addresses the standard range of conceptual and theoretical questions related to European foreign policy. At the same time, in response to the intensity of new policy developments, it endeavours to ensure that it also has a topical flavour, addressing the most important and evolving challenges to European foreign policy, in a way that will be relevant to the policy-making and think-tank communities.

EU–Russia Relations in Crisis
Understanding Diverging Perceptions
Edited by Tom Casier and Joan DeBardeleben

The European Union's Evolving External Engagement
Towards New Sectoral Diplomacies?
Edited by Chad Damro, Sieglinde Gstöhl and Simon Schunz

EU Induced Institutional Change in Post-Soviet Space
Promoting Reforms in Moldova and Ukraine
Ryhor Nizhnikau

The European Union's Approach to Conflict Resolution
Transformation or Regulation in the Western Balkans?
Laurence Cooley

The Proliferation of Privileged Partnerships between the European Union and its Neighbours
Edited by Sieglinde Gstöhl and David Phinnemore

EU–Turkey Relations
Civil Society and Depoliticization
Özge Zihnioğlu

For more information about this series, please visit: www.routledge.com/Routledge-Studies-in-European-Foreign-Policy/book-series/RSEFP

EU–Turkey Relations
Civil Society and Depoliticization

Özge Zihnioğlu

LONDON AND NEW YORK

First published 2020
by Routledge
2 Park Square, Milton Park, Abingdon, Oxon OX14 4RN

and by Routledge
52 Vanderbilt Avenue, New York, NY 10017

Routledge is an imprint of the Taylor & Francis Group, an informa business

© 2020 Özge Zihnioğlu

The right of Özge Zihnioğlu to be identified as author of this work has been asserted by her in accordance with sections 77 and 78 of the Copyright, Designs and Patents Act 1988.

All rights reserved. No part of this book may be reprinted or reproduced or utilized in any form or by any electronic, mechanical, or other means, now known or hereafter invented, including photocopying and recording, or in any information storage or retrieval system, without permission in writing from the publishers.

Trademark notice: Product or corporate names may be trademarks or registered trademarks, and are used only for identification and explanation without intent to infringe.

British Library Cataloguing in Publication Data
A catalogue record for this book is available from the British Library

Library of Congress Cataloging in Publication Data
A catalog record has been requested for this book

ISBN: 978-0-8153-7881-5 (hbk)
ISBN: 978-1-351-22786-5 (ebk)

Typeset in Times New Roman
by Wearset Ltd, Boldon, Tyne and Wear

To Eyşan and Eylül

Contents

List of figures ix
Acknowledgments x
List of abbreviations xii

1 Introduction 1

The current debates and the literature 4
Political conditionality, social learning and civil society 7
Outline of the book 17

2 The recent history of EU–Turkey relations 25

From association to candidacy (1963–1999) 25
Blossoming relations (1999–2004) 27
Period of stagnation (2005–2012) 33
Turbulent years (2013–2019) 38

3 Current issues and challenges in EU–Turkey relations 49

Modernization of the Customs Union 49
Migration crisis and civil society 53
Opportunities and challenges in energy cooperation 56
Reduction of the EU's pre-accession funds to Turkey 59
The EU's many 'crises' 62

4 Revisiting Turkish civil society 69

Diversification of civic actors in the 1980s and 1990s 70
A new narrative on Turkish civil society 72
Turkish civil society today 79

5 Changing landscape of Turkish civil society — 90

The improving legal framework 90
The half-finished reforms 92
The downturn in reforms and the shrinking civic space 93

6 EU civil society support in Turkey — 106

Understanding EU funds in Turkey 107
The functioning of EU funding mechanism 110

7 The impact of EU funds over Turkish civil society — 119

Methods of analysis 120
EU funds for civil society organizations 121
Participation of civil society organizations in public sector projects 132

Conclusion — 137

Depoliticization of civil society and democracy 137
Depoliticization of civil society and Turkey's transformation 140

Appendix 1: list of interviewed civil society organizations — 147
Index — 149

Figures

4.1	Number of active associations according to years (2000–2018)	76
4.2	The distribution of active associations according to their type (1999–2008)	79
4.3	Distribution of associations according to their types	82
7.1	Number of paid-staff in associations in Turkey (2004–2017)	128

Acknowledgments

Writing this book has been a long and sometimes challenging journey. It would not have been possible to complete this book if not for the time, support and encouragement of many people.

This book results from a research project on "European Union Accession Process and the NGO-ization of Turkish Civil Society" (114K774) funded by The Scientific and Technological Research Council of Turkey (TÜBİTAK). I would like to thank Hakan Yılmaz for his supervision, Erhan Akarlar, Büşra Aydın, İmren Borsuk, Ayşegül Helvacıoğlu and Övgü Ülgen for their assistance in this project. They were an important part of this study, and I cannot thank them enough for the pleasure of working with them. The project and later the book benefited from the invaluable input of public officials, EU officials, civil society experts, activists, and the representatives of the civil society organizations I interviewed. I greatly appreciate the time they allocated for interviews, and the information they provided for my empirical study.

While the idea of this book was originally developed during the research phase, the shaping of research findings and my opinions into a book has been a challenge. I am indebted to Julia Adams, Susan Stokes and Hakan Yılmaz who offered much advice and help in developing my ideas into a book format. They helped me broaden my focus and merge my research on Turkish civil society with another research interest, Turkey's relations with the EU. They generously shared their experiences in publishing and with publishers.

Many colleagues and friends have offered invaluable input at various stages of this book. While it is not possible to single out all the individual contributions made, I am particularly grateful to Rahime Süleymanoğlu-Kürüm, and Çağla Gül Yesevi. Despite their busy schedules, they carefully and repeatedly read parts of the manuscript and made valuable comments. Rahime and Çağla also provided steady encouragement and emotional support at times when I felt lost over the course of writing this book. I benefited greatly from discussions with Çisel İleri, Ayhan Kaya, Markus Ketola and Çiğdem Nas. The discussions stimulated my thinking, fed me with ideas and helped me develop the perspective contained in this book.

Finally, I also would like to thank the Routledge editors, and the anonymous reviewers for their constructive criticisms and suggestions to improve the quality of the manuscript. Richard Youngs has been more than a series editor in steering this manuscript to the stage of final publication. I am grateful to his continuous guidance, and patience with me all the way through.

Needless to say, the opinions expressed in the following pages are my own and I take full responsibility for them.

Abbreviations

AfD	Alternative for Germany (*Alternative für Deutschland*)
AKP	Justice and Development Party (*Adalet ve Kalkınma Partisi*)
BusinessEurope	The Confederation of European Business
CDU	Christian Democratic Union of Germany (*Christlich Demokratische Union Deutschlands*)
CFCU	Central Finance and Contracts Unit
CHP	Republican People's Party (*Cumhuriyet Halk Partisi*)
DTP	Democratic Society Party (*Demokratik Toplum Partisi*)
EC	European Community
EEC	European Economic Community
EFTA	European Free Trade Association
EIDHR	European Instrument for Democracy and Human Rights
ESDP	European Security and Defense Policy
EU	European Union
İKV	Economic Development Foundation (*İktisadi Kalkınma Vakfı*)
IPA	Instrument for Pre-Accession Assistance
LGBTI	Lesbian, gay, bisexual, transgender and intersex
MEDA	Euro-Mediterranean Partnership
NAO	National Authorising Officer
NGOs	Non-governmental organizations
NIPAC	National Instrument for Pre-Accession Assistance Coordinator
OECD	Organization for Economic Co-operation and Development
OEEC	Organization for European Economic Co-operation
OSCE	Organization for Security and Co-operation in Europe
PACE	The Parliamentary Assembly of the Council of Europe
PKK	Kurdistan Workers' Party (*Partiya Karkerên Kurdistanê*)
SMEs	Small and medium-sized enterprises
TACSO	Technical Assistance for Civil Society Organisations
TİSK	Turkish Confederation of Employer Associations
TRNC	Turkish Republic of Northern Cyprus
TTIP	Transatlantic Trade and Investment Partnership
TÜSİAD	Turkish Industry and Business Association
USA	United States of America

1 Introduction

In 2017, several EU leaders called for a reduction in pre-accession funds for Turkey due to concerns over its deteriorating democracy. Over the past decade, similar measures, and even terminating the accession negotiations, had been proposed, but the accession process remained largely unaffected. This time, however, it looked different. In keeping with the EU leaders' calls, in late 2017, the European Parliament voted to cut €105 million from the 2018 budget allocated to Turkey. The following year, the Parliament passed a motion to cut another €70 million. Initially, the figures seemed negligible, particularly in comparison to nearly €4.5 billion of pre-accession assistance that the EU allocated to Turkey.[1] This view changed when the EU decided the following year to reduce €146.7 million from the 2019 budget. However, what is even more significant is the symbolic value of this decision. Pre-accession financial assistance is one of the main instruments of the accession process; a measure against the former is a challenge against the latter.

The European Parliament's decision did not come out of the blue. The recent wave of tensions had been building between Turkey and the EU since 2016. In 2017, before the calls to cut the EU funds, German Chancellor Merkel had informed the European Commission that Germany would veto an update to the Customs Union with Turkey, due to concerns over Turkey's rule of law. In justifying her decision to block the talks, Merkel underlined that good ties are linked to respect for the rule of law.

The EU's political criteria have been one of the most challenging pillars of Turkey's accession process – even since before its launch. In recent years, this pillar has been overshadowed by increased cooperation between Turkey and the EU on a range of issues. That said, some of these recent developments bring forward the question of whether democratic norms and values have gained more weight again in Turkey's relations with the EU, and whether there are genuine interests and efforts in the EU to put Turkey's democratic reform process back on track. This normative pillar of EU–Turkey relations and, in particular, the democratic norm transfer to Turkey are what concerns us in this book.

As we will discuss in the next chapter, several internal and external factors have influenced EU–Turkey relations and facilitated their convergence over the decades. While it is difficult to isolate one factor from the rest, Turkey's democratic progress has been a decisive issue in the turning of its relations with the EU. Turkey had to meet a long, albeit ambiguous, list of democratic criteria to start membership talks. In just over two years between 2002 and 2004, Turkey has passed eight 'Harmonization Packages'[2] that amended over 200 articles of 53 laws, covering a wide range of political reforms. During this period, the EU has successfully used its leverage as a 'gatekeeper' to carry through democratic norm transfer to Turkey. In addition, to support its norm transfer efforts, the EU has offered different incentives and benefits, such as financial assistance, in return for Turkey's actions in line with political conditionality.

Indeed, during this period the EU has exercised considerable transformative power over Turkish democracy. The political conditionality was so predominant that discussions on other aspects of the accession process, such as the legislative harmonization in negotiating chapters, have remained limited to the halls of the state bureaucracy. Turkey's accession process has come to be perceived as the democratic reform process by the public at large and was championed for the very effect it had on norm transfer.

Soon enough, the EU membership had turned from a target within reach to an indefinite dream and, in the meantime, the EU has lost its transformative power. Today, the EU lacks such influence over Turkey. Even so, the normative side maintains its importance for EU–Turkey relations for several reasons.

First, Turkey and the EU cooperate on a wide range of issues including, for instance, migration, energy and the fight against terrorism. Their cooperation in tackling the migration crisis has become the flagship of relations in recent years. The arrangement has survived the low points in relations, as well as Turkey's occasional threats to end the deal, accusing the EU of not living up to its commitments. However, numerous areas of cooperation fail to bring Turkey closer to the EU. In essence, these areas are contingent upon defined mutual interest and, in return, such transactional ties are often contextual and bound to be temporary. As the context changes, the need for cooperation may cease or require other partners and partnerships. Trade relations may be an exception to this since Turkish and European economies are already integrated through the EU–Turkey Customs Union. But, as it stands, the customs union between Turkey and the EU is limited in scope. It needs to be modernized to meet today's conditions and remain relevant. All these ties, important as they are, on their own cannot carry EU–Turkey relations into the future. Sound relations and further integration require, not more transactionalism, but the two sides to be bound by common norms and values. This makes the normative side a still crucial part of EU–Turkey relations.

Second, this topic is important for it demonstrates the current challenges of the EU's political conditionality. The EU's enlargement policy mainly works with a conditionality mechanism to influence the existing practices and structures in applicant countries. As detailed below, the EU's political conditionality works through incentives ('rewards') to change an actor's behavior. This mechanism has been a powerful tool in triggering change during Turkey's candidacy and the early years of its accession process. However, political conditionality towards Turkey has clearly not been effective for some time. Exploring the subject of norm transfer to Turkey will address various related questions, such as if and why political conditionality has lost its relevance and how it can be amended or replaced.

Third, the EU often fluctuates between normative objectives and utility considerations in its external policies. It struggles to balance its democracy promotion efforts with counter-terrorism cooperation, commercial interests, energy security concerns and the like. Turkey presents an interesting case because, on the one hand, the EU is bound to impose 'strict conditionality' on Turkey, whose democratic backsliding raises concerns in public opinion across the EU. On the other hand, realist calculations of strategic self-interest also apply to the EU's relations with Turkey, with which trade relations, cooperation on irregular migration and counter-terrorism dominate the agenda.

Finally, democratic norms and values are under attack in the EU itself. In Hungary, Prime Minister Viktor Orbán and his right-wing Fidesz party have been leading the country away from democracy and fundamental rights since 2010. Orbán enacted stringent laws that undermined the country's checks and balances, and secured its dominance in all branches of government, including the judiciary. He has placed loyalists in once independent public bodies, such as the public prosecutor's and the state auditor's offices. Orbán has also cracked down on civil society and attacked universities. He also has increased control over the media. New media laws allow the Prime Minister to appoint his own candidates to lead the country's media regulators, while strengthening the regulators with more power to fine critical news outlets. More recently, the Fidesz party criminalized aiding undocumented migrants. But Hungary is not alone. Poland's right-wing governing party, Law and Justice (PiS), has been following Fidesz's footsteps and mimicking many of its measures since 2015. In 2016, PiS leader Jaroslaw Kaczyński said that Hungarian Prime Minister Viktor Orbán had given an example and that they are learning from his example (Kingsley, 2018).

Both countries are heavily criticized in the EU for the sharp decline in their democracy. In 2017, the European Commission decided to activate Article 7 of the Lisbon Treaty[3] against Poland, which envisages sanctions up to and including suspension of voting. In 2018, this time the European Parliament voted a motion to trigger the same disciplinary procedure against Hungary. While the ultimate sanction of a loss of voting rights is unlikely, as that requires a unanimous vote to go into effect, the Commission is considering other measures, such as tying any new aid to the credibility of the judiciary. Despite all efforts, it seems that the EU cannot forestall the democratic backsliding of Hungary and Poland, whose influence is felt elsewhere in Central and Eastern Europe. The EU has legitimized its political conditionality in other countries, not least in Turkey, by projecting itself as the champion of democratic norms. The question of how the EU can continue to transfer *European* norms outside the EU, when those norms are attacked at home, renders the issue of norm transfer to Turkey all the more important.

The current debates and the literature

Turkey's candidacy to the EU and later the accession process led to a plethora of studies in the 2000s, on various aspects of Turkey's Europeanization and the accession process. This booming academic interest gradually waned in the next decade with the shift in tide in EU–Turkey relations. Since the early 2010s, a limited number of volumes contributed to debates on Turkey's Europeanization (Nas and Özer, 2012; Tekin and Güney, 2015), the accession process (Müftüler-Baç, 2016a; Yeşilada, 2013), and the political conditionality (Müftüler-Baç, 2016b) at length. These studies utilized various conceptual tools in examining how the EU and the accession process shape different policy areas, politics and actors in Turkey. But such efforts have been scarce. Another strand in the literature discusses the reversal of the Europeanization in Turkey's relations with the EU, a process referred by the scholars as de-Europeanization.[4] These studies demonstrate the slowdown and even reversal of EU-induced reforms, as well as how European norms and values cease to inform public debates in Turkey.

More commonly, the recent literature on EU–Turkey relations reflects the current deadlock in the accession process and investigates ways and means to sustain, if not further, the relations under the present circumstances. In these efforts, 'transactionalism' has become the buzzword among scholars and researchers. Transactionalism refers to the efforts to build or sustain the relations on issues based on mutual interests at the time when the relations do not progress towards membership. As such, an important strand of the current literature focuses on one area, or multiple areas, on which Turkey and the EU already cooperate.

One such area is trade relations and economic integration. These studies inevitably focus on the Customs Union between the EU and Turkey. They analyze the EU–Turkey Customs Union, explore its impact on the respective economies, and the gains it produced in the past 20 years (Aytuğ et al., 2016; Togan, 2015). The accelerating negotiations between the EU and the USA for a free trade agreement, the Transatlantic Trade and Investment Partnership (TTIP), in 2015 and 2016, also triggered discussions on the constraints of the Customs Union and different scenarios for its modernization (Altay, 2018; Erzan, 2018; Kirişci, 2015; Long, 2016; Ülgen, 2015). Others argued that the Customs Union's modernization could help spark economic growth on both sides and help preserve the EU–Turkey economic engagement (Ülgen, 2017), while its negotiations could restore the EU's conditionality over Turkey and once again create a constructive momentum (Kirişci and Bülbül, 2017; Hamilton, 2018; Zihnioğlu, 2014). Considering that the EU–Turkey Customs Union entered into force even before Turkey's candidacy, deepening trade and economic relations is seen as a solid ground to further relations. In addition, regional and global developments also make this topic more attractive. On the one hand, the US President Donald Trump's protectionist economic policies have led to what many see as a trade war and threaten European economies. On the other hand, many fear that the UK's planned leave from the EU, Brexit, will cause some major trade disruption in Europe.

The EU's migration crisis in 2015, followed by the EU's efforts to manage the crisis in collaboration with Turkey brought the migration issue high on the agenda in EU–Turkey relations. The Joint Action Plan (2015) and the Statement (2016) between the EU and Turkey, and, in particular, the action points to re-energize the accession process sparked both scholarly and policy debates. Scholars discussed the deal made by the EU and Turkey with its advantages and limitations (Cherubini, 2017; Lehner, 2018; Rygiel et al., 2016), how the deal is framed in the Turkish political scene (Demirsu and Müftüler-Baç, 2017), proposed alternative ways for cooperation (Kirişci, 2016). Other scholars investigated how the migration deal impacted on EU–Turkey partnership on irregular migration (Dimitriadi et al., 2018) and more broadly EU–Turkey relations in general (Ott, 2017).

Several scholars approach functional cooperation in a more holistic way to analyze its implications over EU–Turkey relations. They investigate not only trade and migration, but also energy, the fight against terrorism and even foreign policy. Aydın-Düzgit and Tocci (2015) work with three analytical lenses to understand EU–Turkey relations: Turkey as an enlargement country, as an EU neighbor country and as a global actor. The authors unpack the implications of different areas of cooperation according to each analytical lens. Müftüler-Baç (2017) looks into areas of functional integration and investigates whether alternative models of integration beyond membership are possible. Kirişci (2017) on the other hand, analyzes EU–Turkey cooperation based on Turkey's broader relations with the West. To sum up, the current literature, both those focusing on individual cases of cooperation and also those broader studies consider, explain and analyze the transactional aspects of EU–Turkey relations beyond the accession process.

This book takes a different angle from the transactionalist approaches to EU–Turkey relations and focuses on the hidden but ever-present civil society dimension. In doing so, the book offers an analysis of the limits of socialization through the EU's empowerment of civil society actors in the domestic contexts. The EU's strategy of transnational reinforcement through triggering a debate in the domestic context by empowering civil society actors is based on the logic that civil society actors are well-entrenched and have sufficient access to policy-makers. These assumptions appear void in the context of Turkey. For civil society actors to facilitate social learning, they should also have intensive interactions with their European counterparts. Additionally, such an external connection should be legitimate in domestic contexts. This then links back to the legitimacy of the norms that the EU seeks to promote in third countries – in this case, Turkey.

This book has three pillars. First, it establishes the growing depoliticization of Turkish civil society. It shows the gradual diminishing of critique and contestation in civil society and the tendency among civic organizations to move away from discourse and activities that challenge the policies and practices in their area. While doing so, it explains its transformation and depicts its current picture. It shows that most civic actors have become less political and only certain groups continue rights-based activism.

Second, this book engages with the questions of why and how Turkish civil society depoliticized. This book suggests two main reasons behind this. First is the overall political environment in Turkey. The book discusses how Turkey's retreating democracy, and the intense polarization in Turkish political and social life, make rights-based activism more difficult. It tells the stories of rights-based activists who speak with a lower tone, the civil society organizations that meet new challenges every day; that learn one day they are indicted, only to find out the next day they are closed down. This book examines the transformation from a period when Turkey waited excitedly for the EU's statements, to one where prominent politicians throw EU reports on the floor live on TV. This book discusses how this change and the diminishing leverage of the EU's policies reflect on Turkey's already closing civic space. The second reason is the EU's support to Turkish civil society. An instrument of the EU foreign policy in Turkey, EU funds make up some of the largest financial support Turkish civil society receives. This book shows that EU funds contributed to depoliticization of civil society organizations, by mainly supporting projects that help improve public policies in various areas and rarely rights-based activities.

Finally, this book investigates what implications Turkish civil society's depoliticization bears for Turkey's current and future ties with the EU. For this, it explains why and how EU–Turkey relations deteriorated over the last decade and examines the current stalemate. It explores in detail the current problems, how the relations progress towards a transactional one and discusses why civil society matters. In relation to this, it also addresses the question of how effective depoliticizing civil society could be in transferring European norms.

Despite the ongoing academic interest in EU–Turkey relations, the civil society dimension is largely neglected. Civil society is important for EU–Turkey relations because first, unlike other aspects, it has largely been kept out of daily political conflicts and therefore might act as a communication channel with Turkish society, even when tensions are very high. Second, rights-based activism gains further importance in the face of Turkey's retreating democracy. Explaining the causes of Turkish civil society's depoliticization informs how Turkey's democracy and its relations with the EU will unfold. Finally, with new forms of civic activism more visible since the Gezi Protests of 2013, what comes to define civil society in Turkey is in change. This book is important for understanding the changing outlook of Turkish civil society. It is also a timely contribution to project how the new and traditional civic actors may play out with increasing contextual challenges, particularly since the coup attempt in 2016.

In order to understand the determinants of the EU's impact, positive or negative, in different contexts, the following section will review the literature on Europeanization and its influence mechanisms, which captures both the harmonization of the EU's acquis communautaire through a top-down approach or by triggering a process of socialization from bottom-up.

Political conditionality, social learning and civil society

The question of how the EU induces domestic change has received much academic interest over the past couple of decades. While the early work was limited to the EU's impact on member states, the scope of this literature expanded rapidly with new research directions. With the central and eastern European countries' quest to join the EU and their subsequent membership talks, the literature expanded to accession countries. This was coupled with research on countries with less imminent (Balkan countries and Turkey) and no (European Neighbourhood Policy) membership perspective. As more countries anchored into the EU's orbit, unpacking 'how Europe matters' for their political, economic and social transition has become a central, but challenging issue for politicians, bureaucrats and researchers alike.

The research on the EU's domestic impact is typically part of the broader Europeanization literature. While Europeanization is a fashionable concept in EU studies, what it stands for is still much contested. More commonly, and in a comprehensive understanding, Europeanization is referred to as:

> a process of (a) construction, (b) diffusion, (c) institutionalization of formal and informal rules, procedures, policy paradigms, styles and "ways of doing things" and shared beliefs that are first defined and consolidated in the making of EU decisions and then incorporated in the logic of domestic discourse, identities, political structures and public policies.
> (Radaelli, 2002: 11)

As Bulmer sums up, there are two main understanding of Europeanization. On the one hand, Europeanization means "building European capacity"; on the other hand it refers to "the transfer from 'Europe' to other jurisdictions of policy, institutional arrangements, rules, beliefs, or norms" (2007: 47). Research on the EU's domestic impact follows the latter understanding, exploring the diffusion and institutionalization of EU policies and norms in national settings.

More commonly, the two understandings of Europeanization is captured as a bottom-up or top-down Europeanization, with the direction reflecting the (group of) countries being studied. With old member states, Europeanization is first bottom-up, where member states "upload" their norms and preferences to the EU level, which then add to EU legal structure, norms and practices (Börzel, 2002, 2003). In that sense, Europeanization becomes a "two-way" process (Bulmer and Burch, 2001). In contrast, the EU's interactions with the new member states, accession and other countries are studied as a top-down process; where these countries "download" the rules earlier set by the EU's existing member states (Mikulova, 2014; Radaelli, 2012: 3; Saurugger, 2005). Bottom-up Europeanization is also characterized by asymmetry of power, where the EU exerts its leverage on the target state (Olsen, 2002: 12). In addition, other studies find "sideways" processes within the EU (Wong, 2006), where cross-country interactions lead to "cross-loading" between member

8 Introduction

states (Howell, 2004), suggesting a horizontal Europeanization (Radaelli, 2003: 42).

The literature on the EU's domestic impact is broadly based on insights from new institutionalism. New institutionalism is a school of thought that focuses on the interplay of different institutions within society and explains their impact through studying the institutions' dynamics, rules and norms. New institutionalism mainly argues that the institutions shape outcomes by influencing the norms and the actions of political actors (Przeworski, 2004: 527). It looks at the conditions of their emergence and their existence to understand the institutions and their functioning. Although various theoretical approaches have sprouted from new institutionalism, they all fall into either one of its three main variants: rational choice, sociological (constructivist) and historical institutionalism.

Historical institutionalism accounts for both continuity and change over time in terms of policy or institutional structures (Bulmer, 2007: 50). It is based on the assumption of "path dependency," meaning that existing processes and patterns constrain the options available to political actors and guide their behavior during the policy-making (Thelen, 1999). Historical institutionalists argue that the national institutions would resist the EU's influence to change as a result of path dependency (Cowles and Curtis, 2004: 300; Kay, 2005: 553). Institutions abandon their path and domestic change becomes possible only at the time of "critical junctures," when external forces cause a major disruption in the existing processes and force institutions to adopt to new developments (Krasner, 1984: 234). Historical institutionalism also explains incremental changes (Bulmer and Burch, 1998: 603).

While all variants of new institutionalism have developed conceptual tools and mechanisms to analyze domestic changes taking place in non-member states as a result of their relations with the EU, studies on Europeanization apply rationalist and sociological (constructivist) variants more commonly. Rationalist and sociological institutionalisms identify different mechanisms and stress different factors that facilitate the change of domestic policies and politics (Börzel and Risse, 2003). While the former explains rule adoption with rational calculations for benefit maximization, the latter emphasizes the norms, values and identities. Therefore, we will limit the analysis of the Turkish case to these two variants. Even though the earlier research on candidate countries found conditionality mechanism more successful on non-member states (Schimmelfennig and Sedelmeier, 2005; Sedelmeier, 2011), as we will discuss, rationalist accounts alone have not been enough to analyze the Turkish case.

Rationalist institutionalism and external incentives mechanism

Rationalist institutionalism sees the institutions as "collections of rules and incentives that establish the conditions for bounded rationality" (Peters, 1999: 44). This approach attributes a cost-benefit assessment based on rationality to actors, governmental or civil society, which are exposed to pressures from the EU. In this model, these pressures are conceptualized as a conditionality mechanism. It is argued that actors follow a "logic of consequentialism" (March and

Olsen, 1998) in assessing how they will respond to the EU's calls. Their response is mostly motivated by their desire to maximize their utility. Actors engage in strategic interactions by using their resources to maximize their fixed interests and power. They do this with highly instrumental rationality that presumes extensive cost and benefit calculation. Institutions provide strategic contexts and opportunity structures for this (Börzel and Risse, 2003; Hall and Taylor, 1996: 944–945).

Rationalist institutionalism inspired the external incentives model to explain the domestic change. The external incentives model is developed through explorative case studies, which observed how the EU triggered domestic changes during the accession of central and eastern European countries (Grabbe, 2001, 2003). The model's widespread use and its perceived success in explaining the region's transformation have soon led to new studies of other countries. This framework then expanded significantly; covering case studies from different clusters of countries which includes old and new member states, participants of the European Neighborhood Policy, even countries which signs trade and cooperation agreements with the European Commission (Sedelmeier, 2006, 2011). The model was also used to investigate the post-accession sustainability of the transferred rules in the new member states (Epstein and Sedelmeier, 2008). Each cluster identified different causal pathways to trigger a process of Europeanization, although there are some independent variables which are common to non-members and that are often different from member states. For non-members, treaty-based sanctions can be a useful way of monitoring compliance. Here, the EU's leverage is found to be relatively higher (compared to its leverage on its member states) as the EU keeps a significant carrot at hand: the prospect of full membership. These studies on effective rule transfer from the EU to national level analyze different cases of top-down Europeanization, where these countries "download" the rules and principles set ("uploaded") earlier by the EU's existing member states (Mikulova, 2014; Radaelli, 2012: 3; Saurugger, 2005).

The external incentives model is, in essence, a rationalist bargaining model (Schimmelfennig and Sedelmeier, 2004: 663). The main actors are the target governments and political elites. The actors involved exchange information, threats and promises in the bargaining process to maximize their power and welfare. According to this model, the EU exerts influence in target countries to stimulate domestic policy change through a conditionality mechanism. The EU's conditionality follows the strategy of "reinforcement by reward," where the EU provides external incentives for a target country to comply with its pre-set conditions. The rewards include assistance and institutional ties that range from trade or association agreements, to full membership. This strategy presumes that the target country is committed to the accession process and accepts implied power asymmetry vis-à-vis the EU (Kutter and Trappmann, 2010: 48). This strategy is distinguished from intervening coercively ("reinforcement by punishment") or offering large-scale unconditional assistance ("reinforcement by support") (Schimmelfennig and Sedelmeier, 2004: 664; Schimmelfennig et al., 2003).

10 *Introduction*

Together with the eastern enlargement, the EU's conditionality vis-à-vis the accession countries has developed considerably. At present, it encompasses various tools, processes and means to influence applicant countries' practices and institutional structures. One of the most efficient means of EU conditionality is the EU's 'gate-keeping' role. This refers to the EU's decision-making power to decide when to allow each applicant country to proceed to the next stage in the accession process. Benchmarking and monitoring, which allow the EU to evaluate the applicant countries' progress in a given area through pre-set benchmarks and monitoring procedures, are also equally important conditionality tools. These allow the EU to direct its pressures and offer incentives to change the cost-benefit assessment of the target government in favor of the EU's pressures. Therefore, the EU also frequently uses financial aid, technical assistance, privileged trade access and other incentives to influence the target governments (Grabbe, 2001: 1019–1022).

Conditionality can also affect the target government indirectly through differential empowerment of domestic actors. In this case, the incentives change the domestic opportunity structure in favor of domestic actors and strengthen them vis-à-vis their opponents (Börzel and Risse, 2000: 6–7). Changing opportunity structures are important for "policy entrepreneurs" (Kingdon, 1995). A policy entrepreneur is an individual who promotes policy proposals for a specific problem and advocates his/her idea in various forums to have the policy proposal be placed on the decision agenda. Different actors such as politicians, civil servants, lobbyists or researchers could be policy entrepreneurs. Policy entrepreneurs and their empowerment are important because when opportunities for action, a "policy window," open, they can take advantage of this and propel their policy proposals onto the agenda.

The external incentives model presumes that political elites in the target country engage in a political cost-benefit assessment and that they embark on the reform process if the benefits of EU rewards exceed the domestic adoption costs (Schimmelfennig, 2007; Schimmelfennig and Sedelmeier, 2004: 664, 2005: 19). There is widespread agreement in the literature that several additional factors influence this cost-benefit balance. First is the determinacy of the conditions, meaning that the clarity and formality of EU rules must be clearly set. The rules should be tied to the constitutive norms and values of the EU and the target countries should know exactly what is expected from them. The level of determinacy is higher in policy areas where there is clear and established Community competence. It is equally important that the EU rules have been set through the formal legislative procedures and consistently and coherently applied among the member states. This is not the case with political conditions, both because the EU lacks an institutional template for these (Grabbe, 2003: 319) and also because they are stated in general and vague terms. The EU tries to meet this deficit with a stream of reports during the accession talks that provide detailed information on the shortcomings and achievements of the accession country (Schimmelfennig, 2007: 130). When the EU does not have a clear and determinate policy template, 'informal conditionality' gain precedence, which allows the EU greater leverage to formulate its demands. The research shows that political conditions are not ineffective, but that they do create a weaker impact compared to formal conditionality.

Related to this is the credibility of the EU's threats and promises (Ekiert et. al, 2007; Schimmelfennig, 2008; Schimmelfennig and Sedelmeier, 2004). There should be certainty that the EU will deliver the promised incentives, including the full membership, as the accession country moves forward with the accession criteria and conversely that the EU will withhold them in case of non-compliance. The credibility of the conditionality is related to its consistency (Schimmelfennig, 2008: 921; Schimmelfennig and Sedelmeier, 2004: 671). If the EU were perceived to put forward other political, economic or strategic considerations than those spelled in the Copenhagen European Council, it may hamper the credibility of the membership incentive. In such cases, the accession country may either hope to receive the benefits without fulfilling EU criteria or conclude that it will not receive the rewards at any rate. The latter is true especially for issues with high symbolic value for the applicant country. In both cases, the accession country will fail to comply with the EU's conditions. Equally important is the size and speed of the rewards. In short, if the membership prospect is not explicit, put into doubt during the accession process or will not be provided within a reasonable time period, this will adversely influence the accession country's transition process. Size and credibility of the EU's incentives often move along parallel lines as greater incentives are perceived to be more credible. As the accession process advances, it becomes more costly for the EU to withhold the reward than delivering it (Schimmelfennig and Scholtz, 2008).

Scholars find that domestic factors are equally important in determining the enforcement power of EU conditionality. Given that membership perspective is credible, domestic political costs of adopting the conditionality shapes the political elites' response to EU demands (Schimmelfennig and Sedelmeier, 2004: 663, 669). In particular, issues with high political significance at home or those that relate to national identity entail high domestic costs for the incumbent governments (Schimmelfennig, 2008: 919–920). Reforms expected on these issues would slow down or even block the reform process. In addition, 'receptiveness' of conditions, in other words how well the EU's conditions are compatible with the domestic and foreign policy priorities of the applicant country, influences the domestic political costs (Grabbe, 2001: 1016). In addition, the existence of formal institutions providing actors with resources to exploit the new opportunities may influence the effectiveness of EU conditionality (Börzel and Risse, 2003: 59).

Finally, within the framework developed by Tsebelis, scholars stress the importance of "veto players," and their preferences for domestic change. Tsebelis defines veto players as "individual or collective actors whose agreement is necessary for a change in the status quo" (2002: 19). The number and configuration of veto players determine the possibility of departing from the status quo and the potential for change (ibid.: 2). Veto players are powerful actors as they

12 Introduction

affect the cost-benefit assessment of the target government (Börzel, 2011: 396; Lavenex and Schimmelfennig, 2013: 84; Vachudová, 2005). Potential veto players in a country are the political parties, the electorate, and interest groups (Vachudová, 2001). An equally important group of veto players are the internal institutional templates (Cowles et al., 2001; Dyson, 2007). The bureaucracy is often decisive in determining the pace of implementation, structuring new regulations and communicating them to the public, and therefore play a crucial role whether and how effective EU rules will be transferred (Dyson, 2007: 60).

Veto players may not always use their veto powers, which in return reinforces the Europeanization process. For instance, the Turkish military had expressed its commitment to Turkey's Westernization and EU membership bid on several occasions, prior to candidacy. When the government started carrying out reforms that curbed its own power for democratization and EU membership, the military could not reject these reforms due to concerns that this would have a negative impact on the military's legitimacy and credibility in Turkish society (Sarıgil, 2007: 50). As a result, the military found itself rhetorically entrapped, meaning that its earlier cost-free rhetorical commitment has turned into a costly constraint (Schimmelfennig, 2003: 222).

Discussion on the importance of domestic actors in triggering and facilitating Europeanization always comes with limitations. This is because domestic actors are considered mainly as mediating factors rather than being positioned as the main independent variables (Yılmaz, 2013). There is a growing interest in the literature on the domestic-level factors in examining the case of Turkey with a range of domestic factors and through different units of analysis (see for instance Aydın and Kirişci, 2013; Kaliber, 2014; Mühlenhoff, 2014). Recent research has shown that domestic factors can trigger a process of domestic change even when the EU fails to exert clear conditions and offer significant incentives solely because the EU's demands, even when vaguely defined, can be fully compatible with the positions of the governing parties. In this case, there is a process of domestically-driven Europeanization but still following rationalist calculations (Süleymanoğlu-Kürüm, 2019).

In the EU accession context, scholars have placed more emphasis on EU conditionality as the main motive behind domestic adaptation (Schimmelfennig and Sedelmeier, 2004). Research has shown that the incentives were strong enough to provide the conditions for stimulating change, especially when the EU offered a credible membership prospect. Others, however, question the conditionality hypothesis following the mixed record of the incentive-based approach after enlargement. On the one hand, scholars showed cases of compliance even when EU conditionality was absent in pre- and post-accession periods (Epstein and Sedelmeier, 2008: 796, 802; Süleymanoğlu-Kürüm, 2019). Indeed, the causal link between EU conditionality and successful rule transfer is not necessarily present. This means that while there might be incentives for domestic change, the mechanisms through which accession countries might adopt rules relate to other processes (Schimmelfennig and Sedelmeier, 2004: 662). On the other hand, the EU's conditionality through formal channels has not been always enough to secure a successful transformation. This mechanism proved to be insufficient and lacked implementation, in particular for democratic reforms. Scholars observed backsliding, or selective and shallow Europeanization (Ademmer and Börzel, 2013; Langbein and Börzel, 2013) even after reforms had been carried out. After all, if it was only the membership incentive that drove domestic change, then governments would be expected to roll back politically costly reforms after accession (Epstein and Sedelmeier, 2008: 797).

While the external incentives model is frequently used to study the accession process of candidate counties, it is no longer fit for the Turkish case. As EU–Turkey relations deteriorated, the EU lost its leverage. As discussed in more detail in Chapter 2, it was not only the accession process that soon lost its pace, but also the credibility of the membership reward and other incentives, which began to be questioned by Turkish officials and in public. With that, the domestic adoption costs of the reforms became too high. As a result, the EU's conditionality gradually failed in Turkey. Accordingly, the alternative model of social learning may be more effective in studying Turkey's relations with the EU and explaining the impact, or the lack, of the EU's transformative power.

Sociological (constructivist) institutionalism and social learning

An alternative mechanism to induce reforms in candidate countries is through triggering social learning by empowering domestic groups (Vachudová, 2001), a process that is also referred to in the literature as "transnational social learning" (Schimmelfennig, 2007). The social learning model is rooted in the main tenets of social constructivism and social institutionalism (Schimmelfennig and Sedelmeier, 2004: 667) and is a prominent alternative to rationalist explanations of conditionality (Checkel, 2000; Kahler, 1992). Sociological institutionalism assumes a "logic of appropriateness" (March and Olsen, 1989, 1998). According to this logic, the actors involved are guided by internalized identities, and collective understandings of values and norms (Börzel and Risse, 2003: 65). These identities and understandings define the actors' preferences and behavior. The actors choose the 'appropriate' course of action in order to fulfill social expectations, in contrast to rational institutionalist assumptions that view the actors as utility-maximizers with given preferences.

The social learning model views the EU as a community based on a collective identity, shared norms and values. EU norms and policies exert adaptational pressures on those norms and policies at the domestic level when there is "misfit" between the two (Börzel and Risse, 2003). Accession countries are socialized into these new norms and rules of appropriateness through persuasion and learning and, as a result, they redefine their interests and identities (Börzel and Risse, 2003: 65; Schimmelfennig and Sedelmeier, 2004: 668; Sedelmeier, 2006). Socialization into new norms is a much slower process to use to bring about domestic change, in comparison with incentive-based conditionality. However, the changes are potentially deeper (Diez et al., 2005: 3). Social learning becomes particularly relevant in the implementation phase. Earlier research suggests that rules transferred through social learning are less contested domestically, and in turn result in sustained compliance (Schimmelfennig and Sedelmeier, 2004: 674). In this way, through socialization, one expects to see sustainable positive change in the target country.

Social interaction or regular communication is the key to effective social learning. But even when there is intensive interaction at the elite level, other factors impinge upon the persuasive power of the EU (Schimmelfennig and Sedelmeier, 2004: 668). One important factor is domestic resonance, which includes a lack of domestic rules in the given area, and correspondence of EU rules to domestic preferences and beliefs of good policy, in other words how well the EU rules tie in with the domestic setting (Schimmelfennig and Sedelmeier, 2005: 20). In parallel with this, novelty and prior embeddedness of EU norms in a domestic setting is also important as research suggests that the feeling of domestic actors in a "novel and uncertain environment" helps to ease their socialization (Checkel, 2001). Another key variable is the legitimacy of EU rules. Legitimacy increases with the clarity of rules, adherence to rule hierarchy, the degree of acceptance and the legitimacy of the rule-making procedures; a deliberative quality of the rule-making process and international rule consensus (Schimmelfennig and Sedelmeier, 2005: 19). It decreases, however, if there are special rules for non-member states that are not applied to the member states. A final factor is the identification of domestic political elites and society with the EU community. This means whether the domestic political elites and society see the EU as a community whose norms and values they share, whose recognition they seek and to which they want to belong (Checkel, 2001: 563; Johnston, 2001: 499).

Socialization and learning do not automatically lead to internalization of the new norms and development of new identities. Successful rule and norm transfer require domestic actors with capacities to exploit new opportunities. The actors involved are not only the incumbent governments. Various domestic political and societal organizations may also facilitate social learning. Interactions at the elite level are important in this respect. For instance, scholars demonstrate that day-to-day communication of civil servants in EU-sponsored networks is key to socialization (Meyer-Sahling et al., 2016). "Change agents" or "norm entrepreneurs" make up a key set of facilitating actors. Norm entrepreneurs try to mobilize support at the domestic level to induce change through persuasion and arguing (Risse, 2000). These "norm- and idea-promoting agents" could be epistemic communities of actors who can legitimate new norms by providing scientific knowledge. Or they could be advocacy or principled-issue networks who try to persuade others to reconsider their preferences by appealing to collective identities and shared norms (Börzel and Risse, 2003: 65).

Europeanization literature typically distinguishes between rational calculations (external incentives model) and socialization (social learning model) to explain the EU's domestic impact. Others, however, find the two accounts to be complementary, working with a broader framework to bring the power of incentives and socialization (Diez et al., 2006: 571–574; Epstein and Sedelmeier,

2008: 800; Schimmelfennig and Sedelmeier, 2004: 669–674). They suggest that it is the combined effect of EU conditionality and domestic influence that successfully prompt political elites to pursue domestic change (Spendzharova and Vachudová, 2012).

Civil society organizations are among the much-emphasized group of domestic actors where both approaches intersect. Indeed, they are considered important actors, particularly in the context of transferring the EU's democratic norms and rules. Following insights from both approaches, civil society organizations can act individually or in collaboration with their counterparts in EU countries and are expected to contribute to domestic change in the accession process in several ways. First, civil society organizations can act as "norm entrepreneurs" (Börzel and Risse, 2003; see also Keck and Sikkink, 1998) or norm carriers. They can mobilize at the domestic level and help socialize other domestic actors into these new norms and practices (Checkel, 1999). In this way, they build support in society for the adoption of new EU norms. In the case of interactions of national bureaucracies, a civil society's norm entrepreneurship would complement the social learning at the elite level. Civil society organizations often use persuasion and arguing to induce change (Risse, 2000). Eventually, they may help other actors to redefine their interests and identities and engage in processes of social learning. In that sense, civil society organizations provide a venue through which European norms and practices are diffused to or strengthened in their countries.

Second, civil society organizations have the potential to trigger this social learning process by mobilizing public opinion in favor of the accession and reform process. They can create or frame the issues so that they resonate with local audiences (Way and Levitsky, 2007: 50). Civil society actors can provide indirect communication channels between Brussels and the domestic public and bring in alternative information to that provided by political elites (Haggard and Webb, 1994). This, in turn, would affect the cost-benefit assessment of the target government to encourage more democratic reforms. In addition, the EU can encourage lesson-drawing in the domestic context by empowering domestic actors (Bauer et al., 2007). In either case, this requires civil society organizations to have communication in "EU-sponsored networks" (Bauer et al., 2007). Research suggests that in some cases the communication in these networks may strengthen civil society organizations by also contributing to their advocacy and networking skills, as well as mobilization at home (Dimitrova and Buzogany, 2014).

In addition to vertical interactions between the EU level and the candidate country, civil society organizations can also take part in the horizontal mechanisms of Europeanization (Radaelli, 2003). Research has shown that the transnational interactions and exchanges between civil society organizations in the member states and candidate countries helped to diffuse certain practices and models between countries. This transnational learning, in turn, played an important role in the civil society's empowerment in candidate countries (Wunsch, 2018).

16 Introduction

Beyond the conditionality mechanism and social learning, there is also the "lesson-drawing" model (Rose, 1991). In the lesson-drawing model, non-member states adopt EU rules without incentives or persuasion (Schimmelfennig and Sedelmeier, 2004: 668). Lesson-drawing starts with policy dissatisfaction at the domestic level and searches for a solution abroad. Policy makers then review and evaluate the system of the EU (or its member states) on their suitability for domestic circumstances. This requires EU-centered epistemic communities. If the domestic policy makers expect EU rules to solve domestic policy problems effectively, then they adopt these rules. The transferability of EU rules and veto players are determinative factors.

Civil society organizations may have an additional role to play, particularly in cases where EU conditionality is less effective. This is particularly true in the context of Turkey's accession process, in which EU conditionality and its accompanying EU leverage has eroded considerably over the past decade. In such cases, multiple linkages with the EU through different actors, including civil society organizations, become more important (see Levitsky and Way, 2006; Way and Levitsky, 2007). Turkey has dense economic, political and even some social linkage to the EU and to some individual EU member states. Civil society organizations are important in establishing and maintaining social ties to Europe. These ties have become an important avenue for interaction, especially now that the political connections between the EU and Turkey have been frayed and official channels of communication effectively blocked.

The EU has been supporting and interacting with civil society actors in accession countries with the aim of facilitating the political transition and strengthening democracy. Despite the EU's efforts, several studies question the effectiveness of EU aid and EU-induced policy reform in civil society empowerment (Börzel, 2010; Fagan, 2006; Fagan and Wunsch, 2018; Kutter and Trappmann, 2010). Scholars are critical of the EU's overly instrumental approach to these organizations (Fagan, 2010; O'Brennan, 2013), and demonstrate that the EU's impact on civil society organizations is limited and ambivalent (Kutter and Trappmann, 2010) or at best results in "bounded empowerment" (Sudbery, 2010).

The impact of EU civil society support in Turkey is also a much-studied subject. Earlier studies discussed the issue in relation to Turkey's Europeanization. They examined the empowerment of Turkish civil society in relation to not only financial support and the EU-induced reform process but also the EU's symbolic power (Göksel and Güneş, 2005; Rumelili, 2005). These studies were soon followed by others that adopted a rather critical tone on EU support to Turkish civil society. They criticized the scope of EU funds (Rumelili and Boşnak, 2015) and questioned the impact of EU incentives (Ketola, 2013; Kubicek, 2011; Zihnioğlu, 2013a, 2013b). Scholars found that EU funds create a project culture (Kuzmanovic, 2010), risk undermining volunteerism (Ergun, 2010; Rumelili and Boşnak, 2015) and divert the scarce staff energy to the EU-funded projects only (Paker et al., 2013). More recent research investigated the impact of EU funds in relation to the professionalization, depoliticization and NGO-ization of Turkish civil society (Mühlenhoff, 2014; Zihnioğlu, 2018, 2019).

Introduction 17

This book contributes to the growing body of literature on the EU's domestic impact, EU–Turkey relations and Turkish civil society. The analyses in this book are informed by the main tenets of both rationalist and sociological institutionalism. This book, on the one hand, investigates how EU conditionality and EU leverage have eroded in Turkey's accession process. On the other hand, and more importantly, it shows that social learning has limited potential due to the depoliticization of Turkish civil society. While the existing literature emphasizes normative resonance, interaction, identification or legitimacy as key variables to study social learning, the findings of this book suggests that civil society actors should also be well-entrenched and politicized to have the potential to trigger social learning process.

Outline of the book

This book is divided into eight chapters. Following this introduction in Chapter 1, this book unfolds as follows. Chapter 2 provides a concise overview of Turkey's over-half-a-century-long relation with the EU. To that end, Chapter 2 first explains how the two sides are tied with various economic, political and security concerns starting from Turkey's association to the EU. It shows how the relations assumed a multi-faceted structure over the decades with new dimensions and diverse factors coming into play. This is important for understanding the current course of EU–Turkey relations as this structure shapes the choices of actors on both sides. This chapter then accounts for how the pendulum in relations swung from an intense reform process period to the first stalemate, and then to turbulence of the last two decades. Examining why and how EU–Turkey relations deteriorated will help us understand not only the current stalemate but also why civil society matters. In return, this will inform the discussions on the implications of Turkish civil society's depoliticization over current and future relations.

Chapter 3 follows with broader debates on some of the main issues and current challenges dominating Turkey's relations with the EU in recent years. Accordingly, this chapter, on the one hand, examines the cooperation and integration on economy, trade and energy issues. On the other hand, it addresses the migration crisis, the reduction of the EU's pre-accession assistance to Turkey and the various recent crises that the EU has faced and discusses them in regard to EU–Turkey relations. This chapter is important for two reasons. First, the issues and challenges discussed show how relations have moved beyond the scope of accession negotiations and have increasingly assumed a transactional nature. In return, this may have repercussions on the role civil society can play in these relations. Second, some of the challenges have a direct or indirect effect over Turkish civil society, and a careful study of these challenges may inform us on the future course of this.

The purpose of the next chapter is to show and account for the depoliticization of Turkish civil society. In parallel with the context of the book, Chapter 4 traces the changes that Turkish civil society has gone through, in particular over the last three decades. For this, it first shows how Turkish civic space diversified with new groups from the 1980s until the early 2000s. Then, in considering the following decade, this chapter critically engages with discussions on the literature on Turkish civil society. Finally, this chapter examines the changes in Turkish civil society since the early 2010s and discusses its current state. It shows how traditional civic organizations increasingly shy away from overtly political activities and take on less political discourse. This chapter also introduces the new civic activists, how they confront Turkey's current challenging environment and the place they gain in the changing outlook of Turkish civil society.

Chapter 5 examines how domestic developments in Turkey and the changing course of EU–Turkey relations reflect on Turkey's civic space. This chapter analyzes how the legal framework on freedom of association and its implementation evolved from the early 2000s until today. For this, it first briefly overviews the improving framework between 2001 and 2006 and discusses the half-finished reform process. Based on the context outlined in Chapter 2, this chapter then examines the closing civic space and, particularly after 2013, increasing repression against civic actors. It discusses how the diminishing leverage of the EU's policies towards Turkey, and Turkey's political and social polarization impact on the closing civic space. Finally, it discusses the broader contextual challenges influencing Turkish civil society since the failed coup attempt in July 2016.

Chapter 6 examines the EU's civil society support as an instrument of its policies towards Turkey. For this purpose, the chapter provides a detailed picture of the aims, scope, structure and functioning of the EU-funding machinery for civil society actors in Turkey. It also introduces the major actors managing these funds. In addition, this chapter discusses the problems raised on the functioning of pre-accession assistance and the recent changes made. While the focus is on the funding coming through the EU's pre-accession assistance to Turkey, other major venues are also mentioned.

This is followed in Chapter 7 with an analysis of the impact of the EU's civil society support in Turkey. This chapter, on the one hand, shows that EU funds contributed to the depoliticization of civil society organizations by mainly supporting projects that help improve public policies in various areas and rarely rights-based activities. On the other hand, it argues that the professionalization impact of the funds is far more limited. The findings in this chapter draw from an extensive database of the author's interviews with representatives of civil society organizations in Turkey. This chapter is important as it challenges the conventional wisdom on the EU's civil society support as an instrument of its foreign policy.

The concluding chapter, discusses the wider implications of Turkish civil society's gradual depoliticization on Turkey's relations with the EU. This chapter reiterates that civil society matters for EU–Turkey relations. In the light of the framework drawn in the introductory chapter and perspectives offered in prior chapters, this chapter discusses how the diminishing of rights-based groups and activities adversely affect the norm transfer and undermine Turkey's already faltering democracy.

Notes

1 Under the Instrument for Pre-Accession Assistance II, the European Union allocated €4.5 billion for the period 2014–2020. For more details on EU financial assistance to Turkey, see Chapter 6.
2 During the reform process, a 'harmonization package' has come to refer to a draft law consisting of a collection of amendments to different laws. Each package was designed to amend more than one code or law at a time, which was then voted in a single session in the Parliament. The packages introduced political reforms to bring the legislation in line with EU standards.
3 Article 7 of the Lisbon Treaty is an internal mechanism to punish any of the member states posing "clear risk of a serious breach" of the "values of respect for human dignity, freedom, democracy, equality, the rule of law and respect for human rights, including the rights of persons belonging to minorities."
4 See South European Society and Politics special issue on de-Europeanization (volume 21, issue 1).

Bibliography

Ademmer, E. and Börzel, T. (2013) Migration, Energy and Good Governance in the EU's Eastern Neighbourhood, *Europe-Asia Studies*, 65(4), pp. 581–607.

Altay, S. (2018) Toward a "Privileged Partnership": The EU, Turkey and the Upgrade of the Customs Union, *Insight Turkey*, 20(3), pp. 179–198.

Aydın, U. and Kirişci, K. (2013) With or Without the EU: Europeanisation of Asylum and Competition Policies in Turkey, *South European Society and Politics*, 18(3), pp. 375–395.

Aydın-Düzgit, S. and Tocci, N. (2015) *Turkey and the European Union*. London: Palgrave Macmillan.

Aytuğ, H., Mavuş Kütük, M., Oduncu, A. and Togan, S. (2016) Twenty Years of the EU–Turkey Customs Union: A Synthetic Control Method Analysis, *Journal of Common Market Studies*, 55(3), pp. 419–431.

Bauer, M., Knill, C. and Pitschell, D. (2007) Differential Europeanization in Eastern Europe: The Impact of Diverse EU Regulatory Governance Patterns, *Journal of European Integration*, 29(4), pp. 405–424.

Börzel, T. (2002) Member State Responses to Europeanization, *Journal of Common Market Studies*, 40(2), pp. 193–214.

Börzel, T. (2003) Shaping and Taking EU Policies: Member State Responses to Europeanisation, *Queen's Papers on Europeanisation*, No. 2.

Börzel, T. (2010) Why You Don't Always Get What You Want: EU Enlargement and Civil Society in Central and Eastern Europe, *Acta Politica*, 45(1), pp. 1–10.

Börzel, T. (2011) When Europe Hits … Beyond Its Borders: Europeanisation and the Near Abroad, *Comparative European Politics*, 9(4/5), pp. 394–413.

Börzel, T. and Risse, T. (2000) When Europe Hits Home: Europeanization and Domestic Change, *European Integration Online Papers*, 4(15), available at http://eiop.or.at/eiop/texte/2000-015a.htm.

Börzel, T. and Risse, T. (2003) Conceptualising the Domestic Impact of Europe, in K. Featherstone and C. M. Radaelli (eds), *The Politics of Europeanisation*. Oxford: Oxford University Press.

Bulmer, S. (2007) Theorising Europeanisation, in P. Graziano and M. P. Vink (eds), *Europeanisation: New Research Agendas*. Basingstoke: Palgrave Macmillan, pp. 46–58.

Bulmer, S. and Burch, M. (1998) Organising for Europe: Whitehall, the British State and European Union, *Public Administration*, 76(3), pp. 601–628.

Bulmer, S. and Burch, M. (2001) The Europeanization of Central Government: The UK and Germany in Historical Institutionalist Perspective, in G. Schneider and M. Aispinwall (eds), *The Rules of Integration: Institutional Approaches to the Study of Europe*. Manchester: Manchester University Press.

Checkel, J. T. (1999) Social Construction and Integration, *Journal of European Public Policy*, 6(4), pp. 545–560.

Checkel, J. T. (2000) Compliance and Conditionality, *ARENA Working Papers 00/18*. Oslo: ARENA.

Checkel, J. T. (2001) The Europeanization of Citizenship, in M. G. Cowles, J. Caporaso and T. Risse (eds), *Transforming Europe*. Ithaca: Cornell University Press.

Cherubini, F. (2017) The "EU–Turkey Statement" of 18 March 2016: A (Umpteenth?) Celebration of Migration Outsourcing, in S. Baldin and M. Zago (eds), *Europe of Migrations: Policies, Legal Issues and Experiences*. Trieste: Edizioni Università di Trieste.

Cowles, M. G. and Curtis, S. (2004) Developments in European Integration Theory: The EU as "Other," in M. G. Cowles and D. Dinan (eds), *Developments in the European Union 2*. Basingstoke: Palgrave.

Cowles, M. G., Caporaso, J., and Risse, T. (eds) (2001) *Transforming Europe: Europeanization and Domestic Change*. Ithaca and London: Cornell University Press.

Demirsu, İ. and Müftüler-Baç, M. (2017) The Turkish–EU Cooperation on the Refugee Crisis: The Turkish Perceptions in the Parliamentary Debates, *PACO Working Paper No. 07*.

Diez, T., Agnantopoulos, A. and Kaliber, A. (2005) Turkey, Europeanisation and Civil Society, *South European Society and Politics*, 10(1), pp. 1–15.

Diez, T., Stetter, S. and Albert, M. (2006) The European Union and Border Conflicts: The Transformative Power of Integration, *International Organization*, 60(3), pp. 563–593.

Dimitriadi, A., Kaya, A., Kale, B. and Zurabishvili, T. (2018) EU–Turkey Relations and Irregular Migration: Transactional Cooperation in the Making, *FEUTURE Online Paper 16*. www.feuture.uni-koeln.de/sites/feuture/user_upload/FEUTURE_Online_Paper_No_16_D6.3.pdf.

Dimitrova, A. and Buzogany, A. (2014) Post-Accession Policy-Making in Bulgaria and Romania: Can Non-state Actors Use EU Rules to Promote Better Governance? *Journal of Common Market Studies*, 52(1), pp. 139–156.

Dyson, K. (2007) *Enlarging the Euro Area: External Empowerment and Domestic Transformation in East Central Europe*. Oxford: Oxford University Press.

Ekiert, G., Kubik, J. and Vachudová, M. A. (2007) Democracy in the Post-Communist World: An Unending Quest?, *East European Politics and Societies*, 21(1), pp. 7–30.

Epstein, R. A. and Sedelmeier, U. (2008) Beyond Conditionality: International Institutions in Postcommunist Europe after Enlargement, *Journal of European Public Policy*, 15(6), pp. 795–805.

Ergun, A. (2010) Civil Society in Turkey and Local Dimensions of Europeanization, *Journal of European Integration*, 32(5), pp. 507–522.

Erzan, R. (2018) Customs Union between EU and Turkey: A Success Story to be Nurtured, *Working Papers 2018/03*, Bogazici University, Department of Economics.

Fagan, A. (2006) Transnational Aid for Civil Society Development in Post-socialist Europe: Democratic Consolidation or a New Imperialism?, *Journal of Communist Studies and Transition Politics*, 22(1), pp. 115–134.

Fagan, A. (2010) *Europe's Balkan Dilemma: Paths to Civil Society or State-Building?* London: I.B. Tauris.

Fagan, A. and Wunsch, N. (2018) Fostering Institutionalisation? The Impact of the EU Accession Process on State-Civil Society Relations in Serbia, *Acta Politica*. DOI: 10.1057/s41269-018-0093-1.

Göksel, D. N. and Birden Güneş, R. (2005) The Role of NGOs in the European Integration Process: The Turkish Experience, *South European Society and Politics*, 10(1), pp. 57–72.

Grabbe, H. (2001) How Does Europeanization Affect CEE Governance? Conditionality, Diffusion and Diversity, *Journal of European Public Policy*, 8(6), pp. 1013–1031.

Grabbe, H. (2003) Europeanization Goes East: Power and Uncertainty in the EU Accession Process, in K. Featherstone and C. M. Radaelli (eds), *The Politics of Europeanisation*. Oxford: Oxford University Press.

Haggard, S. and Webb, S. B. (1994) Introduction, in S. Haggard and S. B. Webb (eds), *Voting for Reform: Democracy, Political Liberalization, and Economic Adjustment*. New York: Oxford University Press.

Hall, P. A. and Taylor, R. C. (1996) Political Science and the Three New Institutionalisms, *Political Studies*, 44(5), pp. 936–957.

Hamilton, D. S. (2018) Getting Back on Track with Turkey, *Intereconomics* 53, pp. 242–243. DOI: 10.1007/s10272-018-0757-0.

Howell, K. E. (2004) *Europeanization, European Integration and Financial Services: Developing Theoretical Frameworks and Synthesising Methodological Approaches*. London: Palgrave Macmillan.

Johnston, A. I. (2001) Treating International Institutions as Social Environments, *International Studies Quarterly*, 45(4), pp. 487–515.

Kahler, M. (1992) External Influence, Conditionality, and the Politics of Adjustment, in S. H. Kaufman (ed), *The Politics of Economic Adjustment*. Princeton: Princeton University Press.

Kaliber, A. (2014) Europeanisation in Turkey: In Search of a New Paradigm of Modernisation, *Journal of Balkan and Near Eastern Studies*, 16(1), pp. 30–46.

Kay, A. (2005) A Critique of the Use of Path Dependency in Policy, *Public Administration*, 83(3), pp. 553–571.

Keck, M. E. and Sikkink, K. (1998) *Activists beyond Borders: Advocacy Networks in International Politics*. Ithaca: Cornell University Press.

Ketola, M. (2013) *Europeanization and Civil Society: Turkish NGOs as Instruments of Change?* Basingstoke: Palgrave Macmillan.

Kingdon, J. W. (1995) *Agendas, Alternatives, and Public Policies* (2nd ed.). New York: HarperCollins.

Kingsley, P. (2018) As West Fears the Rise of Autocrats, Hungary Shows What's Possible, *New York Times* (10 February), www.nytimes.com/2018/02/10/world/europe/hungary-orban-democracy-far-right.html.

Kirişci, K. (2015) TTIP's Enlargement and the Case of Turkey, *Turkey Papers*. Istanbul: IPC, Washington, D.C.: Wilson Centre.

Kirişci, K. (2016) Europe's Refugee/Migrant Crisis: Can "Illiberal" Turkey Save "Liberal Europe" while Helping Syrian Refugees? European Policy Centre (16 February).

Kirişci, K. (2017) *Turkey and the West: Fault Lines in a Troubled Alliance*. Washington, D.C.: Brookings Institution Press

Kirişci, K. and Bülbül, O. (2017) The EU and Turkey Need Each Other. Could Upgrading the Customs Union Be the Key?, Brookings Institution (29 August).

Krasner, S. (1984) Approaches to the State: Alternative Conceptions and Historical Dynamics, *Comparative Politics*, 16(2), pp. 223–246.

Kubicek, P. (2011) Political Conditionality and European Union's Cultivation of Democracy in Turkey, *Democratization*, 18(4), pp. 910–931.

Kutter, A. and Trappmann, V. (2010) Civil Society in Central and Eastern Europe: The Ambivalent Legacy of Accession, *Acta Politica*, 45(1), pp. 41–69.

Kuzmanovic, D. (2010) Project Culture and Turkish Civil Society, *Turkish Studies*, 11(3), pp. 429–444.

Langbein, J. and Börzel, T. A. (2013) Explaining Policy Change in the European Union's Eastern Neighbourhood, *Europe-Asia Studies*, 65(4), pp. 571–580.

Lavenex, S. and Schimmelfennig, F. (eds) (2013) *Democracy Promotion in the EU's Neighbourhood: From Leverage to Governance?* Abingdon: Routledge.

Lehner, R. (2018) The EU–Turkey-"Deal": Legal Challenges and Pitfalls, *International Migration*. DOI: 10.1111/imig.12462.

Levitsky, S. and Way, L. A. (2006) Linkage versus Leverage. Rethinking the International Dimension of Regime Change, *Comparative Politics*, 38(4), pp. 379–400.

Long, C. (2016) The Opportunity Space of Overlapping Trade Regimes: Turkey, the Customs Union, and TTIP, *Global Politics*, 7(3), pp. 360–369.

March, J. G. and Olsen, J. P. (1989) *Rediscovering Institutions: The Organizational Basis of Politics*. New York: Free Press.

March, J. G. and Olsen, J. P. (1998) The Institutional Dynamics of International Political Orders, *International Organizations*, 52(4), pp. 943–969.

Meyer-Sahling, J.-H., Lowe, W. and Stolk, C. (2016) Silent Professionalisation: EU Integration and the Professional Socialisation of Public Officials in Central and Eastern Europe, *European Union Politics*, 17(1), pp. 162–183.

Mikulova, K. (2014) Potemkin Europeanisation?, *East European Politics and Societies and Cultures*, 28(1), pp. 163–186.

Müftüler-Baç, M. (2016a) *Divergent Pathways: Turkey and the European Union: Re-Thinking the Dynamics of Turkish-European Union Relations*. Berlin: Budrich Publishers.

Müftüler-Baç, M. (2016b) The Pandora's Box: Democratization and Rule of Law in Turkey, *Asia Europe Journal*, 14(1), pp. 61–77.

Müftüler-Baç, M. (2017) Turkey's Future with the European Union: Alternative Modes of Differentiated Integration, *Turkish Studies*, 18(3), pp. 416–439.

Mühlenhoff, H. (2014) Funding Democracy, Funding Social Services? The European Instrument for Democracy and Human Rights in the Context of Competing Narratives in Turkey, *Journal of Balkan and Near Eastern Studies*, 16(1), pp. 102–118.

Nas, Ç. and Özer, Y. (eds) (2012) *Turkey and the European Union, the Process of Europeanization*. London: Routledge.

O'Brennan, J. (2013) The European Commission, Enlargement Policy and Civil Society in the Western Balkans, in V. Bojičić-Dželilović, J. Ker-Lindsay and D. Kostovicova (eds), *Civil Society and Transitions in the Western Balkans*. Basingstoke: Palgrave Macmillan.

Olsen, J. P. (2002) The Many Faces of Europeanisation, *Journal of Common Market Studies*, 40(5), pp. 921–952.

Ott, A. (2017) EU–Turkey Cooperation in Migration Matters: A Game Changer in a Multi Layered Relationship?, *CLEER Paper Series, 2017/4*, T.M.C. Asser Institute for International & European Law 2017-4. Available at SSRN: https://ssrn.com/abstract=3118921.

Paker, H., Adaman, F., Kadirbeyoğlu, Z. and Özkaynak, B. (2013) Environmental Organisations in Turkey: Engaging the State and Capital, *Environmental Politics*, 22(5), pp. 760–778.

Peters, G. (1999) *Institutional Theory in Political Science: "The New Institutionalism."* London: Pinter.
Przeworski, A. (2004) Institutions Matter? *Government and Opposition*, 39(4), pp. 527–540.
Radaelli, C. M. (2002) The Domestic Impact of European Union Public Policy: Notes on Concepts, Methods, and the Challenge of Empirical Research, *Politique Europénne*, 1(5), pp. 105–136.
Radaelli, C. M. (2003) The Europeanization of Public Policy, in K. Featherstone and C. M. Radaelli (eds), *The Politics of Europeanization*. Oxford: Oxford University Press.
Radaelli, C. M. (2012) Europeanisation: The Challenge of Establishing Causality, in T. Exadaktylos and C. M. Radaelli (eds), *Research Design in European Studies*. Basingstoke: Palgrave Macmillan.
Risse, T. (2000) "Let's Argue!" Communicative Action in International Relations, *International Organization*, 54(1), pp. 1–39.
Rose, R. (1991) What is Lesson-Drawing?, *Journal of Public Policy*, 11(1), pp. 3–30.
Rumelili, B. (2005) Civil Society and the Europeanization of Greek–Turkish Cooperation, *South European Society and Politics*, 10(1), pp. 45–56.
Rumelili, B. and Bosnak, B. (2015) Taking Stock of Europeanization of Civil Society in Turkey: The Case of NGOs, in A. Tekin and A. Güney (eds), *The Europeanization of Turkey: Polity and Politics*. London: Routledge.
Rygiel, K., Baban, F. and Ilcan, S. (2016) The Syrian Refugee Crisis: The EU–Turkey "Deal" and Temporary Protection, *Global Social Policy*, 16(3), pp. 315–320.
Sarıgil, Z. (2007) Europeanization as Institutional Change: The Case of the Turkish Military, *Mediterranean Politics*, 12(1), pp. 39–57.
Saurugger, S. (2005) Europeanisation as a Methodological Challenge: The Case of Interest Groups, *Journal of Comparative Policy Analysis*, 7(4), pp. 291–312.
Schimmelfennig, F. (2003) *The EU, NATO and the Integration of Europe: Rules and Rhetoric*. Cambridge: Cambridge University Press.
Schimmelfennig, F. (2007) European Regional Organizations, Political Conditionality, and Democratic Transformation in Eastern Europe, *East European Politics and Societies*, 21(1), pp. 126–141.
Schimmelfennig, F. (2008) EU Political Accession Conditionality after the 2004 Enlargement: Consistency and Effectiveness, *Journal of European Public Policy*, 15(6), pp. 918–937.
Schimmelfennig, F. and Scholtz, H. (2008) EU Democracy Promotion in the European Neighbourhood: Political Conditionality, Economic Development and Transnational Exchange, *European Union Politics*, 9(2), pp. 187–215.
Schimmelfennig, F. and Sedelmeier, U. (2004) Governance by Conditionality: EU Rule Transfer to the Candidate Countries of Central and Eastern Europe, *Journal of European Public Policy*, 11(4), pp. 661–679.
Schimmelfennig, F. and Sedelmeier, U. (2005) Introduction: Conceptualizing the Europeanization of Central and Eastern Europe, in F. Schimmelfennig and U. Sedelmeier (eds), *The Europeanization of Central and Eastern Europe*. Ithaca and London: Cornell University Press.
Schimmelfennig, F., Engert, S. and Knobel, S. (2003) Costs, Commitment and Compliance: The Impact of EU Democratic Conditionality on Latvia, Slovakia and Turkey, *Journal of Common Market Studies*, 41(3), pp. 495–518.
Sedelmeier, U. (2006) Europeanisation in New Member and Candidate States, *Living Reviews in European Governance*, 1(3).

Sedelmeier, U. (2011) Europeanisation in New Member and Candidate States, *Living Reviews in European Governance*, 6(1).
Spendzharova, A. B. and Vachudová, M. A. (2012) Catching Up? Consolidating Liberal Democracy in Bulgaria and Romania after EU Accession, *West European Politics*, 35(1), pp. 39–58.
Sudbery, I. (2010) The European Union as Political Resource: NGOs as Change Agents? *Acta Politica*, 45(1), pp. 136–157.
Süleymanoğlu-Kürüm, R. (2019) *Conditionality, the EU and Turkey: From Transformation to Retrenchment*. London: Routledge.
Tekin, A. and Güney, A. (eds) (2015) *The Europeanization of Turkey Polity: and Politics*. London: Routledge.
Thelen, K. (1999) Historical Institutionalism in Comparative Politics, *Annual Review of Political Science*, 2, pp. 369–404.
Togan, S. (2015) The EU–Turkey Customs Union: A Model for Future Euro-Med Integration, in R. Ayadi, M. Dabrowski and L. De Wulf (eds), *Economic and Social Development of the Southern and Eastern Mediterranean Countries*. Cham: Springer.
Tsebelis, G. (2002) *Veto Players: How Political Institutions Work*. Princeton: Princeton University Press.
Ülgen, S. (2015) A New Era for the Customs Union and the Business World, *TÜSİAD Publication No: T/2015, 10–568*. İstanbul: TÜSİAD.
Ülgen, S. (2017) *Trade as Turkey's EU Anchor*. Washington: Carnegie Endowment for International Peace.
Vachudová, A. M. (2001) The Leverage of International Institutions on Democratising States: Eastern Europe and the European Union, *San Domenico: RSCAS Working Paper No. 2001/33*. Italy: European University Institute.
Vachudová, A. M. (2005) *Europe Undivided: Democracy, Leverage and Integration after Communism*. Oxford: Oxford University Press.
Way, L. A. and Levitsky, S. (2007) Linkage, Leverage, and the Post-Communist Divide, *East European Politics and Societies*, 21, pp. 48–66.
Wong, R. Y. (2006) *The Europeanization of French Foreign Policy: France and the EU in East Asia*. Basingstoke: Palgrave Macmillan.
Wunsch, N. (2018) Transnational Learning and Civil Society Empowerment in the EU Enlargement Process, *Journal of Common Market Studies*. DOI: 10.1111/jcms.12808.
Yeşilada, B. (2013) *EU–Turkey Relations in the 21st Century*. London: Routledge.
Yılmaz, G. (2013) It is Pull-and-Push that Matters for External Europeanisation! Explaining Minority Policy Change in Turkey, *Mediterranean Politics*, 19(2), pp. 1–21.
Zihnioğlu, Ö. (2013a) *European Union Civil Society Policy and Turkey: A Bridge Too Far?* New York: Palgrave Macmillan.
Zihnioğlu, Ö. (2013b) The "Civil Society Policy" of the European Union for Promoting Democracy in Turkey: Golden Goose or Dead Duck? *Journal of Southeast European and Black Sea Studies*, 13(3), pp. 381–400.
Zihnioğlu, Ö. (2014) Bringing the European Union Back on the Agenda of Turkish Foreign Policy, *Insight Turkey*, 16(3), pp. 149–164.
Zihnioğlu, Ö. (2018) European Union Funds and the Assumed Professionalization of Turkish Civil Society Organizations, *Turkish Studies*. DOI: 10.1080/14683849.2018.1555754.
Zihnioğlu, Ö. (2019) European Union Civil Society Support and the Depoliticisation of Turkish Civil Society, *Third World Quarterly*, 40(3), pp. 503–520.

2 The recent history of EU–Turkey relations

The long history of Turkey's relations with the EU is not only a sum of successive steps of convergence and alienation. Over more than half a century, relations have assumed a multi-faceted structure with new dimensions and diverse factors coming into play. Examining the current course of EU–Turkey relations and explaining the challenges facing the relations today requires an understanding of this increasingly sophisticated structure and how it influences the choices of different actors in Turkey and in the EU.

From association to candidacy (1963–1999)

From the very beginning in the late 1950s, multiple interests and concerns, stretching beyond mere trade ties, brought Turkey and the EEC closer. For Turkey, association with the EEC was ideological, and an extension of its policy to be part of the Western political and security structure. In the post-war years, Turkey sought membership in Western institutions. Turkey became a member of the OECD (then OEEC) in 1948, the Council of Europe in 1949, and NATO in 1952. Aiming for Western institutions was not only a natural extension of Turkey's Westernization, but also integrating with these institutions would minimize the reversal potential of its modernization. In that sense, association with the EEC came to be seen as an *anchor* of its long-sought Westernization (Uğur, 2004: 2–3). Application to the EEC was also a strategic decision as Turkey sought to maintain its competitive position vis-à-vis Greece, who had just applied for association. On the other hand, the EEC welcomed Turkey's application for it as an acknowledgement of the EEC's importance in its competition against EFTA.

Turkey's unsteady political and economic structure has become a major factor impacting upon its relations with the Community since the initial years. Both the military takeover in 1960 (leading to occasional suspension of negotiations and frequent changing of Turkish delegations) and the EEC's concerns over the potential severe impact of the Turkish economy slowed down the negotiations (Çalış, 2016: 63–64). Under such adverse circumstances, what made the Association Agreement in 1963 possible was probably the Cold War conditions and West Germany's persistence not to alienate Turkey (Tekeli and İlkin, 1993: 143).

The Ankara Agreement set out a plan for the gradual establishment of a customs union between the EEC and Turkey in three stages. The preparatory stage provided for Turkey to strengthen its economy, while receiving economic support and accessing EEC markets without assuming obligations. During the transitional stage, Turkey and the EEC would further align their economies and progressively lift barriers to trade, which would culminate in a customs union in the final stage. The agreement was carefully worded to also keep the door open for free movement of capital, services and workers, as well as Turkey's future membership aspirations, while not making any definite promises. As such, the agreement amounted to an acknowledgement of its Western identity for Turkey's political and bureaucratic elite who, almost uniformly,[1] acclaimed the Ankara Agreement (Çalış, 2016: 95).

Despite the early enthusiasm, the relations quickly soured and became increasingly thorny in the 1970s. In late 1970s, the EEC and Turkey signed the Additional Protocol to the Association Agreement, which marked the passage from the preparatory stage to the transitional stage. But even that did not help relations. One reason behind this was Turkey's still volatile economy. Failure to adjust the Turkish economy resulted in the extension of the preparatory stage until 1970. The 1970s proved only worse for the Turkish economy: the heavy obligations Turkey had to assume during the transitional stage, coupled with the adverse effects of the 1973 oil crisis. The ensuing shrinking of world trade further weakened Turkish economy. When the USA imposed sanctions following the intervention in Cyprus in 1974, the Turkish economy came to the brink of collapse. Consequently, in 1978, on the basis of Additional Protocol Article 60, Turkey asked the EEC to postpone its obligations.

Starting with the 1970s, domestic political setting also became a decisive factor in EC/EU–Turkey relations. The consensus on Turkey's integration with the EC did not last long, and different segments of bureaucracy and politics started to voice their opposition as early as the late 1960s. The prevailing political uncertainty, despite the 1971 Turkish military memorandum, only exacerbated the cleavages, rendering relations with the EC a tool for Turkish domestic political disputes. The EC's strong reaction against Turkey's intervention in Cyprus in 1974 (European Commission, 1974a, 1974b; European Parliament, 1974) fueled the opposition and added the 'Cyprus factor' to relations.

EU–Turkey relations witnessed a big shift towards the end of 1970s. One reason was the change in international conjuncture itself. The end of détente, the Soviet invasion of Afghanistan and the Iranian revolution, all reminded the Europeans of Turkey's strategic importance (Aydın-Düzgit and Tocci, 2015: 14). In addition, throughout the 1970s, the EC extended preferential tariff agreements and economic aids to countries Turkey competed with commercially. With its Global Mediterranean Policy in 1972, the EC negotiated a series of bilateral trade and cooperation agreements with several Mediterranean countries (European Institute for Research on Mediterranean on Euro-Arab Cooperation, 2017).[2] Losing its privileged access to European markets put pressures on Turkey. Finally, Greece's acceptance to full membership in 1979 prompted the

Turkish foreign minister to call for a membership application to preempt the difficulties Greece may raise in the future. As this initiative failed due to Turkey's domestic political conflicts, Greece entered EU–Turkey relations as a decisive factor (Çalış, 2016: 174).

Despite the pro-Western discourse of the junta regime following the 1980 military takeover, the EC reacted to Turkey's deteriorating democracy and human rights record and suspended the association in March 1982 (ibid.: 193). The relations have gradually eased in the coming years with the return to democracy. Turkey, driven partly by its now neoliberal economy's need for new markets and aid, applied for full membership in 1987. This was rejected based on the Commission's negative opinion, citing economic and political reasons, especially in the face of the forthcoming single market (European Commission, 1989). Turkey embarked on completing the customs union offered by the EU in its stead, considering it a step to full membership. However, the announcement at the Essen European Council in 1994 that the next enlargement would include Cyprus caused serious disappointment.

The European Commission (1997) has laid out its perspective for the EU's future and, in particular, for enlargement in a document titled "Agenda 2000: For a Stronger and Wider Union." In this document, the European Commission allocated a separate section on the relations with Turkey, where it underlined that the Customs Union has been working satisfactorily. However, due to the political conditions in the country as well as the Cyprus issue, Turkey is left outside of the second wave of enlargement. The decisions of the ensuing Luxembourg Summit reflected by and large the contents of the Agenda 2000. Considering the political and economic conditions of some of the eastern European candidates, Turkey's singling out in the Luxembourg Summit in 1997 was seen in Ankara as clear discrimination and brought relations almost to end of the road.

On the eve of the twenty-first century, EU–Turkey relations became increasingly multifaceted. Not only were the two sides tied with various economic, political and security concerns, but different interests stretching from domestic politics to regional issues and international setting, were influencing relations. With so many moving parts at the same time, Turkey's accession process to the EU came to resemble a Rubik's Cube.

Blossoming relations (1999–2004)

In retrospect, the initial years of Turkey's candidacy until the mid-2000s, is the period when Turkey's relations with the EU have been the most vivid. Turkey has undertaken intense reforms and EU membership has never been so within reach. However, it would be misleading to assume that a steady convergence characterized relations during this period. Widespread hope and optimism in Turkish society overshadowed the bumps in the road. Several issues converged and clouded relations in the following years.

Despite the negative outcome at the Luxembourg Summit, the EU was well aware that it could not alienate Turkey for a long time. Instability in southeast

Europe was influential during this period (Aydın-Düzgit and Tocci, 2015: 18–19). Turkey's active efforts for peace and stability in the Balkans throughout the 1990s, lent credibility to arguments highlighting Turkey's potential contribution to the EU's ESDP.

Political changes in several EU countries also had a significant effect on Turkey's EU bid. In Germany, the CDU, which was largely against Turkey's EU membership, was replaced with a more supportive coalition of the SPD and the Green Party. Equally important was the change in Greece's position towards Turkey. Greece shifted from a veto player to a strategic actor that aimed to resolve its bilateral disputes with Turkey under the EU's conditionality, and therefore supported Turkey's accession process in principle. Although there has been diplomatic tension between 1996 and 1999, relations took an unexpected turn in 1999. Earthquakes and other humanitarian disasters in both countries, not only set the scene for an intense dialogue, but also provided the pretext for a major policy shift. This was reflected in Greece's support for Turkey's candidacy at the Helsinki Council in late 1999 (Tocci, 2004: 127).

During this period Turkey also enjoyed the Clinton administration's active support for its EU candidacy. Prior to the Helsinki Council, the Clinton administration exerted considerable pressure on the EU through formal and informal channels, including phone calls to EU leaders (Sayarı, 2003: 168). On numerous occasions, such as his speech at the OSCE Summit in Istanbul and his speech at the Turkish Grand National Assembly in 1999, President Clinton emphasized Turkey's strategic importance to the West. The Clinton administration's support is considered crucial in turning the tide in favor of Turkey.

Positive signs for Turkey's candidacy came as early as 1998. Following the Cardiff European Council, the European Commission included Turkey to the screening process for accession countries and launched its first Regular Report in November 1998.[3] The Parliament, too, was actively involved in debates on Turkey. Two reports that the European Parliament published on Turkey in late 1998[4] suggest supporting the integration process. While heavy criticisms against Turkey's democracy are abound in these reports, they also emphasize that Turkey's future membership will contribute to peace and security in Europe. In sum, with the removal of the Greek veto and the support of major players, Turkey was granted a candidacy status at the Helsinki Summit in December 1999.

Without delay, in 2000, Turkey established a Secretariat General for EU Affairs[5] for the planning and internal coordination of the harmonization efforts of public institutions. Soon after, Turkey announced its National Programme in 2001 to meet the priority areas identified in the EU's Accession Partnership Document in 2000. While both documents addressed all aspects of the Copenhagen criteria, it was the section on political reforms that attracted the most attention. For that, the National Programme was promising. It set out an ambitious roadmap addressing freedom of thought, expression, assembly, anti-discrimination, human rights and rule of law. And yet, this major societal project did not stay only on paper, but became the first step of an unprecedented reform process.

Over the next five years, Turkey has amended 42 articles of its Constitution in total; 32 articles in 2001, two articles in 2002 and 10 articles in 2004.[6] The constitutional amendments have been accompanied by packages of political reforms, commonly known as the 'Harmonization Packages.' Between February 2002 and July 2004, eight Harmonization Packages have amended 218 articles of 53 laws covering a wide range of political reforms. The packages included several reforms on politically sensitive issues such as the lifting of the death penalty, the removing of obstacles to education and broadcasting in Kurdish. Incentives for the reform process increased in 2003 and 2004, as Turkey struggled to gain a date from the EU to begin accession negotiations.

In 2006, the Parliament passed a final Harmonization Package, amending a further nine laws including the laws on foundations, Ombudsman and the establishment of a Political Ethics Commission in the Parliament. In addition, the Turkish Parliament ratified several international and European conventions during the early 2000s. These include, inter alia; Protocol No. 6 to the European Convention on Human Rights concerning the abolition of the death penalty; International Covenant on Civil and Political Rights; the International Covenant on Economic, Social and Cultural Rights; Council of Europe Criminal Law Convention on Corruption; European Agreement relating to persons participating in proceedings of the European Court of Human Rights and the UN Convention on the Fight Against Corruption. This intense reform period is considered to be Turkey's 'silent revolution' (Independent Commission on Turkey, 2004: 6).

The announcement of Turkey's candidacy provided new dynamics for resolving the Cyprus question as well. For one thing, particularly with the Accession Partnership Document of 2001, there was now a clear linkage between the progress of EU–Turkey relations and the political settlement of the conflict. The political elite in Turkey not only had stronger motives but also more opportunities to make maneuvers on politically sensitive issues. Therefore, Turkey backed the Annan Plan[7] and expressed support for a positive vote prior to referendum in TRNC. However, the Plan collapsed following the 'no' vote of the Greek side.

Turkey's efforts did not go unnoticed in the EU. In 2001, the European Parliament adopted Alain Lamassoure's report on Turkey, in which the Parliament has welcomed the initiation of the constitutional reform process and supported Turkey's right to be involved in the future of Europe debate (European Parliament, 2009: 6). Around the same time, at the Laeken European Council, EU leaders welcomed the progress Turkey has made, in particular on political criteria, and brought forward the prospect of opening accession negotiations (European Council, 2001: par. 12). However, the Seville European Council in June 2002 pointed to the Copenhagen European Council at the end of the year for a possible decision on the next stage of Turkey's candidature. The outcome of the Copenhagen European Council was yet another disappointment for Turkey. Despite Turkey's intense reform efforts, in 2002, EU leaders postponed further the decision on the opening of accession negotiations to the European Council in December 2004. The decision was also made conditional on the Commission's recommendation and on Turkey's fulfilling of the Copenhagen political criteria

(European Council, 2002: par. 19). That said, the Council suggested deepening the EU–Turkey Customs Union and significantly increasing the pre-accession financial assistance to Turkey (ibid.: par. 20). The Commission's Progress Report and its Recommendation on Turkey's progress towards accession were favorable. After a detailed assessment, the Commission concluded that Turkey sufficiently fulfilled the political criteria and accordingly recommended the Council to open the accession negotiations (European Commission, 2004c). EU leaders took this recommendation into consideration and decided that accession talks could begin, but only on October 2005.

The domestic environment in Turkey has been an important parameter determining the pace and direction of EU–Turkey relations. As such, the early 2000s require a more detailed look as those years marked a turbulent period in both Turkey's political and economic situation. The dramatic changes of these years have been decisive in shaping Turkey's abovementioned reforms process.

From 1999 up until 2002, Turkey was ruled by a three-party coalition government. Prime minister's Democratic Left Party (*Demokratik Sol Parti*, DSP) had its reservations on Turkey's accession to the EU due to the customs union and the Cyprus problem. The right-wing coalition partner, Nationalist Action Party (*Milliyetçi Hareket Partisi*, MHP), was even more skeptical with the EU due to its demands on fundamental rights. Only the other coalition partner, Motherland Party (*Anavatan Partisi*, ANAP), openly supported this process. This was an uneasy coalition for Turkey's EU bid. Some of the issues raised as part of the political criteria, especially those pertaining to cultural rights and the abolishing of death penalty, has drawn nationalist reactions. Such issues were still sensitive to different sectors of Turkish society and political actors, as the Kurdish rebel leader was just captured in 1999. These reactions were not limited within the two coalition partners and their constituencies. At the time still an influential actor in Turkish political life, the military was also uncomfortable; especially after the EU made its demands more concrete with its Accession Partnership document. Then Commander of the War Colleges stated that:

> the European Union's demands from us and the demands of the separatist terrorist organization match up with one another. If we accept the EU's demands as they are, Turkey will become incapacitated due to being occupied with problems of reactionism and separatism.
>
> (Hürriyet, 2001)

The coalition, nevertheless, took a number of politically risky decisions, passed the initial harmonization packages and established the EU General Secretariat. However, under the circumstances, it was not easy for this three-party coalition to keep delivering the ambitious reforms necessitated by the accession process. This precarious balance between coalition partners soon shattered with the two major economic crises in November 2000 and February 2001. These crises have several implications extending to Turkey's relations with the EU. First, the crises revealed the deep structural flaws in the Turkish economy.

During the initial years following the crises, the heavy debt burden and its management no doubt had a negative impact on the EU's approach to Turkey. However, the appointment of former Vice President of the World Bank, Kemal Derviş in 2001 as the Minister of Economy and the series of economic reforms he initiated (held by ensuing governments) contributed to the Turkish economy's recovery. The economic success of the following years boosted Turkey's accession.

Equally important was the dramatic change Turkish politics underwent. The existing parties lost substantial power in general elections in November 2002. The newly established Justice and Development Party (*Adalet ve Kalkınma Partisi*, AKP) won 34.4 percent of the votes and 65 percent of the parliamentary seats. Such a majority allowed the AKP to establish a single party government. This was a major breakthrough in Turkish politics, where coalition or minority governments are the rule and single party governments are an exception. The elections results were important not only for bringing political stability to a country that still experienced the hardships of economic crises, but they were also important for enabling the AKP to pursue a reform agenda more rigorously.

The accession process provided various opportunities for the AKP. While the AKP was officially established only in the summer of 2001, many of its members were from Turkey's long-established Islamist political line. The party's founding and current leader, Recep Tayyip Erdoğan, was a former mayor of İstanbul and has been active in politics since the 1970s. The accession process and the reform agenda allowed the AKP to shake off its Islamist reputation in Turkey and in the EU. Therefore, on the one hand, the party attracted liberals and widened its base in Turkey. On the other hand, the promise of more religious freedom and curbing the power of military in political life preserved its traditional conservative base (Aydın-Düzgit and Tocci, 2015: 28). With the accession process, the AKP could consolidate its place vis-à-vis the secularist establishment within a politically acceptable framework. In addition, the AKP enjoyed widespread public support for its reform process as the EU membership bid has become a goal of different sectors of the Turkish society and a unifying project in the country. This gave the AKP the power to pass the politically sensitive reforms rather more easily. Finally, the AKP leadership adopted a new nation-branding for Turkey's partly Western and partly Eastern liminal identity (Rumelili and Süleymanoğlu-Kürüm, 2017). Starting from the early 2000s, Turkish policy-makers have combined representations of Turkey as both Western and Eastern, with an approach to identify Turkey's foreign policy as well as other activities. Accordingly, Turkey started catering to the West in the West and the East in the East. Turkey's EU candidacy and its relations with the EU in this respect have become an important site for this branding.

During this period, the signals the EU sent to Turkey on accession were mixed at best. On the one hand, Turkey was pursuing the common path to full membership, albeit more slowly than the rest. On the other hand, some EU leaders have long been approaching Turkey's accession with suspicion. Probably the strongest and most explicit statements voicing doubts on Turkey came from former French President Giscard d'Estaing. Time and again, d'Estaing stated that Turkey was not a European country, underlined the dissimilarity of Turkey's values to the West, and even claimed that Turkey's entry to the EU would be "the end of Europe" (BBC, 2002).

If it was only the suspicious attitude of some EU leaders, this may have been balanced with more positive statements from other EU leaders and institutions. However, Turkey was also consistently treated separately from the other 12 accession countries. Although Turkey's candidacy coincided with or shortly followed the others, its accession process was singled out from the eastern enlargement. This is clearly visible in the Council's presidency conclusions where the accession process of other countries is considered as one issue, while Turkey's accession process as another. The Council's approach on the distinctiveness of Turkey's accession was reflected to other documents. For instance, Pascal Fontaine's *A New Idea for Europe* also singled Turkey out from the other 12 countries and did not even count it as one of the candidate countries (2000: 25).

The separate treatment of Turkey was not only on paper but was soon accompanied by differences in the accession process. Unlike the other 12 countries that started entry talks soon after the announcement of their candidacy, Turkey waited for a 'date' for its accession negotiations to begin. And even when EU leaders decided, on December 2004, that Turkey sufficiently fulfilled the Copenhagen criteria, they decided on a start date 10 months later. At first, the expectation to start accession negotiations helped sustain the momentum for the reforms. However, the EU's postponing of the decision for two more years caused a big disappointment and left the reformers in Turkey alone. This problem became more acute with the decision to start entry talks. The EU's absorption capacity, somehow the forgotten aspect of the Copenhagen Criteria, was launched again with Turkey's Negotiating Framework in 2004 and later with the European Commission's Enlargement Strategy in 2005. Likewise, the open-ended nature of accession negotiations, though applied to central and eastern European countries, was not underlined as much during the eastern enlargement as it was during Turkey's accession process. Finally, the EU's emphasis in the Negotiating Framework that there may be "long transitional periods, derogations, specific arrangements or permanent safeguard clauses … in areas such as freedom of movement of persons, structural policies or agriculture" (European Council, 2004: par. 12) was discouraging for many of the reformers in Turkey.

The cautious wording of the Negotiating Framework was a reflection of an increasing skepticism towards Turkey's accession. While such skepticism has long existed, the skeptics diversified and became louder as Turkey moved closer to accession negotiations. Various EU leaders now talked about Turkey's economic underdevelopment and its potential impact on EU funds or Turkey's different culture. Others, like the former Christian Social Union (CSU) chairman Edmund Stoiber, argued that there must be a limit to the EU enlargement which is not the Iraqi borders (Peel and Notz, 2002). With the Iraqi war in 2003, as the region destabilized, Turkey came to be seen as a potential importer of instability.

The emphasis on the EU's integration capacity, exit options in the Negotiating Framework and possibility to put future enlargements to referendum in some of the EU countries were also partly a result of the 'enlargement fatigue' after 2004. Whatever the reason was, however, such criteria brought more uncertainty to Turkey's accession prospects and less credibility to the process. References to issues that were not directly related to Copenhagen Criteria and have high symbolic value for Turkish national identity (for example, peaceful settlement of disputes with Armenia and Cyprus) clouded the relations (see Schimmelfennig, 2008 for more debate; European Commission, 2004a, 2004b, 2004c; European Council, 2004). These messages do not only show us that the EU does not see Turkey's destiny unambiguously in the EU (Aydın-Düzgit and Tocci, 2015: 3). More importantly, they provided legitimization for arguments that Turkey could not become an EU member no matter what. In return, this sense of rejection contributed to the slowing down of the reform process.

This change in attitude towards Turkey's accession process was also a reflection of the change of discourse on European foreign policy in the early 2000s. There was now an emphasis on "the need to draw definite borders for the EU" (Cebeci and Schumacher, 2017: 8–9). Further enlargement has come to be perceived as a threat to the European integration. Only a few months before the inception of the Wider Europe initiative, the European Commission's then President Prodi's statement (2002) that the EU "cannot go on enlarging forever," which he considered would "water down the European political project and turn the European Union into just a free trade area on a continental scale," clearly reflects this change in perception vis-à-vis enlargement.

Period of stagnation (2005–2012)

EU–Turkey relations both peaked and reversed in 2005. On the positive side, the start of accession negotiations on 3 October 2005 was welcomed with joy and excitement by most sectors of Turkish politics and society. EU membership was now not a dream but had become an objective within reach. This is because the negotiations were regarded as a final stage preparing the candidate country for accession, the last critical juncture before membership. As then Prime Minister Erdoğan expressed "we passed the most important phase in our 40 years long EU objective" (Hürriyet, 2005).

The negotiations were launched in 2005, with the screening process; the analytical examination of the EU's acquis to identify the areas where progress is needed. The actual negotiations to harmonize Turkey's legislation with the EU's acquis began in 2006. The negotiations are by and large a technical process managed by the Commission officials and the accession country's bureaucrats. However, the opening of each chapter requires a unanimous decision of the Council, which makes the progress of the negotiations a political decision.

During the first couple of years, hopes were still alive, and the negotiations proceeded, albeit slowly. After opening one chapter in 2006, five chapters were opened in 2007, four in 2008 and two in 2009. As it will be discussed in Chapter

6, this is also the period when the EU emphasized the role of civil society organizations as important actors in Turkey's accession process. In parallel with this, Turkey has taken limited steps to involve civil society organizations in the negotiations. Once the screening process was completed, the Chief Negotiator called selected civil society organizations to submit a sample Negotiation Position Paper.[8] Those who submitted a paper were then invited to a meeting at the General Secretariat for EU Affairs once the final position paper was completed. While this may suggest a degree of consultation, in reality, civil society organizations' involvement in the accession process was very limited. First, the meetings at the General Secretariat for EU Affairs took place once Turkey's Position Paper was completed. Therefore, there were no further discussions on the paper. Second, as the final position papers had to be confidential, it was not possible to assess whether or to what degree the opinions of civil society organizations were taken into account. Third, the invitations were usually sent with only a few days' notice, giving hardly any time to prepare. Finally, there were no defined procedures as to which civil society organizations were included in this process (Zihnioğlu, 2013: 80).

On the negative side, as of 2005 the 'Cyprus factor' started to affect the course of EU–Turkey relations. In 2005, Turkey had to extend the Ankara Association Agreement with an Additional Protocol to those countries that acceded to the EU in 2004. However, in conjunction with the Additional Protocol, Turkey made a declaration that the signing of the Additional Protocol does not mean the recognition of the 'Republic of Cyprus' by any means. The Commission's Progress Report on November 2006 underlined that Turkey does not fulfill its commitments under the Additional Protocol by denying access to its ports to vessels flying the Republic of Cyprus flag or applying similar restrictions in the field of air transport (European Commission, 2006: 24). Following this report and the Commission's recommendation on November 29, the General Affairs and External Relations Council decided to suspend negotiations on eight chapters[9] relevant to Turkey's restrictions and to not close the other chapters until Turkey fulfills its commitments. The European Council endorsed the Council's conclusions on Turkey as they are (European Council, 2006: point 10). This became the breaking point in EU–Turkey relations. From this point onwards, Turkey gradually estranged itself from the EU and relations never became as lively again as they had been during the early 2000s.

The shadow of the Council's 'Cyprus decision' was not the only issue souring relations. Several other factors, issues and developments from both sides contributed to Turkey's eventual estrangement. First, the shy skepticism towards Turkey's accession during the early years of its candidacy started to be expressed more loudly. Several EU politicians from Austria, the Netherlands, Germany and more joined in this chorus. Especially, Merkel's election in Germany in 2005 and Sarkozy in France in 2007, added a different dimension to this skepticism.

A prominent matter of debate during these years was privileged partnership. While the former French President Valéry Giscard d'Estaing had earlier suggested privileged partnership with Turkey as an alternative to its membership to the Union (Lannes, 2000), it was with Merkel that the issue came to the fore. Although Germany officially supported Turkey's EU bid under Schröder's administration, his successor and the leader of the German Christian Democrats (CDU) was not of the same opinion. In her letter to other center-right leaders in the EU in September 2004, Chancellor-to-be Merkel called the leaders to block Turkey's full membership and to offer instead a privileged partnership (Carter, 2004). Merkel renewed her call for privileged partnership in the coming years as well.

Chancellor Merkel's calls were reciprocated by the French President Sarkozy. Skepticism to Turkey's EU membership had already been prevalent among French politicians before Sarkozy. However, it was President Sarkozy who systematically opposed Turkey's full membership, starting from his election campaign, and he took actual steps to block it once in power. In a televised interview in December 2004, following the EU's decision to start accession negotiations with Turkey, President Sarkozy repeated his proposals for privileged partnership instead of full membership and notoriously said that "If Turkey was European, we would know it."[10] In the following years, he continued his discourse and argued that "Turkey has no place in the European Union because it is not a European country" (Sarkozy, 2007). In 2007, Sarkozy blocked the opening of negotiations on five chapters on the grounds that they are directly related with membership,[11] and proposed to take Turkey's entry to referendum.

Others in the EU joined Merkel and Sarkozy in their bid to block Turkey's membership. Austria's Freedom Party adopted the slogan, "No to Turkey," while Bulgaria's National Union Attack Party used anti-Turkish slogans in its campaign. Hans-Gert Pöttering, at the time of his Presidency of the European Parliament, stated that "politically, culturally, financially and geographically, it would be too much to have Turkey as a member of the European Union" (Dempsey, 2009). In addition, starting from 2004, the EU stopped inviting Turkey to the Summits. Finally, on December 2009, Cyprus declared that it would block the opening of six further chapters[12] (Republic of Turkey Ministry of Foreign Affairs, 2013). As a result, the accession negotiations reached a stagnation point. But more importantly, Turkish officials and the public began to question both the EU's will and the credibility of the membership reward.

The reform process continued on and off during these years. The EU commended the Kurdish opening, followed by several improvements in cultural rights, as well as opening to Armenia in 2009. However, the reform process had lost its pace. The slowdown and at times regression in democratic principles also blurred the relations. For instance, the closure case against the AKP in 2008 received strong reactions from across the board in the EU. Commissioner for Enlargement, Olli Rehn, said the EU may review Turkey's negotiating process "in case of a serious and persistent breach of EU political and human rights criteria" (Hürriyet, 2008), insinuating in an unprecedented way that the accession process may be suspended.

It is important to remember that the years following 2004 have been turbulent for the EU as well. There is no doubt that the several challenges the EU have faced since then have had impact on its approach to Turkey. First, the 'big-bang' accession in 2004 led to an enlargement fatigue among some member states as well as EU institutions. The failure of the Constitutional Treaty in 2005 accompanied this. This was followed by the subsequent efforts to first draft and then ratify the Lisbon Reform Treaty. Finally, the financial crisis that hit a number of EU countries revealed the shortcomings of the Eurozone. In return, the EU has become introverted.

With the start of negotiations, Turkey's interest in the accession process gradually waned as well. The reforms slowed down considerably after 2005. In addition, some of the leading members of the governing AKP were very critical of the EU and even adopted an anti-EU discourse. While then-Prime Minister Erdoğan acknowledged this slowdown in his meetings with his European counterparts (Çalış, 2016: 408–410), he did not do much to revive the reform process. In a way, the AKP's policies and discourse during the second half of the 2000s, rather favored the freezing of relations (Aydın-Düzgit and Tocci, 2015: 29). During this period, Erdoğan and other government officials frequently said that they would change the name of the Copenhagen Criteria to the Ankara Criteria and continue with the reforms even if the EU does not take in Turkey. Although this rhetoric on the surface may suggest the political leadership's commitment to the reform process, its repeated use implies that the main goal is not EU membership.

Several reasons contribute to this policy change. First, it is during these years that Turkish foreign policy began to change with openings to its neighborhood, especially to the Middle East and Africa (Cop and Zihnioğlu, 2017). Turkey increasingly started to spend more time, energy and resources in improving its relations with various countries in these regions, with a growing tension of Europeanization and Euro-Asianism in Turkish foreign policy (Öniş and Yılmaz, 2009). Ironically, Turkey declared 2005, the year it started accession negotiations with the EU, as the 'Year of Africa.' Indeed, as a result of this, starting from 2007, these openings triggered a new debate in Turkey questioning whether the main orientation of Turkish foreign policy has changed. In domestic discussions, the term "shift of axis" was coined. This term suggested a shift from the traditional Western oriented foreign policy that had been hallmark of Turkish foreign policy to the east, in particular to former Ottoman territory.

Second, the AKP became immersed in a number of domestic problems directly involving itself. In 2007, as the incumbent President Sezer's term in office drew to an end, the question of who his successor will be dominated the political agenda. The AKP's nomination of then Foreign Minister Abdullah Gül as the presidential candidate got strong reactions from the secular establishment and led to a months-long crisis. The main opposition CHP boycotted the vote in the Parliament and then appealed to the Constitutional Court for the annulment of the vote. The Constitutional Court upheld the CHP's claim that a quorum of 367 attendees was required for the first round to be valid, as opposed to a normal legislative quorum of 184. In the meantime, the General Staff released a controversial statement, branded as an e-memorandum or e-coup by critics. The statement said the military had been watching the presidential election with concern and reminded the politicians that the military was the ultimate guardian of secularism. The nomination and the likely election of Abdullah Gül aroused secular sectors of Turkish society and led to mass protests in support of state secularism. These protests, known as, Republican Rallies (*Cumhuriyet Mitingleri*) took place in several Turkish provinces[13] in April and May 2007, gathering "hundreds of thousands of people" (BBC, 2007). The AKP has overcome this opposition by calling an early general election, winning a landslide victory and then re-nominating Gül.

The problems for the AKP continued in 2008, when Turkey's chief prosecutor filed a lawsuit claiming that the AKP became the focal point of anti-secular activities, demanded its closure and the banning of several officials, including Prime Minister Erdoğan and President Abdullah Gül. The Constitutional Court remained one vote short of necessary consensus to bring the party's closure, but instead decided to cut the state funding to the AKP. These crises not only shifted the AKP's focus away from the accession process but, more importantly, challenged by several actors of the secular establishment, the AKP's domestic priority became the consolidation of its place in the political system rather than pursuing the reform process.

Third, in the 2007 general elections the AKP increased its votes from 34 to 46 percent. It has been argued that with this electoral victory, the AKP emerged even stronger both in society and against the secularist establishment (Öniş, 2010: 9). Accordingly, the AKP eventually felt more self-confident and less dependent on the EU and the reform process in widening and strengthening its base in the country.

During this period Turkish society's support in joining the EU fell steadily. Those who thought Turkey's membership in the EU will be something good fell from 71 percent in 2004, to around 50 percent in 2006 and 2007, and to 42 percent by 2008. On the other hand, almost one in every three people (29 percent) thought EU membership will be something bad (Eurobarometer, 2008: 20). The reasons for this fall might be multiple. For example, politically sensitive issues becoming part of the accession process, the subsequent anti-EU statements of politicians across the board, slowing down of the accession process or the media's loss of interest. What is important is that with public support steadily shrinking, it became easier for the AKP to shelve Turkey's EU bid.

Starting from this point, EU–Turkey relations no longer moved forward with its own dynamics. In the following years, Turkey's relations with the EU remained at a low profile, with few exceptions like the initiation of a visa liberalization process. Even though the AKP embraced the EU as "the biggest modernization move since the founding of the Republic" in its new government programme (Turkish Grand National Assembly, 2011), relations were routinized after the 2011 general elections: The Commission would publish its annual progress report, then Turkey would respond, sometimes react and if necessary make counter arguments. The media interest would be short-lived and especially if it involved strong reactions like tossing the report out in a live broadcast.

38 *The recent history of EU–Turkey relations*

In the hopes of breaking through the stagnation of Turkey's accession process, the European Commission launched a new process called Positive Agenda in May 2012. The Positive Agenda aimed at complementing the accession process through potential cooperation areas such as political reforms, energy, visa liberalization and the fight against terrorism. In addition, in June 2012, foreign ministers of the 16 EU member states published a jointly signed article in the Turkish daily *Hürriyet*. In this article, the foreign ministers underlined the shared interests in the region, the mutual responsibilities and the need to improve dialogue (Çalış, 2016: 438). However, both initiatives remain symbolic. The EU took no concrete step to move Turkey's accession forward. After the single chapter opened for negotiations in 2010, no new chapters would be opened until late 2013.

Turbulent years (2013–2019)

Starting from 2013, EU–Turkey relations are marked by a series of sharp ups and downs. This is because relations have been straying away from the membership objective. In the following years, even the extra efforts of the EU (Positive Agenda in 2011) and Turkey (New EU Strategy in 2014) could not succeed to revive the accession process. The relations are now increasingly viewed in a transactional manner. In return, the external factors are becoming more determinative in shaping the relations, which leads to sudden rapprochement and still more sudden estrangement.

Turkey's disinterest in EU membership has become explicit in Erdoğan's statements during this period. In a meeting with journalists in early 2013, Erdoğan said,

> The EU wants to forget us, but it holds back, it cannot forget us. However, if they make public [that they do not want us], we will be relieved. Instead of wasting our time, make it public, so that we get on.
>
> (Hürriyet, 2013)

This disinterest has become more evident as Erdoğan made successive calls for Turkey to be allowed into the Shanghai Cooperation Organisation (SCO). In a joint press conference with the Russian President Putin, Erdoğan repeated his request and told Putin to "save us from the trouble" of trying to enter the EU (Hürriyet Daily News, 2013). Whether or not Turkey's membership in the SCO is a realistic objective, it is noteworthy that Erdoğan presents the SCO as an alternative to the EU.

Relations were further shaken by EU leaders' strong reactions condemning excessive and disproportionate use of police force during the Gezi protests in May and June 2013. The Commission's annual progress report and the European Parliament's resolution expressed similar concern, calling authorities to guarantee freedom of expression, peaceful assembly and peaceful protest. However, hard feelings were put aside when Turkey and the EU launched a visa liberalization dialogue and signed a readmission agreement in December 2013. Under the readmission agreement, Turkey accepted taking back those irregular immigrants that reached the EU through Turkish territory and repatriate them to their country of origin. But for Turkey, readmission was linked with membership to the EU. Turkey declared that it would not sign or implement the agreement unless the EU takes steps towards visa liberalization to Turkish citizens. Therefore, the readmission agreement went together with a visa liberalization dialogue that aims to eliminate the visa obligation currently imposed on Turkish citizens. The dialogue is based on a roadmap that lists the criteria Turkey needs to meet. The readmission agreement and the roadmap are very concrete in what is expected from Turkey, while visa liberalization is not based on a foreseeable schedule. In addition, the process is open ended. Nonetheless, Turkey considered this a breakthrough in the relations.

The importance attached to the visa liberalization process is not without reason. Research (Economic Development Foundation, 2018) suggests that close to 40 percent of those who support Turkey's accession to the EU do so because they want to benefit from the free movement to, the right of settlement and educational opportunities in the EU. This process is important not only because of the value Turkish people attach to mobility to and within the EU. In addition, all accession countries, except for Turkey, enjoy visa-free travel to Schengen countries and accordingly visa liberalization is commonly considered a step for all accession countries. The value that government officials have attached to the start of the visa liberalization process stem from its significance in relation to both the accession process and the public opinion.

Turkey declared 2014 as the 'Year of Europe' and in a new government programme then Prime Minister Davutoğlu designated 2023 (the Republic's 100th anniversary) as the target date for full membership. Soon after, Turkey also announced the New EU Strategy to accelerate the accession process. With its focus on political reforms, socio-economic change and a communications strategy directed towards both Turkish and EU citizens, the New Strategy was in fact bringing forward those issues that were already under way.

However, the positive winds in the direction of the EU were not blowing strong enough. For much of 2014, Turkish politics, media and society were occupied with presidential elections, where Erdoğan became the first popularly elected president. In 2014, the EU itself was busy with European parliamentary elections and later the formation of the Commission. Even worse for EU–Turkey relations was that Juncker's new Commission acknowledged there will be no enlargement of the Union for the next five years. To emphasize the five-year hold on enlargement, DG Enlargement changed its name to 'European Neighbourhood Policy and Enlargement Negotiations.' All in all, no progress has been achieved in accession negotiations in 2014. In 2015, the European Parliament's report describing the 1915 events as genocide resulted in a short crisis and Turkey canceled the Joint Parliamentary Committee's meeting early the next year.

Further developments in 2015 show us how EU–Turkey relations are increasingly treated as transactional by both sides (see Chapter 3 for a more detailed discussion). The World Bank's evaluation of and suggestions on the EU–Turkey Customs Union led to new efforts on its revision. Turkey already had growing concerns over the expected impact of the then-discussed free trade agreement between the EU and the USA, while the EU saw the potential benefit of an upgraded customs union with Turkey. As a result, the EU and Turkey agreed to start preparations for future talks to modernize the EU–Turkey Customs Union. While Turkey's entry to the EU would have alleviated Turkey's concerns and satisfied the EU's expectations, the discussions on the revision of the Customs Union gradually detached themselves from the accession process. Since then the modernization talks have become a separate item in the agenda of EU–Turkey relations.

An even more important development in 2015 was the massive influx of migrants and refugees into Europe. More than one million people arrived in the EU in 2015, fleeing from war in Syria, but also conflict and hardship elsewhere in the Middle East and Africa. This sparked a crisis in the EU over how best to resettle these people, while countries struggled to deal with the thousands arriving at their shores or borders every day. At this point, all eyes turned to Turkey, as Turkey emerged as a principal transit country. Commissioners Timmermans, Hahn and Avramopoulos's visit in October was followed by Chancellor Merkel a week later. There were also claims in the press that Commission President Juncker stepped in to delay the publishing of the 2015 progress report three times to keep Erdoğan on board with the plans to stem migration (Barker and Wagstyl, 2015; Hürriyet, 2015).

This rapprochement suited the AKP as well. At home, Turkey was in the midst of a political deadlock after the general elections in June and in the run-up to new elections in November. Abroad, the rift with Russia over Syria was widening. Turkey's shooting down of a Russian jet near the Turkish–Syrian border in late November triggered a major crisis between the two countries. As a result, "the swing of Erdoğan's foreign policy pendulum between Brussels and Shanghai for the first time after years was oscillating in the direction of Brussels" (Çalış, 2016: 490).

The EU and Turkey held the first Summit in the context of the migration crisis on 29 November 2015. In the Joint Statement of the Summit, Turkey and the EU agreed to revitalize the accession process (one chapter opened to negotiations two weeks after), to hold EU–Turkey Summits twice a year and political dialogues at the ministerial level. The EU also pledged three billion euro of financial assistance to be used for Syrians under protection in Turkey.

A bigger deal came with the Statement as a result of the third Summit on 18 March 2016. With this Statement, Turkey agreed to take back all new irregular migrants crossing from Turkey into five Greek islands starting from 20 March 2016. In return, for every Syrian being returned to Turkey, one Syrian from Turkey will be resettled to the EU based on the UN Vulnerability Criteria. The EU also accepted to mobilize an additional three billion euro of funding for Syrians in Turkey. In addition, the two sides agreed to accelerate the visa liberalization efforts, repeated their commitment to revitalize the accession process (one other chapter opened to negotiations in June 2016) and welcomed the ongoing work on modernizing the customs union.

This deal eventually worked for the EU and the number of irregular immigrants transiting through Turkey dropped from thousands to a few per day. This was a pragmatic bargain between the EU and Turkey. The EU stopped the migration before it reaches its borders and EU politicians enjoy the political benefits of reducing the flow of migrants. On the other hand, Turkey needs the earmarked funds and wants the other benefits. Indeed, although Turkey's expectations on visa liberalization and reinvigorating the accession process have not been fulfilled and even with relations having worsened in the following years, the deal remains in place because both sides find continuation of the deal in their interest. However, EU–Turkey relations are no more a broader rules-based relationship anchored in the accession process. It is now a transactional relationship in areas of mutual interest and for as long as those interests are considered valid. This was made explicit in the words of Merkel, who, ahead of her visit in October 2015, said that Turkey's help was needed to stop the refugee flow, but that this had not changed her view on Turkey's EU bid. "I have always been against EU membership, President Erdoğan knows this, and I still am" (Hürriyet Daily News, 2015).

In July 2016, Turkey was shaken by a military coup attempt. While the elected government thwarted the putsch for the first time in Turkey's modern history, the ensuing developments heightened tensions between Turkey and the EU. First, soon after the coup attempt, EU leaders and officials expressed their full support to Turkey's democratically elected government. However, their rather slow reaction to the events unfolding on the night of the coup attempt, rather than an outright condemnation of the putsch, has been a subject of criticism by Turkish officials.

More alarming for the EU and individual member states were the extraordinary measures that the government adopted after the failed coup. Less than a week after, on 20 July, the Turkish Parliament declared a state of emergency, which allowed the President to rule by decree and the authorities to restrict civic space by banning gatherings. A state of emergency was adopted initially for three months,[14] to investigate the coup attempt and coup plotters in a more efficient way. The government holds the Muslim cleric, Fethullah Gülen, who lives in self-imposed exile in the USA, responsible for the attempted coup. However, as the crackdown expanded in the following months in a massive purge of civil servants, military officials, academicians and civil society organizations, many in the EU became concerned that it extended beyond coup plotters and had become a tool to silence or intimidate critics. The tensions increased especially when EU citizens were put behind bars.

It is important to remember that several EU member states, including France, Germany and the Netherlands have had elections in 2017. Turkey held a referendum in 2017 and general elections in 2018. The use of strong language against one another during the electoral and referendum campaigns added further tension to the already strained relations. As a result, Turkey's relations with a number of

EU member states hit rock bottom in 2017 and through most of 2018, while relations with many others faltered.

In 2017, Turkey's relations with Germany have slid into unchartered waters of crisis. On the one hand, in January, the news that 40 Turkish military officials had applied for asylum in Germany sparked a year-long conflict between the two countries. More news followed in the coming months of hundreds of other people seeking asylum in Germany and of whom Turkey accused of playing a role in the failed military coup. Germany's decision to grant asylum to some military officials has further heightened tensions (Toksabay, 2017; Deutsche Welle, 2017). On the other hand, the German daily *Die Welt* journalist Deniz Yücel's detention in February has spurred strong reaction in Berlin. In the following months, dozens of other German citizens were detained in Turkey on charges of links to terrorist groups and terrorist propaganda. Relations between the two countries deteriorated sharply in the run-up to the referendum in Turkey in mid-April.

Germany did not give permission for political rallies of Turkish government officials to address the Turkish diaspora ahead of the referendum. In reaction to this, President Erdoğan accused Germany of Nazi-style practices. Turkey also featured in Germany's electoral campaigns in fall 2017. The SPD leader Martin Schulz's call for an end to accession talks with Turkey prompted Chancellor Merkel to call for a suspension of the talks (Sloat, 2018). Amid coalition negotiations in late 2017, Foreign Minister Gabriel said, "alternative forms of closer cooperation" (Saeed, 2017) were needed if full membership is not an option and suggested post-Brexit UK can be a model for Turkey.

In May, Turkey prevented a German parliamentary delegation from visiting the German troops stationed at the NATO's İncirlik base in Turkey – which led Germany to withdraw its troops from Turkey. The row over access to the base in Konya was resolved after NATO Secretary General Jens Stoltenberg intervened. However, in July, with Germany blocking Erdoğan's rally to address the Turks on the sidelines of the G20 Summit in Hamburg and the detention of Peter Steudtner in İstanbul with other human rights activists, relations have sunk from bad to worse. In the months that followed, Germany took further steps, such as blocking the modernization of the Customs Union, calling to reduce pre-accession assistance and to be more selective in European Investment Bank loans. The tensions eased over in the fall, especially after the former Chancellor Gerhard Schröder visited President Erdoğan at the request of the German Foreign Minister Gabriel to broker Steudtner's release from jail in Turkey. Other German detainees were also released later in 2017.

Relations with other EU countries were also strained in 2016 and 2017, with EU leaders calling the EU to end the accession process. Most prominently, Austria reacted strongly to a crackdown following the coup attempt and urged the EU to end the membership talks with Turkey. Some others in the EU, however, disagree. For instance, Foreign Ministers from Finland, and Lithuania argue that the suspension of the membership talks would not be helpful and that the negotiations should continue (BBC, 2017).

There has been diplomatic tension between Turkey and the Netherlands shortly before the Dutch general elections and the Turkish referendum. The Dutch authorities refused to give the Turkish Foreign Minister Çavuşoğlu's plane the permission to land ahead of a rally and blocked the Turkish Family and Social Policies Minister Sayan Kaya from entering the Turkish consulate. Erdoğan called the Dutch authorities "Nazi remnants" for keeping the government officials from campaigning to Turkish diaspora. The level of diplomatic representation was lowered in both countries.

In addition, the European Parliament also toughened its stance towards Turkey in 2016, following the detention of members of parliament from the HDP and the arrests at *Cumhuriyet* daily, including its editor-in-chief. In November 2016, the European Parliament issued a resolution calling on the Commission and the member states for "a temporary freeze of the ongoing accession negotiations with Turkey" (European Parliament, 2016: point 1). In 2017, the European Parliament has voted to cut €105 million from the 2018 budget of the pre-accession assistance allocated to Turkey (see Chapter 3 for a more detailed discussion). It also decided to place another €70 million in reserve. In October 2018, the Parliament passed a motion to transfer this €70 million earmarked for Turkey to European Neighbourhood Instrument and to fulfill part of the EU pledge for Syria.

The EU was not alone in its concerns and criticisms against the recent developments in Turkey. In April 2017, the Parliamentary Assembly of the Council of Europe (PACE) adopted a resolution where it expressed serious concerns "about the respect for human rights, democracy and the rule of law" (Council of Europe Parliamentary Assembly, 2017: point 28). With this resolution, PACE reopened the monitoring procedure against Turkey, a process it had closed in 2004, until these concerns "are addressed in a satisfactory manner." In addition, the Venice Commission under the Council of Europe has set out its concerns in a report on the proposed constitutional changes before the constitutional referendum. The Commission concluded that the changes would "lead to an excessive concentration of executive power in the hands of the president and the weakening of parliamentary control of that power" (Venice Commission, 2017: point 47).

Bilateral relations were on the move in 2018, although the results were mixed. In September President Erdoğan made his first official visit to Germany in four years. Although much of the differences between two leaders remained unsolved, many regarded this visit as the beginning of a normalization process. This was followed by the German Economy Minister's visit to Ankara. After the meetings, economy ministers from both countries decided on measures to accelerate the bilateral economic relations.

In January 2018, President Erdoğan visited France to improve bilateral relations, where French President Macron expressed discouraging remarks for Turkey's EU bid. President Macron noted that currently, the accession process "does not allow for an outcome in the coming years" (France 24, 2018). He suggested, therefore, that the EU should develop a 'partnership' with Turkey instead of full membership. In 2018, Turkey's relations with the Netherlands have been normalizing following high-level dialogue, and with both countries reinstating their ambassadors in Ankara and the Hague.

Since 2018, Turkey's relations with several EU countries are on the mend, although the accession process has effectively come to a standstill. No new chapters have been opened since June 2016. The Council "notes that Turkey has been moving further away from the European Union" and therefore "no further chapters can be considered for opening or closing" (General Affairs Council, 2018: point 35). The focus in Turkey's relations with individual EU countries has been on bilateral issues, such as trade and economy, rather than Turkey's EU bid. When EU relations are brought to the agenda, the emphasis is often on cooperation and dialogue in certain areas, other than membership talks. Turkey is seen as a key partner, rather than an accession country. Even if EU leaders may be uncomfortable with Turkey's deteriorating democracy, it does not seem that they will let this overshadow the bilateral relations and cooperation with the EU. As we will discuss in more detail in the next chapter, the approach to the current issues and challenges between Turkey and the EU has become increasingly a transactional one.

This overview shows us that there is now a wide range of factors that influence EU–Turkey relations. As the membership perspective becomes blurred, the EU's leverage diminishes, and the relations are more exposed to the influences of these factors. As a result, the trajectory of relations have become less predictable with sharp ups and downs. Civil society is important because it can provide a consistent avenue of dialogue and interaction at a time when the relations have been frayed and official channels of communication are neither stable nor effective. The civil society dimension is particularly important during times of crisis, when the political elite at both sides adopt either anti-Western or anti-Turkish discourse.

This chapter also demonstrates how the EU anchor lost its significance in Turkey and, with that, norm-based relations gave way to one that is utility-based. As the EU lost its normative appeal, there is an ever more need for norm-carriers in Turkey – a role that strong, rights-based civic groups may be a candidate for.

Notes

1 During these early years, the only major group opposing the agreement was the left leaning Workers Party of Turkey.
2 As part of the Global Mediterranean Policy, the EEC signed agreements with Israel in 1975; with Morocco, Algeria and Tunisia in 1976; and with Egypt, Jordan, Lebanon and Syria in 1977.
3 The Regular Report was renamed first as Progress Report and later as Report.
4 McMillan-Scott Report (16 September 1998) and Swoboda Report (3 December 1998).
5 The Secretariat General for EU Affairs was replaced with Ministry for EU Affairs in 2011. The Ministry for EU Affairs was subsumed under the Ministry of Foreign Affairs as a Directorate in 2018.
6 Articles 38 and 87 have been amended twice, once in 2001 and later in 2004.
7 The Annan Plan was revealed by the UN Secretary-General Kofi Annan on 11 November 2002. It was subsequently revised several times. The final version was voted in separate referenda on both sides of the island on 24 April 2004.

8 The Negotiation Position Paper for a given chapter outlines the accession country's level of harmonization, harmonization efforts foreseen as well as the timeline and financing.
9 These chapters are: Chapter 1: Free Movement of Goods; Chapter 3: Right of Establishment and Freedom to Provide Service; Chapter 9: Financial Services; Chapter 11: Agriculture and Rural Development; Chapter 13: Fisheries; Chapter 14: Transport Policy; Chapter 29: Customs Union and Chapter 30: External Relations.
10 See http://discours.vie-publique.fr/notices/043003247.html for the text of the interview with Nicolas Sarkozy.
11 Agriculture and Rural Development (it had been blocked also due to Additional Protocol); Economic and Monetary Policy; Regional Policy and Coordination of Structural Instruments; Financial and Budgetary Provisions; Institutions. The vetoes on Regional Policy and Coordination of Structural Instruments and Economic and Monetary Policy were later lifted and the negotiations on these two chapters started in 2013 and 2015, respectively.
12 Freedom of Movement for Workers; Energy; Judiciary and Fundamental Rights; Justice, Freedom and Security; Education and Culture; Foreign, Security and Defence Policy.
13 Ankara (14 April), İstanbul (29 April), Manisa (5 May), Çanakkale (5 May), İzmir (13 May), Samsun (20 May), Denizli (26 May).
14 A state of emergency was extended seven times and remained in force for two years.

Bibliography

Aydın-Düzgit, S. and Tocci, N. (2015) *Turkey and the European Union*. London: Palgrave Macmillan.
Barker, A. and Wagstyl, S. (2015) EU Sidelines Critical Turkey Report as it Seeks Migration Deal, *Financial Times* (16 October) www.ft.com/content/1b4044b8-7415-11e5-bdb1-e6e4767162cc.
BBC. (2007) Huge Rally for Turkish Secularism, (29 April) http://news.bbc.co.uk/2/hi/6604643.stm.
BBC. (2002) Turkey Entry "Would Destroy EU" *BBC News World Edition* (8 November) http://news.bbc.co.uk/2/hi/europe/2420697.stm.
BBC. (2017) AB'de Türkiye ile müzakerelerin durdurulmasý çaðrýlarýna kim, ne diyor? (8 September) www.bbc.com/turkce/haberler-dunya-41193397.
Çalýş, Þ. (2016) *Türkiye – Avrupa Birliði Ýliþkileri: Kimlik Arayýþý, Politik Aktörler ve Deðiþim* (5th ed.). Ankara: Nobel Yayýnlarý.
Carter, R. (2004) Top German Conservative Rallies Centre-Right Opposition to Turkey, *EU Observer* (17 September) https://euobserver.com/enlargement/17312.
Cebeci, M. and Schumacher, T. (2017) The EUs Construction of the Mediterranean (2003–2007) *Medreset Working Papers No. 3*.
Cop, B. and Zihnioğlu, Ö. (2017) Turkish Foreign Policy under AKP Rule: Making Sense of the Turbulence, *Political Studies Review*, 15(1), pp. 28–38.
Council of Europe Parliamentary Assembly. (2017) *The Functioning of Democratic Institutions in Turkey*. Resolution 2156 (25 April 2017). Strasbourg: Council of Europe.
Dempsey, J. (2009) Merkel's Party Eases Anti-Turkish Stance, *New York Times* (2 June) http://query.nytimes.com/gst/fullpage.html?res=9500E5D9143AF931A35755C0A96F9C8B63.
Deutsche Welle. (2017) Kriz Yýlý Sona Eriyor ... Peki ya Kriz? (22 December) www.dw.com/tr/kriz-y%C4%B1l%C4%B1-sona-eriyor-peki-ya-kriz/a-41895079.

Economic Development Foundation. (2018) *Türkiye Kamuoyunda AB Desteği ve Avrupa Algısı [Perception of Europe and Support for EU Membership in Turkish Public Opinion]*. Public Opinion Survey 2017. Publication No: 295. İstanbul: Economic Development Foundation.

Eurobarometer. (2008) *Eurobarometer 70 Fall 2008 National Report Turkey.*

European Commission. (1974a) *Statement on Cyprus by the European Commission.* Information Bulletin of Community Spokesman No 182 of 17.7.1974.

European Commission. (1974b) *Statement on Cyprus by the Ministers of Foreign Affairs of Nine.* Information Bulletin of Community Spokesman No. 188 of 23.7.1974.

European Commission. (1989) *Opinion on Turkey's Request for Accession to the Community.* Brussels: European Commission.

European Commission. (1997) *Agenda 2000: For a Stronger and Wider Union.* Luxembourg: European Communities.

European Commission. (2004a) *Turkey 2004 Regular Report*, SEC (2004) 1201, Brussels: European Commission.

European Commission. (2004b) *Issues Arising from Turkey's Membership Perspective*, SEC (2004) 1202, Brussels: European Commission.

European Commission. (2004c) *Communication from the Commission to the Council, the European Parliament, Recommendation of the European Commission on Turkey's Progress Towards Accession.* Brussels: European Commission.

European Commission. (2006) *Commission Staff Working Document Turkey 2006 Progress Report*, Brussels (8 November). SEC (2006) 1390.

European Council. (2001) Presidency Conclusions European Council Meeting in Laeken 14 and 15 December 2001. Brussels.

European Council. (2002) *Copenhagen European Council 12 and 13 December 2002 Presidency Conclusions.* Brussels.

European Council. (2004) *Brussels European Council, 25–26 March, Presidency Conclusions*, 9048/04, Brussels: European Council.

European Council. (2006) *Presidency Conclusions, 14–15 December 2006*, 16879/06, Brussels: European Council.

European Institute for Research on Mediterranean on Euro-Arab Cooperation. (2017) *Euro-Mediterranean Cooperation (Historical)* www.medea.be/en/themes/euro-mediterranean-cooperation/euro-mediterranean-cooperation-historical/.

European Parliament. (1974) *Steps to Safeguard the Independence and Freedom of Cyprus-Association with Cyprus.* EP Docs. 243/74 and 245/74 of 13.9.1974.

European Parliament. (2009) *Information Note on the Work of the EU–Turkey Joint Parliamentary Committee.* www.europarl.europa.eu/cmsdata/121561/D-TR%20history%20through%202009.pdf.

European Parliament. (2016) *Resolution of 24 November 2016 on EU–Turkey Relations* (2016/2993(RSP)).

Fontaine, P. (2000) *A New Idea for Europe, European Documentation Series.* Luxembourg: Office for Official Publications of the European Communities.

France 24. (2018) Macron Suggests "Partnership" with EU for Turkey, not Membership, (5 January) www.france24.com/en/20180105-french-president-macron-suggests-partnership-deal-turkey-eu-not-membership-erdogan.

General Affairs Council. (2018) *Council Conclusions on Enlargement and Stabilisation and Association Process as adopted. 26 June 2018.* No. prev. doc. 10374/18. 10555/18.

Hürriyet. (2001) Bölücüyle AB'nin İstekleri Örtüşüyor, (13 January), www.hurriyet.com.tr/bolucuyle-abnin-istekleri-ortusuyor-39216168.

Hürriyet. (2005) Erdoğan: Türkiye Dev Bir Adım Daha Atmıştır, (3 October) http://webarsiv.hurriyet.com.tr/2005/10/03/hurriyetim.asp.
Hürriyet. (2008) Rehn warns Turkey on Closure Case Against Ruling Party, (29 March) www.hurriyet.com.tr/rehn-warns-turkey-on-closure-case-against-ruling-party-8574883.
Hürriyet. (2013) Şangay Beşlisi'ne alın AB'yi unutalım, (26 January) www.hurriyet.com.tr/sangay-beslisine-alin-abyi-unutalim-22448548.
Hürriyet. (2015) Avrupa Birliği Türkiye İlerleme Raporu'nu Yaýnladı, (10 November) www.hurriyet.com.tr/dunya/ve-ab-turkiye-raporunu-yayinladi-40012192.
Hürriyet Daily News. (2013) Turkish PM Erdoğan to Putin: Take us to Shanghai, (22 November) www.hurriyetdailynews.com/turkish-pm-erdogan-to-putin-take-us-to-shanghai-58348.
Hürriyet Daily News. (2015) Merkel Shifts EU–Turkey Stance upon Migrant Crisis, (18 October) www.hurriyetdailynews.com/merkel-shifts-eu-turkey-stance-upon-migrant-crisis-90028.
Independent Commission on Turkey. (2004) *Turkey in Europe: More than a Promise*, Report of the Independent Commission on Turkey, British Council and Open Society Institute, www.emmabonino.it/campagne/turchia/english.pdf.
Lannes, S. (2000) Entretien avec le Président Valéry Giscard d'Estaing: l'Europe met la Turquie en porte-à-faux, *Géopolitique*, 69, pp. 5–8.
Öniş, Z. (2010) Contesting for the "Center": Domestic Politics, Identity Conflicts and the Controversy over EU Membership in Turkey, *Working Paper No. 2*. İstanbul: İstanbul Bilgi University European Institute.
Öniş, Z. and Yılmaz, Ş. (2009) Between Europeanization and Euro-Asianism: Foreign Policy Activism in Turkey during the AKP Era, *Turkish Studies*, 10(1), pp. 7–24.
Peel, Q. and Notz, A. (2002) Stoiber Warns Against Continual EU Enlargement, *Financial Times* (17 May), www.ft.com.
Prodi, R. (2002) A Wider Europe: A Proximity Policy as the Key to Stability, *Speech delivered at the "Peace, Security and Stability: International Dialogue and the Role of the EU" Sixth ECSA World Conference* (SPEECH/02/619), Brussels, 5–6 December, http://europa.eu/ rapid/press-release_SPEECH-02–619_en.htm.
Republic of Turkey Ministry of Foreign Affairs (2013) www.mfa.gov.tr/relations-between-turkey-and-the-european-union.en.mfa
Rumelili, B. and Süleymanoğlu-Kürüm, R. (2017) Brand Turkey: Liminal Identity and Its Limits, *Geopolitics*, 22(3), pp. 549–570.
Saeed, S. (2017) Sigmar Gabriel: Post-Brexit Britain Can Be Model for Turkey and Ukraine, *Politico* (26 December 2017) www.politico.eu/article/sigmar-gabriel-post-brexit-britain-can-be-model-for-turkey-and-ukraine.
Sarkozy, N. (2007) Toulon Speech (February 2007), http://discours.vie-publique.fr/notices/073000533.html.
Sayarı, S. (2003) The United States and Turkeys Membership in The European Union, *The Turkish Yearbook of International Relations*, 34.
Schimmelfennig, F. (2008) EU Political Accession Conditionality after the 2004 Enlargement: Consistency and Effectiveness, *Journal of European Public Policy*, 15(6), pp. 918–937.
Sloat, A. (2018) *The West's Turkey Conundrum*. Brookings Institute. www.brookings.edu/wp-content/uploads/2018/02/fp_20180212_west_turkey_conundrum.pdf.
Tekeli, İ and İlkin, S. (1993) *Türkiye ve Avrupa Topluluğu, Ulus Devletini Aþma Çabasýndaki Avrupa'ya Türkiye Yaklaþýmý*. Ankara: Ümit Yaýncýlýk.
Tocci, N. (2004) *Accession Dynamics and Conflict Resolution: Catalyzing Peace or Consolidating Partition in Cyprus?* Aldershot: Ashgate.

Toksabay, E. (2017) Germany Granting Asylum to Suspected Coup Plotters Further Strains Ties, Turkey PM Says, *Reuters* (16 May) www.reuters.com/article/us-turkey-germany-coup-idUSKCN18C16U.

Turkish Grand National Assembly. (2011) *Third Erdoğan Government Program* www.tbmm.gov.tr/hukumetler/HP61.htm.

Uğur, M. (2004) *Avrupa Birliği ve Türkiye Bir Dayanak/ İnandırıcılık İkilemi.* İstanbul: Agora Kitaplýðý.

Venice Commission. (2017) *Turkey Opinion on the Amendments to the Constitution Adopted by the Grand National Assembly on 21 January 2017 and to Be Submitted to A National Referendum on 16 April 2017.* Opinion No. 875/2017 (13 March 2017). Strasbourg.

Zihnioğlu, Ö. (2013) *European Union Civil Society Policy and Turkey: A Bridge Too Far?* New York: Palgrave Macmillan.

3 Current issues and challenges in EU–Turkey relations

Chapter 2 has shown in detail how Turkey's relations with the EU have grown sophisticated over the decades, with new issues and actors. It is mainly because of this sophisticated structure that in today's EU–Turkey relations, crises can rapidly alternate and even co-exist with cooperation. Over the past decade, this structure has come to define EU–Turkey relations. On the one hand, relations have lurched from one crisis to the next. At times, relations have faced multiple challenges at the same time. Relations have suffered from these crises and, with each crisis, the political elite with common sense on both sides have had to implement creative methods to put relations back on track.

On the other hand, in certain policy issues such as trade, migration or energy, cooperation is possible, feasible and, at times, even necessary. In these areas, there is a growing cooperation, and even functional integration, between Turkey and the EU. Given the deadlock in accession negotiations, the willingness of both Turkey and the EU to cooperate in these areas introduces a window of opportunity for relations to progress. However, the development of such a transactional relationship bears the risk of degrading the framework of relations from the accession process to these specific areas of interest only. In addition, a transactional relationship assumes Turkey and the EU to be equal partners. This contradicts the implied power asymmetry of the EU's conditionality. While some issues, such as visa liberalization, have a conditionality of its own, this cannot substitute for the overall conditionality of the accession process.

Accordingly, this chapter overviews the major challenges and issues that have come to define or affect Turkey's relations with the EU. This chapter discusses the background and the current state of relations in the given issue. More importantly, it identifies how these issues and challenges impact the accession process, and more broadly EU–Turkey relations. In doing that, this chapter pays special attention to what, if any, these issues and challenges may have on the role civil society can play in EU–Turkey relations.

Modernization of the Customs Union

Economic and trade relations are among the oldest and well-integrated pillars between Turkey and the EU. The Ankara Association Agreement of 1963 is, in essence, an economic agreement, which laid out the principles, stages and timetables for establishing a customs union between the two sides. The Customs Union entered into force on 1 January 1996 through the EU–Turkey Association Council Decision 1/95, covering industrial goods and processed agricultural commodities but excluding the European Coal and Steel Community (ECSC) products. However, contrary to general opinion, strong economic ties between Turkey and the EU started long before that. The EC provided an 'entry permit' for some Turkish goods to its markets during the stages prior to the creation of the Customs Union. As stipulated in the Ankara Association Agreement, the EC opened its market to Turkey following the Additional Protocol in 1970, and gradually reduced industrial tariffs in the following years. By the early 1990s, only limited tariff barriers were left on a few sensitive products. Indeed, the EC has been Turkey's key trading partner since its inception in the late 1950s (Ülgen and Zahariadis, 2004: 2).

The entry into force of the Customs Union still constitutes a milestone for economic and trade ties between Turkey and the EU. With the Customs Union, all customs duties, quantitative restrictions, charges with an equivalent effect to customs duties and all measures with an equivalent effect to quantitative restrictions in the trade of industrial goods and processed agricultural commodities were removed. In addition, with the Customs Union, Turkey has modernized its customs administration and adopted new legislation in line with the EC's Customs Code. The changes include harmonization of standards with European and international standards, harmonization of technical legislation with that of the EU, establishing the quality infrastructure comparable to that of the EU and developing a market surveillance and import control system similar to that of the EU. Finally, Turkey has been implementing the rules and regulations of the EU's trade policy since the formation of the Customs Union. These reforms resulted in decreased trade costs and better market access conditions for goods on both sides to enter each other's market (Aytuğ et al., 2017: 421). These have contributed to 'trade creation,' meaning that the elimination of the tariffs resulted in additional trade. In addition, these reforms also paved the way for a closer integration between Turkey and the EU in economic and trade matters, even before the start of membership talks.

However, public opinion on the Customs Union's impact on Turkish economy is far from uniform. Ever since its inception, a considerable part of Turkish public opinion has been suspicious of the Customs Union with the EU and its contribution to Turkish economy. Indeed, the Customs Union at times has served as a rallying point that brought together anti-EU groups in Turkey (ibid.: 420). One main reason for this is Turkey's consistent net trade deficit with the EU. The other reason is the requirement under the Customs Union for Turkey to adopt the EU's Common Customs Tariff on third country imports and all preferential trade agreements the EU had concluded and would conclude afterwards with third countries. The main issue with this is the inherent asymmetry because, unless there was a separate arrangement, similar conditions do not automatically apply to Turkey, meaning that the tariff barriers with the rest of the world remained high for Turkish goods. This resulted in 'trade diversion,' as it became difficult for Turkey to replace lower cost imports coming from third countries into Turkey with additional trade with the EU (Ülgen and Zahariadis, 2004: 3–4).

On the trade and welfare impact in Turkey of the Customs Union, scholars have presented conflicting results. In the earlier ex-ante studies, Harrison et al. (1997) argued that the Customs Union would generate welfare gains for Turkey, while Mercenier and Yeldan (1997) concluded that the Customs Union would reduce welfare in Turkey if not accompanied by extensive reforms. More recent ex-post studies, such as Nowak-Lehmann et al. (2007), Ülgen and Zahariadis, (2004) and Aytuğ et al. (2017), argue that the Customs Union has had a positive economic impact. Others, such as Antonucci and Manzocchi (2006) and Bilici et al. (2008), however, are more skeptical and have found that the Customs Union does not promote additional trade between Turkey and the EU.

As the Customs Union deepened bilateral economic ties, it also increased Turkey's reliance on the EU as a trading partner. Turkey has opened its trade towards new markets and diversified its trading partners starting from the second half of the 2000s. Although, this has slightly decreased the EU's share in Turkey's imports, on the whole, the EU and individual EU member states, such as Germany, the UK, Italy and France, are among Turkey's top trading partners (Zihnioğlu, 2014).

A turning point in the EU–Turkey Customs Union was the plans for establishing a free trade area between the EU and the USA, known as the Transatlantic Trade and Investment Partnership (TTIP). While the idea of a transatlantic trade partnership dates to the mid-1990s, the idea was reinvigorated earlier this decade and talks started in July 2013, with the goal of achieving a broad and comprehensive free trade agreement (Palmer, 2013). The TTIP has been troubling for Turkey due to the asymmetric nature of its Customs Union with the EU. As in other free trade agreements the EU signs with third countries, the TTIP would result in US products being able to enter Turkey without facing tariffs. Turkish products could not enjoy the same rights unless Turkey becomes a party to the TTIP or they hold a separate agreement with the USA. However, during the time when the talks were still on, neither of the two sides were willing to also have Turkey on-board, nor did the US administration want to negotiate a separate agreement with Turkey. Changing the terms of the Customs Union with the EU appeared to be Turkey's only option.

Despite the suspension of the TTIP, the asymmetric structure has been at the center of Turkey's complaints about the Customs Union. At the time of the Customs Union's signature, the number of countries that had free trade agreements with the EU was limited and their economic impact on Turkey was negligible. Turkish diplomats who had negotiated the Customs Union were well-aware of the pitfalls of the arrangement. However, they expected the costs to be temporary since Turkey was on course for full membership (Aydın-Düzgit and Tocci, 2015: 96). Over the years, as Turkey's full membership to the EU has been delayed, the EU continued to sign free trade agreements with numerous countries including large economies such as Canada,[1] Mexico, South Africa, South Korea and Japan. This has become a growing concern for Turkey's trade policy.

At the European Commission's request, the World Bank conducted a study on the problems encountered during the implementation of the Customs Union. The report of this study was published in 2014 with the World Bank's assessments of the EU–Turkey Customs Union's positive and negative effects. The report praised the Customs Union's contribution to the growth of bilateral trade. However, it also underlined the problems stemming from its asymmetric structure and other flaws in its design. The report suggested widening and deepening the Customs Union and implementing further reforms to ensure continued growth of trade and maximize the benefit.

In addition, economic developments both in Turkey and in global trade since the inception of the EU–Turkey Customs Union also necessitated its revision. The modernization of the Customs Union is one area where Turkish civil society, in particular the major interest groups, have been very active. For instance, TÜSİAD and TİSK have been consistently lobbying EU institutions and politicians on this issue. These organizations are also active at Business-Europe, an umbrella organization at the European level for business organizations. This gives them the opportunity to convey their messages to EU officials and across EU capitals through their European counterparts. As a result of these concerns and based on a mutual will between Turkey and the EU, a series of technical meetings were held. In the meantime, the two sides drafted a framework of negotiations. The modernization package has foreseen expanding the Customs Union's scope to include services, public procurement and furthering agricultural concessions. In May 2015, the bilateral technical discussions came to an end and the two sides announced the political understanding that officially initiated the modernization of the Customs Union. After the Impact Assessment Process was concluded in December 2016, the European Commission asked the Council for a mandate to launch negotiations with Turkey to modernize the customs union. However, a number of EU countries, most notably Germany, has been blocking the giving of this mandate to the Commission due to recent heightened tensions and concerns over Turkey's rule of law. In June 2018, the General Affairs Council reiterated the Commission's point that Turkey is moving away from the EU and underlined that "no further work towards the modernization of the EU–Turkey Customs Union is foreseen" (2018: point 35).

At present, the Customs Union has significance for EU–Turkey relations in two respects. First, despite its flaws, the Customs Union has been successfully implemented for over two decades. It has become the backbone of bilateral trade relations, and a key pillar for relations. As membership talks are de facto on halt, there is an increasing political and scholarly interest in the Customs Union, and it is considered as the main pillar that keeps relations on their feet. After all, the Customs Union is a rules-based system that is in the interest of both sides. This idea has merits, and it is possible and understandable for one area to come to the forefront. However, if the Customs Union becomes the defining framework of relations it bears the risk of being seen as an alternative to the accession process.

Second, in principle, both Turkey and the EU prefer the modernization of the Customs Union, although to sell the revision of the Customs Union at home would probably be difficult for some EU countries. However, its aforementioned asymmetric structure and Turkey's greater dependence on EU markets makes the modernization an urgent topic for Turkey. This gives the EU a leverage in its relations with Turkey. Indeed, the EU has started to instrumentalize the modernization of the Customs Union as part of its conditionality mechanism. This was most visible when the General Affairs Council decided in 2018 not to move forward with modernization negotiations by pointing to democratic conditions in Turkey. While this may be a positive step to reinstituting the political conditionality of the accession process, tying the modernization to other issues, such as the arrangement for the irregular migrants (see below) waters down the prospects for conditionality.

Migration crisis and civil society

Migration has become one of the key issues in EU–Turkey relations over the past couple of years. The course of the migration crisis has been a decisive factor. In addition, the management of the crisis between Turkey and the EU has been by and large trouble-free. However, the migration issue is also important for its impact on EU–Turkey relations, Turkish civil society and the role civic actors may assume in the coming years.

Soon after the outbreak of the Syrian Civil War in 2011, Syrian immigrants entered Turkey's agenda. As early as 2014, according to official figures, the number of Syrian immigrants in Turkey was well over a million. By then the issue had already been part of daily life not only in southeastern provinces, but also in major cities in Turkey because many of the Syrians had not been living in camps.

The issue of immigrants centered on EU–Turkey relations, with the migration crisis spilling into Europe in 2015. The EU has not been a stranger to irregular migration from the Middle East and Africa, and EU countries have long been a destination for asylum applications from neighboring regions. Since the early 1990s, the EU tried to manage irregular migration through focusing on its containment to the periphery and returns (Dimitriadi et al., 2018: 1). However, the numbers escalated sharply in 2015. There was a six-fold increase in illegal border crossing in comparison with 2014, and a 17-fold increase compared to the year before.[2] The numbers arriving at the EU's border reached around 1.8 million and those filing an asylum claim to more than 1.3 million (BBC, 2016).

This near-exponential surge in the spring and summer of 2015 was driven by a mix of factors. First, the ongoing conflict, violence and instability in the region not only precipitated further mass immigrant flows but also rendered return, at least in the near future, impossible. Second, neighboring Jordan, Lebanon and Turkey were overwhelmed by protection responsibilities and their capacities started wearing thin. These countries resisted either granting formal legal status or giving immigrants the rights that would have encouraged their long-term integration. The ongoing lack of opportunities and limited rights coupled with, especially, German Chancellor Merkel's welcome for immigrants. These became a major driver for immigrants' westward movement. More importantly was the change of route for immigrants. The central Mediterranean route from Libya, Tunisia or Egypt to Italy and Malta had dominated migration flows until 2015. This route lost its dominance in 2015, partly because of increasing instability in Libya due to the civil war. In addition, huge numbers of immigrants, particularly those coming from Syria, discovered the eastern Mediterranean route. The relatively short boat trip from Turkey's western coasts to Greek islands made this route easier, safer and also cheaper (Banulescu-Bogdan and Fratzke, 2015).

The shifting of the main immigration route from the central Mediterranean to the eastern Mediterranean coincided with a spike in illegal crossings. At its peak, thousands of new immigrants per day arrived on Greek shores and new tent camps mushroomed across Germany. There was a sense of chaos in several European countries. An equally important problem was the growing deep internal division between EU member states on who was responsible for those arriving and how best to handle the surging numbers of immigrants. With what was soon to become the EU's migration crisis, and Turkey's position in the eastern Mediterranean route, EU–Turkey relations took a new turn. Calls for a reinforced dialogue with Turkey at all levels increased over the summer and fall. With the escalation of the crisis, EU and Turkish leaders met in a summit on 29 November 2015 and issued the EU–Turkey Statement. Leaders activated the Joint Action Plan[3] to step up their cooperation on irregular immigration management and help Turkey address the consequences of the Syrian conflict. The EU committed to provide an initial three billion euro of additional resources to Turkey to help it cope with Syrian immigrants in the country. The EU established the Facility for Refugees in Turkey to facilitate the mobilization of resources. The Statement also included issues not related to the migration crisis. The leaders agreed to re-energize Turkey's accession process by opening a new chapter for negotiations, organize summits twice a year to reinforce high level dialogue and complete the visa liberalization process to lift the visa requirement for Turkish citizens' entry to the Schengen zone.

On 18 March 2016, the EU and Turkey issued another EU–Turkey Statement, which included additional action points. The most important new actions concerned those new immigrants who crossed from Turkey into the Greek islands and whose application was considered unfounded or inadmissible in accordance with the EU's Asylum Procedures Directive. Turkey agreed to take back all such new irregular migrants starting from 20 March 2016. For every Syrian returned to Turkey from the Greek islands, another Syrian will be resettled from Turkey to the EU, taking into account the UN Vulnerability Criteria. The EU pledged to mobilize an additional three billion euro of funding for the Facility for Refugees up to the end of 2018. As in the 2015 EU–Turkey Statement, this Statement also included Turkey's demands and expectations on other issues not related to migration. The Statement noted that the visa liberalization roadmap will be accelerated, reconfirmed their commitment to re-energize the accession process with opening new chapters for negotiations, and welcomed the ongoing work on the upgrading of the EU–Turkey Customs Union (European Council, 2016).

Although relations deteriorated soon after the Statement until 2018 and Turkey has, at times, threatened to pull out of this 'deal,' it has survived to this day. This is mainly because the deal is one of convenience, meeting the interests of both sides. On the one hand, the migration issue is the EU's soft belly and the arrangement in the Statement has since successfully stemmed the flow of irregular immigrants. The flow of migrants across the EU's southeastern corridor seems to be under control for now. On the other hand, Turkey needs the additional funds for the 3.5 million Syrians it is now hosting. Turkey also briefly re-energized its accession process, even though the funds were slow in arriving,[4] the lifting of visa requirements for Turkish citizens and the modernization of the Customs Union have not materialized. In a way, as *The Economist* (2016) put it, it was "a messy but necessary deal."

Both Statements have been controversial from the very start. For one, despite the references made to the principle of non-refoulement and the protection of migrants in accordance with relevant international standards, the return agreement has been heavily criticized for running counter to the United Nation's 1951 Refugee Convention. Others criticized EU leaders for giving in to Turkey too much in the face of the country's staggering democracy and its deteriorating relations with several EU member states. EU leaders could partly stand up to these criticisms by disbursing the committed funds to contracted projects specifically addressing the needs of the Syrians in Turkey[5] instead of handing the funds directly over to Turkish state. Some Europeans also noted that the arrangement has given President Erdoğan a pressure point he can use against the EU at will. That being true, in return, Erdoğan has an interest in the deal's survival.

Necessary as they may be, the funds disbursed for Syrians' needs may be controversial as well. Despite the welcoming of Syrians by Turkish society, some incidents revealed potential tensions against immigrants in the country. With straining economic conditions in Turkey and already limited opportunities for the host communities, if projects are seen as addressing Syrians' needs and improving their conditions only, this may lead to new tensions in the future. Funds should be distributed with a community method where the development projects should embrace the host region and the community as a whole. While important responsibility falls to contracting organizations, public authorities and local administrations, civil society organizations can also play a part in better communicating projects to society. This is not to suggest a bigger role for civic actors in dispersing funds or carrying out the projects, as this would only enhance their role as service providers. But several local or national organizations have been on the field since the early days of migration flows to Turkey. Not only does civil society have vast experience on the ground, but some of these organizations have established strong communications channels with Turkish and Syrian communities. Civil society organizations can use these

56 *Current issues and challenges in relations*

channels to shape public opinion, which in return could help reduce potential tensions in society.

What is equally important is that with the migration crisis and the ensuing operational cooperation, EU–Turkey relations and more specifically the accession process took a new turn. As was detailed in Chapter 1, the accession process mainly works through a conditionality mechanism that is based on the EU's Copenhagen criteria. Until recently, the EU has carefully linked proceeding in accession talks with progress on these criteria. However, with the two Statements following the migration crisis, the EU placed accession talks with Turkey outside of its conventional frame. The EU for the first time has opened a chapter for negotiations with a country that has not shown any progress with respect to its criteria and at a time when EU officials were criticizing Turkish leaders for behavior that is transgressive of EU norms. The transactional design of this cooperation based on continuous give and take, has drawn a coach-and-four through the credibility of the Copenhagen criteria and invalidated the conditionality mechanism. Transactionalism had been introduced previously when the signing of the readmission agreement was linked with the starting of the visa liberalization process. However, the Statements encouraged the Turkish leadership to further instrumentalize migration in relation to the EU and eventually undermined the conditionality mechanism.

Opportunities and challenges in energy cooperation

The EU and Turkey share a mutual strategic interest in the area of energy, since both sides face common challenges and share common objectives, such as reducing import dependency, diversifying energy routes and sources and increasing efficiency and productivity. In the light of recent developments in the region, energy has become a multi-dimensional area affecting relations with both opportunities and challenges.

The first major issue is the EU's heavy dependence on energy imports and Turkey's role as a key transit country due to its geographical location at the crossroad of the Middle East, Caucasus and Europe. The EU has a net energy import dependency, although its dependency has stabilized in recent years, fluctuating between 52 percent and 55 percent since 2005. However, in the case of natural gas, its net dependency increased from 57.1 percent to 70.4 percent in 2016. Of the EU member states,[6] 24 are net gas importers. In 16 of these states, this dependency exceeds 90 percent with about half of them fully reliant on gas imports (European Commission, 2017: 34).

Ensuring stable, secure and affordable energy supplies is central to EU energy strategy. Regional geopolitical dynamics require the EU to diversify supplying countries and routes. This is particularly important for central and south-eastern European countries that are heavily dependent on Russia for most or all their natural gas. As early as the 2000s, Russian–Ukraine conflicts and the two crises in 2005–2006 and 2009 interrupted gas deliveries and showed just how vulnerable the energy supply to some EU countries is to political turmoil and Russian disruptions. Such crises and conflict with Russia enhanced the importance of alternative routes for supplying energy to the EU.

As a result, one of the four priority gas corridors identified in the Trans-European Networks for Energy (TEN-E) Strategy is the Southern Gas Corridor. The Southern Gas Corridor is a term used for planned infrastructure projects for the transmission of gas from the Caspian Basin, Central Asia, the Middle East and eastern Mediterranean to the EU. In the Southern Gas Corridor, Turkey plays an important role as a transit country and this Corridor promotes Turkey's goal to be an energy hub. Turkey has already been transmitting gas via the Turkish-Greek natural gas interconnector, and oil via the Baku–Tbilisi–Ceyhan oil pipeline (Yesevi and Yavuz Tiftikçigil, 2015). But Turkey's role as a transit country and its integration into the EU energy market will be enhanced through the Trans-Anatolian Natural Gas Pipeline Project (TANAP). The TANAP was opened in June 2018 and it carries Azerbaijan's natural gas and other resources from Shah Deniz through Turkey to Europe. Initially, the TANAP pipeline network will deliver 16 bcm per year (6 bcm to Turkey and 10 bcm to Europe once it is connected to the Trans Adriatic Pipeline by 2020) and is extendable up to 32 bcm per year. These figures are small in comparison to the EU's over 400 bcm natural gas need each year. However, this project is politically important as it enables the EU to bypass Russia as a supplier of natural gas. At the institutional level, Turkey is a member of the Southern Gas Corridor Advisory Council, which brings together countries involved in different projects at the Southern Gas Corridor. This Council is an opt-in arrangement in the energy sector for non-member countries (Müftüler-Baç, 2017: 430).

Due to the mutual strategic interest, as well as existing and potential areas of cooperation, energy has been regarded as one of the key pillars of Turkey's accession process. Turkey has taken important steps in restructuring its energy sector and harmonizing its legal framework on electricity and gas markets, renewable energy and energy efficiency with the EU, starting from the early 2000s (Karbuz, 2014: 8). Since the early 2000s, Turkey has undertaken serious efforts to liberalize its energy sector. Accordingly, Turkey has enacted several new laws, reviewed others and established new regulatory authorities in order to establish a liberal and competitive energy market. However, marketing and distribution in this area continues to be a mixture of state control and private sector ownership, and there is still room for more legislative and regulatory improvement and alignment with the acquis. Further harmonization and Turkey's integration into the EU energy market have also come up as part of the modernization of the EU–Turkey Customs Union.

Another way to integrate Turkey further into to the EU energy framework is through the Energy Community. The Energy Community is an international organization, which brings together the EU and its neighbors with the aim of creating an integrated and competitive pan-European energy market. The Energy Community was established in 2005 and Turkey joined the following year with an observer status (Ministry of Foreign Affairs, 2011). Turkey's further integration into the Energy Community necessitates the adoption by Turkey of the EU's relevant legislation on energy, environment and competition (Müftüler-Baç, 2017: 430). However, absent the full membership probability, further adoption of the EU's legislation in these areas is costly for Turkey. Progress on this could be possible should the energy chapter in the accession negotiations be opened. However, this is unlikely considering that the opening of this chapter is unilaterally blocked by Cyprus. Opening of this chapter would enhance energy market integration between Turkey and the EU.

Despite the limits to Turkey's progress on the energy chapter, avenues for further cooperation and even integration between Turkey and the EU may still be available. One such area is the institutional engagement of Turkey's national energy institutions into the relevant EU institutions. For instance, in April 2015, the Turkish Electricity Transmission Company (TEIAS) signed a long-term agreement with the European Network of Transmission System Operators for Electricity (ENTSO-E), which represents 43 transmission system operators from 36 countries. This agreement formed the legal basis for Turkey's electricity system's permanent operation with Continental Europe's electricity grid and provided an important step in Turkey's physical and permanent integration into the EU electricity markets. Relations were taken to a higher level with an agreement in January 2016, which incorporated TEIAS into ENTSO-E as an observer member (TEIAS, 2017; Ministry of Foreign Affairs, 2015). This interconnectedness is not only important for Turkey's integration into the EU electricity markets. Equally important, this interconnectedness enhances Turkey's cross-border trade and energy cooperation with its EU neighbors, Greece and Bulgaria (Müftüler-Baç, 2017: 430).

The European Commission and Turkey also launched the High Level Energy Dialogue in March 2015, for deeper integration in relevant energy sectors such as electricity, gas, nuclear, renewables and also issues including energy efficiency and climate action.[7] Both sides have reiterated that the High Level Energy Dialogue is not a substitute to, but complements and supports, Turkey's accession process. However, given Cyprus's unilateral veto in opening negotiations in the energy chapter and the overall deadlock in the accession process, cooperation and integration in this policy area constitutes a differentiated integration, where a non-member country complies with the EU rules and opts-in in a functional policy area (ibid.: 431).

An important challenge before Turkey's further cooperation with the EU in the energy sector is the dominance of national policies vis-à-vis EU level initiatives. The EU is far from acting with a single voice in this policy area. Despite the work undertaken establishing the Energy Union, it is largely national priorities that determine national energy policies. The South Stream pipeline had been hugely controversial among some EU member states until Putin announced in late 2014 that Russia had abandoned the project. In a similar way, Germany received huge reactions not only from within the EU, but also from the USA in regards to the North Stream pipelines, but continued with plans anyway (Yesevi, 2018).

New hydrocarbon reserves that have been discovered in the Eastern Mediterranean, and the issue of how to monetize these reserves, create new opportunities and challenges in this area for Turkey and the EU (Yorucu and Mehmet,

2018: 87). There are three new sources of natural gas that have been confirmed. These are: (1) Israel's Tamar and Leviathan offshore fields, (2) Aphrodite field off the coast of South Cyprus, and (3) the Egyptian Zohr gas field. There are good prospects that potentially rich gas and oil reserves also exist in the region.

Aphrodite gas field was discovered in 2011. Pumping the gas through a pipeline from Cyprus to Turkey and then to Europe was calculated to be the most cost-efficient way to transport the gas to Europe (ibid.: 91). This would also provide an opportunity to revive the reunification talks in Cyprus and potentially unblock the energy chapter in Turkey's accession process. However, soon after the discovery of the gas field, the Cypriot government embarked on a unilateral programme to explore the natural gas. As the discovery of gas reserves were much below the original expectations, the Cypriots considered cooperative deals with Greece, Egypt and Israel. These options seem more diplomatic than economic. The Cypriot government's unilateral actions and negotiations excluding Turkey, has antagonized Turkey and Turkish Cypriots as Turkey claims that portions of the exclusive economic zone established by Cyprus lies within its own continental shelf. Tensions escalated as Turkish officials announced Turkey's intention to carry out gas exploration in the region and as both sides accelerated their seismological research and drilling activities. With renewed tensions in 2018, it looks unlikely for there to be a reconciliation over the exclusive economic zone or cooperation in gas transportation, without progress on the political settlement of the Cyprus problem, which, for now is a dim prospect.

Reduction of the EU's pre-accession funds to Turkey

The calls to cut the EU's pre-accession funds to Turkey were first articulated in 2017, due to concerns over the country's deteriorating democracy. At the start of the EU summit in October 2017, German Chancellor Angela Merkel has said that "the entire rule of law in Turkey is moving in the wrong direction," in reference to the large-scale purges after the failed coup in July 2016, and that she would back a reduction in pre-accession funds. Germany was not alone on this issue. Other EU countries, including the Netherlands and Belgium, also backed the idea to divert part of the pre-accession funds Turkey receives. Others, such as Austria, demanded not just the freezing of pre-accession funds, but also an end to membership talks, while many others opposed this idea. EU leaders soon found a common ground and agreed to ask the European Commission "to make recommendations on changing and reducing the pre-accession aid" as they seek dialogue with Turkey (Emmott and Barkin, 2017).

EU leaders' calls found support also from the European Parliament. Siegfried Muresan, the European Parliament's chief budget negotiator underlined that they cannot finance Turkey with EU funds, while Turkey "is drifting further away from European democratic standards" (Emmott, 2017). During the budgetary negotiations in November 2017, the European Parliament decided to cut €105 million from the 2018 budget of pre-accession funds for Turkey. The European Parliament decided to place another €70 million in reserve. The funds in reserve would be released under the condition that "Turkey makes measurable, sufficient improvements in the fields of rule of law, democracy, human rights and press freedom, according to the annual report of the Commission." However, the European Commission, in its next annual report published on April 2018 concluded that "Turkey has been significantly moving away from the European Union, in particular in the areas of the rule of law and fundamental rights and through the weakening of effective checks and balances in the political system." This was followed by the European Parliament's motion to support the draft amending budget in October. The motion proposed transferring €70 million in pre-accession funds earmarked for Turkey to the European Neighbourhood Instrument and to fulfil part of the EU pledge for Syria. With increasing criticisms focused on the deterioration of fundamental human rights and freedoms in Turkey, the motion was passed by a landslide majority with 544 members of European Parliament voting in favor, while 28 were against and 74 abstained (European Parliament, 2018). EU officials repeatedly underline that these cuts exclude the funds allocated to civil society programmes. This means less funds are available to programmes opened to public institutions.

The calls of political leaders raised the issue of whether the EU can reduce or even suspend pre-accession assistance as this practice was unprecedented. This issue was also taken up by the European Court of Auditors (2018) in its special report on EU pre-accession assistance to Turkey. On the point of reducing pre-accession aid, the Court underlined the EU legislator's power to reduce future assistance as the budgetary authority. Suspension of pre-accession aid, however, is a different matter. Under the IPA I (2007–2013), the Council had the possibility of suspending financial assistance if the principles of democracy and rule of law had not been complied with.[8] The Council could do this without the need to suspend the accession negotiations. This is not the case under IPA II (2014–2020) as the relevant legislation[9] does not explicitly provide for such a possibility. In a 2017 resolution, the European Parliament called for a suspension of all pre-accession funds to Turkey, if accession negotiations are suspended (2017: point 25). In view of the relevant legislation, however, the EU legislator no longer has the right to implement this suspension of funds.

The reduction of the pre-accession assistance to Turkey was not a one-time thing and further reductions followed in the 2019 budget. During the negotiations of the 2019 budget, the EU decided to reduce pre-accession funds for Turkey vis-à-vis the financial programming in view of the situation as regards democracy, rule of law and human rights in Turkey. The cut from the 2019 budget of pre-accession funds is €146.7 million (European Council, 2018). As in the 2018 budget, EU officials underlined that this reduction will not be reflected to funds allocated to civil society.

The decision to make cuts in the pre-accession assistance is first and foremost a highly symbolic stand. With this decision, the EU for the first time has cut the pre-accession assistance allocated to a candidate country. That said, the amount of the cuts is not negligible. Initially, there was a tendency to play down the amount as the figures cut from the 2018 budget were not that high in comparison to the nearly €4.5 billion of EU pre-accession assistance allocated to Turkey during the period 2014–2020. However, given that there were further reductions from the 2019 budget, it is likely that the reductions will continue in the coming years as well. In addition, the cuts made should be compared in relation to the amount allocated for each year's budget, rather than the seven-year budget. All that taken into account, the amount of the reduced funds is becoming increasingly remarkable.

In a nutshell, the EU provides pre-accession assistance to candidate countries to promote structural reforms necessary to transform sectors and bring them up to EU standards. These sectors may cover a wide range of areas linked to the enlargement strategy including political, economic and social reforms. In a way, pre-accession funds prepare the candidate country, its institutions, policies, practices and the people, for an anticipated accession. Turkey's accession process has long been de facto on halt. Turkey's accession is not present even in the EU's long-term plans, while Turkey has not taken any serious steps towards accession in years, beyond the political elite's rhetoric. No wonder EU leaders and officials question the use or need for pre-accession funds, with growing doubts on Turkey's eventual accession and Ankara's commitment to democracy and fundamental freedoms.

Turkey's stalled bid to join the bloc also hinders the EU's conditionality mechanism. The tools of the EU's conditionality, including the pre-accession assistance, are meaningful only if they can influence the existing practices and structures in applicant countries. Where these tools are not effective is in bringing the candidate country closer to EU standards, and almost taken for granted, it is more appropriate to question not only the tools (for example, pre-accession assistance), but the very conditionality mechanism itself. In a way, the EU has lost much of its leverage over Turkey. Making cuts to pre-accession assistance can be seen as a political deal that could appease the discontented public at home, while at the same time sending a message to Turkey without disrupting the relations.

In that sense, it is important to view whether these cuts are the start of a longer-term reduction of pre-accession assistance to Turkey, as some EU officials suggest. If, in the coming years, the cuts reach a substantial sum and the flow of pre-accession assistance is regularly disrupted, this may be the sign that the EU is willing (and may be ready) to change the rules of the game for Turkey's accession.

It is not clear what new tools and mechanisms the EU would employ in its relations with Turkey should the EU decide to change the rules of the game. As it stands, the pre-accession assistance is an important tool for the EU to interact with both the officials and the public through programmes aimed at Turkish institutions and policies, as well as civil society. The funds allow for the EU to keep a dialogue open with Turkey at different levels. Crippling this tool substantially would have adverse effects on the EU's dialogue with Turkish society. As the EU reduces its pre-accession assistance, the onus to sustain the dialogue will fall to civil society groups, considering that high-level political dialogue is susceptible to recurring potential crisis. Therefore, civil society will need to play a greater role in the EU's efforts to reach out to Turkish society. At this point, it is important that the EU officials carefully underline that pre-accession cuts will not affect civil society funds. Some officials even suggest that these funds should be directed to programmes for Turkish civil society, although this is not what the EU has decided to do.

Ascribing new and greater roles to Turkish civil society requires caution. Despite the growing numbers of groups with increased visibility, it is unrealistic to assume a strong organized civil society sector with wide and deep connections to society. Researchers are more critical of the euphoria on a flourishing civil society of the last decade. In particular, following the developments over the past couple of years (see Chapter 5), civil society groups holding up European norms and values are increasingly turning upon themselves. Any new role ascribed to Turkish civil society organizations, including their future norm entrepreneurship, will have to keep in mind its changing dynamics.

The EU's many 'crises'

The highs and lows of European integration have often had repercussions on the EU's policy towards Turkey. Recent developments, starting with the Eurozone crisis in 2008, failed to foster an enabling environment for membership talks to progress in a meaningful way. The multiple crises the EU has faced over the past decade and the current state of affairs at the political and social level across the continent is not conducive for any favorable development for Turkey's accession. The purpose of this section is not to give a detailed account of these multiple crises, but rather to provide a brief overview of the major issues of the past decade in the context of their implication on the EU's relations with Turkey.

Scholars often point to the European debt crisis as the spark that started this new period. The so-called Eurozone crisis broke out in 2009 and revealed serious deficiencies in the institutional design of the monetary union. In addition, the crisis had extant effects on intra-EU relations. The efforts to keep the Eurozone intact required compromise, cooperation and joint action. But this could not hide the growing distrust between (actual and potential) debtor countries and other countries, as well as their diverging opinions on how to tackle structural challenges. The EU has yet to address these challenges. The troubles of the monetary union are not directly related to Turkey's accession nor to the EU's enlargement policy in general. However, EU member states are likely to be more reluctant to move ahead with the accession of as large and 'problematic' a country as Turkey, before resolving the uncertainty over the monetary union's future.

In recent years, the debate on the future of the monetary union has veered toward one on the future of the Union itself. No doubt that a major reason behind this shift is the UK's decision to leave the Union, known as 'Brexit.' Almost everyone agrees that Brexit is a momentous event in the EU's history. However, there is much difference of opinion on Brexit's implications for the European integration process, ranging from political union to disintegration. With many scholars, politicians, EU officials and civic actors actively engaged in this debate, there has been no shortage of models, plans and ideas on which direction the European integration should be heading. One line of argument sees Brexit as an opportunity that will enable the EU to craft a stronger Union. Whilst the UK was a key actor in the EU, it held quite a few reservations (for example, the monetary union, the Social Charter, 2011 veto on budget rules). With Brexit, the EU will be able to move forwards to a deeper integration without its initiatives being blocked by the UK. In addition, concerned about not opening the way for other member states to question the EU's existing structures, some EU leaders insist on limiting the scope of EU's flexibility (Youngs, 2017: 17).

Emmanuel Macron's election to the French presidency in May 2017 has contributed to this positive mood. Since his election campaign, Macron has been assertive in advocating for a united Europe. Macron's vision for the post-Brexit EU provided much food for thought in the months following his Sorbonne speech in September, where he laid out his plans.

Not everyone in the EU shares this Euro-enthusiasm and Brexit has also opened the way for expressing contrasting views. Some purported the limited flexible arrangements in the EU as the reason for the UK's decision to leave and argued that the more ambitious countries should slow down their process of European integration. While Brexit is a result of British concerns, many consider it to symbolize the problems within the EU's system of governance and the EU inability to react in a flexible way (ibid.: 18). These arguments are supported with a plethora of differentiated integration models.

It is difficult to estimate which direction this debate will go and what the outcome will be. Important as this debate may be for the EU, it is likely to shift more of the EU's energy to the restructuring of post-Brexit EU. The EU will likely keep the door shut on Turkey's membership bid until the dust has settled.

Another new test for the EU is regional nationalism rising simultaneously in different European countries. In regions such as Catalonia, Scotland, Corsica, calls for independence or more autonomy may lead to political crises. While some individual member states are no stranger to regional or ethic nationalism, its prevalence is new to the EU and the tension it creates may have an adverse effect on the EU's enlargement policy.

The migration crisis detailed above has been one of the most important critical junctures for the EU in recent years. What aggravated its impact was multiple terrorist attacks occurring at various locations in Europe in around the same period and the resulting security concerns. These deadly attacks hit major European cities such as Berlin, Brussels, Manchester, Nice and Stockholm during its peak between 2015 and 2017. Accordingly, the migration crisis's impact went beyond the massive influx of immigrant and refugees stretching the EU's asylum system to the breaking point. Several member states introduced border controls one after the other and even built border fences. With the state of panic and security concerns, member states have started retiring into their own shell and defied the EU's ethos. Others transformed their migration policy. Germany, known as having high recognition rates, is an important example. Due to concerns over the refugees' integration and together with the rise of the right-wing, radical political party Alternative for Germany (AfD), Germany has shifted course since 2016. This change resulted in fewer positive recognition of asylum applications from nationalities like the Afghans and Nigerians. In addition, family reunification was put on hold for approximately two years for most cases (Dimitriadi, 2018: 12–13).

The immigration issue has been central to the discourse of right-wing populist political parties in Europe. Their hostile discourse is not only towards the recent wave of migrants but also their own settled Muslim communities. Indeed, since the 9/11 attacks, public skepticism towards Muslims has been growing in Europe. With laws against the hijab and the burqa in France, in 2004 and 2011 respectively, Islamophobia has been legalized and thus normalized.[10] Muslim-origin migrants came to be seen as burdens to their home countries and often associated with illegality, crime, violence and fundamentalism (Kaya, 2015). While the debate on the end of multiculturalism has been roaming in Europe for some time, "failure of multiculturalism" has become the catchphrase of not only extremist right-wing parties but also of centrist parties (Kaya, 2010: 80).

Right-wing populist parties and movements are on the rise across Europe. They are in power in Hungary and Poland but also have substantial political representation in several other EU countries. However, their power should not be measured by their parliamentary seats, as they can often influence public and political debates and even discourse, irrespective of their voting rate.

The strengthening of right-wing populist parties and movements affect Turkey's accession process in two ways. First, where these parties are in power, they pose a direct challenge to democratic norms and principles. In Hungary, Orbán's right-wing Fidesz party systematically dismantled the country's checks and balances by enacting stringent laws and placing loyalists in critical positions. Orbán's attacks on the judiciary, media, civil society, universities and migrants have been widely criticized and led to increased tensions with the EU. The Polish government has been worrying the EU as well. Commission Vice President Frans Timmermans said that the 13 new laws enacted over the past couple of years by Poland's right-wing governing party Law and Justice (PiS) "can systematically interfere with the composition, powers, the administration and the functioning" of the judiciary (Deutsche Welle, 2017).

The European Commission's decision to trigger Article 7 of the Lisbon Treaty against Poland in 2017, and the Parliament's vote for the same procedure against Hungary the next year are welcoming steps. To institute democratic norms and principles outside its borders, the EU must guard them at home in the first place. Otherwise, the EU risks both the legitimacy and the credibility of its political conditionality. This applies to Turkey's accession process as well. However, it is still unclear how the EU can reinstitute democratic norms and rules in Hungary and Poland and if the EU's recent measures will deter other EU leaders that look to Orbán as a role model. The EU is at a crossroads in maintaining the democratic norms that it stands for, the result of which will impact on its relations with Turkey.

Second, Turkey is much affected from this changing political landscape, as a Muslim majority country. A recent study[11] demonstrates that the supporters of right-wing populist parties in Europe consider Turkey's EU membership impossible. Their fear of mass migration from Turkey is coupled with the presumed failure of Turkish migrant workers' integration and the presumed incompatibility of Islam to European civilization. While migration- and integration-related fears are not new, they are now exploited by Europe's right-wing populist parties. For instance, the United Kingdom Independence Party (UKIP) capitalized on the fear of mass migration of Turks during the Brexit campaign in 2016.

In addition to problems of Turkey's own making, the continuing rise of right-wing populist parties will cause a further decrease in support for Turkey's accession to the EU. Turkey might not have too many options at its disposal. The rise of right-wing populist parties and xenophobic nationalist sentiments will continue to shape the EU's future in the short- to mid-term. The prevailing atmosphere in EU countries will have repercussions on both discourses and policy choices of political leaders and will push them further away from Turkey's accession. It is unlikely that right-wing populist parties will end all dialogue with Turkey. More likely is that they will push for a transactional relation with Turkey, based exclusively on issues of mutual interest. This would limit Turkey's relations with the EU to issues such as trade, migration, energy and security.

This pessimistic scenario, although likely, need not necessarily prevail. Political leaders, parties and movements may emerge and override populist calls – as we have seen with Macron during French presidential elections. But in either case, to maintain its EU bid, Turkey will have to stick to its formal accession process. Equally important, Turkey will also have to reach out to the European public to overcome prejudices, concerns and fears. Even without this pessimistic scenario, Turkey needs to explain itself clearly more than ever before.

Notes

1 The Comprehensive Economic and Trade Agreement (CETA) between the EU and Canada entered into force provisionally in September 2017, meaning that most of the agreement now applies. However, before CETA can take full effect, national parliaments in EU member states – and in some cases regional ones too – will need to approve it.
2 See the European Parliament Research Service's website: www.europarl.europa.eu/thinktank/infographics/migration/public/index.html?page=migration.
3 The EU–Turkey Joint Action Plan was agreed on 15 October 2015. The Action Plan identifies a series of collaborative actions to be implemented by both sides. One of the most prominent actions foreseen in the Plan is for the EU to mobilize new funds to Turkey outside of the pre-accession funds. In return, Turkey would step up its patrolling activity, search and rescue capacity and implement policies to facilitate Syrian access to public services. For a full list of actions of the Joint Action Plan, see europa.eu/rapid/press-release_MEMO-15-5860_en.pdf.

66 *Current issues and challenges in relations*

4 As of October 2018, the first tranche of the three billion euro planned for 2016–2017 period had been fully contracted and €1.94 billion had been disbursed. From the second tranche of three billion euro planned for the 2018–2019 period, €450 million has been committed so far. https://ec.europa.eu/neighbourhood-enlargement/news_corner/migration_en.
5 The EU Facility for Refugees covers both humanitarian, development (education, health, socio-economic support) actions and migration management (costs incurred in the management of returns).
6 Cyprus and Malta do not use natural gas; Denmark and the Netherlands are net gas exporters.
7 The High Level Dialogues are ministerial level meetings on a regular basis, at least once a year. Following the meeting of the EU heads of state or government with Turkey on November 2015, a series of high-level dialogues on economy, energy and transport were established.
8 Council Regulation (EC) No 1085/2006, Article 21 on suspension of assistance:

> Where a beneficiary country fails to respect these principles [of democracy, the rule of law and for human rights and minority rights and fundamental freedoms] or the commitments contained in the relevant Partnership with the EU, or where progress toward fulfilment of the accession criteria is insufficient, the Council, acting by qualified majority on a proposal from the Commission, may take appropriate steps with regard to any assistance granted under this Regulation.

9 See Regulation (EU) No 231/2014 of the European Parliament and of the Council of 11 March 2014 establishing an Instrument for Pre-accession Assistance; Commission Implementing Regulation (EU) No 447/2014 on the specific rules for implementing Regulation (EU) No 231/2014; Framework Agreement of 11 February 2015 regarding IPA II between the Republic of Turkey and the European Commission. See also European Parliament's statement on the suspension of assistance granted under the financial instruments on p. 25 attached to Regulation (EU) No 231/2014 of the European Parliament and of the Council of 11 March 2014 establishing an Instrument for Preaccession Assistance (IPA II) (OJ L 77, 15.3.2014, p. 11).
10 See Ayhan Kaya (2018) for a detailed discussion on the rise of Islamophobia, its relation to right-wing populist political parties in Europe and how this relates to Turkey's accession bid to the EU.
11 Fieldwork was conducted in 2017 with the supporters of Germany (Alternative für Deutschland, AfD), France (Front National), Italy (Movimento Cinque Stelle [Five Star Movement]), Greece (Golden Down) and the Netherlands (The Partij voord de Vrijheid [The Freedom Party]).

Bibliography

Antonucci, D. and Manzocchi, S. (2006) Does Turkey have a Special Trade Relation with the EU? A Gravity Model Approach, *Economic Systems*, 30(2), pp. 157–169.
Aydın-Düzgit, S. and Tocci, N. (2015) *Turkey and the European Union*. Basingstoke: Palgrave Macmillan.
Aytuğ, H., Mavuş Kütük, M., Oduncu, A. and Togan, S. (2017) Twenty Years of the EU–Turkey Customs Union: A Synthetic Control Method Analysis, *Journal of Common Market Studies*, 55(3), pp. 419–431.
Banulescu-Bogdan, N. and Fratzke, S. (2015) Europe's Migration Crisis in Context: Why Now and What Next? *Migration Policy Institute*, www.migrationpolicy.org/article/europe%E2%80%99s-migration-crisis-context-why-now-and-what-next.
BBC. (2016) Migrant Crisis: Migration to Europe Explained in Seven Charts, (4 March) www.bbc.com/news/world-europe-34131911.

Bilici, Ö., Erdil, E. and Yetkiner, İ. H. (2008) The Determining Role of EU in Turkey's Trade Flows: A Gravity Model Approach, *Izmir University of Economics Working Papers in Economics*. İzmir: İzmir University of Economics.

Deutsche Welle. (2017) European Commission Triggers Article 7 against Poland, (20 December) www.dw.com/en/european-commission-triggers-article-7-against-poland/a-41873962.

Dimitriadi, A., Kaya, A., Kale, B. and Zurabishvili, T. (2018) EU–Turkey Relations and Irregular Migration: Transactional Cooperation in the Making, *FEUTURE Online Paper 16*. www.feuture.uni-koeln.de/sites/feuture/user_upload/FEUTURE_Online_Paper_No_16_D6.3.pdf.

Economist. (2016) Europe's Migrant Crisis A Messy but Necessary Deal, (12 March) www.economist.com/leaders/2016/03/12/a-messy-but-necessary-deal.

Emmott, R. (2017) In Warning to Ankara, EU Cuts Funds for Turkey's Membership Bid, *Reuters* (20 November) www.reuters.com/article/us-eu-turkey/in-warning-to-ankara-eu-cuts-funds-for-turkeys-membership-bid-idUSKBN1DU2D4.

Emmott, R. and Barkin, N. (2017) Merkel Praises Allies to Cut Funds for Turkey's EU Bid, *Reuters* (19 October) www.reuters.com/article/us-eu-turkey-summit-merkel/merkel-presses-allies-to-cut-funds-for-turkeys-eu-bid-idUSKBN1CO1V5.

European Commission. (2017) Second Report on the State of the Energy Union, *Commission Staff Working Document Monitoring Progress towards the Energy Union Objectives – Key Indicators*. Brussels. 01.02.2017, SWD(2017) 32 final.

European Council. (2006) *Council Regulation (EC) No 1085/2006 of 17 July 2006 Establishing an Instrument for Pre-Accession Assistance (IPA)*. https://eur-lex.europa.eu/LexUriServ/LexUriServ.do?uri=OJ:L:2006:210:0082:0093:EN:PDF.

European Council. (2016) *EU–Turkey Statement, 18 March 2016*. www.consilium.europa.eu/en/press/press-releases/2016/03/18/eu-turkey-statement.

European Council. (2018) *Council Endorses Agreement on EU Budget for 2019*, www.consilium.europa.eu/en/press/press-releases/2018/12/11/council-endorses-agreement-on-eu-budget-for-2019.

European Court of Auditors. (2018) *EU Pre-Accession Assistance to Turkey: Only Limited Results So Far*. Special Report No 7, www.eca.europa.eu/Lists/ECADocuments/SR18_07/SR_TURKEY_EN.pdf.

European Parliament. (2017) *Resolution of 6 July 2017 on the 2016 Commission Report on Turkey (2016/2308(INI))*.

European Parliament. (2018) Turkey: *MEPs Cut Support by €70m Due to No Improvement in Respect for EU Values*. Press Release, (2 October) www.europarl.europa.eu/news/en/press-room/20180926IPR14407/turkey-meps-cut-support-by-EU70m-due-to-no-improvement-in-respect-for-eu-values.

General Affairs Council. (2018) Council Conclusions on Enlargement and Stabilisation and Association Process as Adopted (26 June) No. prev. doc. 10374/18. 10555/18.

Harrison, G. W., Rutherford, T. F. and Tarr, D. G. (1997) Economic Implications for Turkey of a Customs Union with the European Union, *European Economic Review*, 41(3), pp. 861–870.

Karbuz, S. (2014) EU–Turkey Energy Cooperation: Challenges and Opportunities, *IAI Working Papers 14*.

Kaya, A. (2010) Migration Debates in Europe: Migrants as Anti-citizens, *Turkish Policy Quarterly*, 10(1), pp. 79–91.

Kaya, A. (2015) Islamophobism as an Ideology in the West: Scapegoating Muslim-Origin Migrants, in A. Amelina, K. Horvath and B. Meeus (eds), *International Handbook of Migration and Social Transformation in Europe*. Wiesbaden: Springer.

Kaya, A. (2018) Right-wing Populism and Islamophobism in Europe and Their Impact on Turkey–EU Relations, *Turkish Studies*, DOI: 10.1080/14683849.2018.1499431.

Langbein, J. and Börzel, T. A. (2013) Explaining Policy Change in the European Union's Eastern Neighbourhood, *Europe-Asia Studies*, 65(4), pp. 571–580.

Mercenier, J. and Yeldan, E. (1997) On Turkey's Trade Policy: Is a Customs Union with Europe Enough?, *European Economic Review*, 41(3), pp. 871–880.

Ministry of Foreign Affairs. (2011) *Turkey's Energy Profile and Strategy*. www.mfa.gov.tr/turkeys-energy-strategy.en.mfa.

Ministry of Foreign Affairs. (2015) *Turkey Signed Long-Term Agreement with the European Network of Transmission System Operators for Electricity (ENTSO-E)*. www.ab.gov.tr/49931_en.html.

Müftüler-Baç, M. (2017) Turkey's Future with the European Union: An Alternative Model of Differentiated Integration, *Turkish Studies*, 18(3), pp. 416–438.

Nowak-Lehmann, F., Herzer, D., Martinez-Zarzoso, I. and Vollmer, S. (2007) The Impact of a Customs Union between Turkey and the EU on Turkeys Exports to the EU. *Journal of Common Market Studies*, 45(3), pp. 719–743.

Palmer, D. (2013) After Long Buildup, U.S.-EU Free Trade Talks Finally Begin, *Reuters*, (8 July). www.reuters.com/assets/print?aid=USL2N0F71XS20130708.

TEIAS. (2017) ENTSO-E (European Network of Transmission System Operators for Electricity). www.teias.gov.tr/en/node/221.

Ülgen, S. and Zahariadis, Y. (2004) The Future of Turkish–EU Trade Relations Deepening vs Widening, *Centre for European Policy Studies, EU–Turkey Working Papers*, No. 5.

World Bank. (2014) Evaluation of the EU–Turkey Customs Union, *World Bank Report No. 85830-TR*.

Yesevi, Ç. G. (2018) Considering Pipeline Politics in Eurasia: South Stream, TurkStream and TANAP, *Bilge Strateji*, 10(18), pp. 11–52.

Yesevi, Ç. G. and Yavuz Tiftikçigil, B. (2015) Turkey-Azerbaijan Energy Relations: A Political and Economic Analysis, *International Journal of Energy Economics and Policy*, 5(1), pp. 27–44.

Yorucu, V. and Mehmet, Ö. (2018) The Southern Energy Corridor, *Lecture Notes in Energy Volume 60*. Switzerland: Springer.

Youngs, R. (2017) *Europe Reset: New Directions for the EU*. London: I.B. Tauris.

Zihnioğlu, Ö. (2014) Bringing the European Union Back on the Agenda of Turkish Foreign Policy, *Insight Turkey*, 16(3), pp. 149–164.

4 Revisiting Turkish civil society

The previous chapters have revealed the current limitations of the EU's political conditionality in Turkey and its diminishing impact. As detailed in the first chapter, an alternative to the conditionality mechanism to induce reforms in candidate countries is through triggering transnational social learning by empowering domestic groups. The EU considers civil society actors as an important domestic group for this purpose in several countries, including Turkey.

An important question is whether and how well Turkish civil society can trigger social learning and carry out the roles attributed for this process. This requires not only a thorough understanding of Turkish civil society today, but also of the changes that civil society has gone through. Indeed, throughout Turkey's modern history, civil society has simultaneously embodied and reflected continuity and change. On the one hand, the political environment at home and abroad has changed. The legal framework has gradually improved but occasionally relapsed. New actors and issues have entered civil society, while others drifted away. On the other hand, certain key features of Turkish civil society and associationalism has remained constant. This chapter traces Turkish civil society's current depoliticization based on these dynamics in its recent history.

It is widely acknowledged that a strong state tradition shapes civil society in Turkey. Scholars depict an 'almighty state' actively engaged in extensive social and political engineering. Accordingly, the state has not allowed for an independent civil society outside its remit and control. Therefore, the state hampered any bottom-up dynamic that it considered might unfold. Yet others questioned the very strength of the Turkish state. For Kalaycıoğlu (2002: 250–261) the Turkish state lacks regulatory, extractive and distributive capacity, which renders the political elite fearful about collectively expressed discontent. It is due to this weakness that the state impedes the development of civil society. The elite's distrust of the people further complicates this. Both perceptions add up to the same thing; what is commonly referred to as the 'Papa State.' The state, be it strong or weak, is benevolent and allows for civil society, so long as they co-operate with state or complement its work. When it is challenged though, it becomes repressive.

As will be discussed in more detail later in this chapter, this perception has also been well-accepted among the public and civil society organizations. With

70 *Revisiting Turkish civil society*

the state being permissive 'within limits,' associationalism developed in Turkey after World War II. Religious groups, local and regional solidarity groups, cultural initiatives have become part of Turkish society as early as the 1950s (Kalaycıoğlu, 2002: 268). Following the growth of the private industrial sector in the 1960s, organizations representing both business groups and workers, in the form of economic associations, trade unions and chambers mushroomed throughout the 1970s (Ahmad, 2000: 132, 143, 2003: 120). Rigid and secularly-oriented social engineering narrowed the scope for civil society's development during this period. Nevertheless, on the eve of military takeover in 1980, there were over 38,000 associations in Turkey (Şimşek, 2004: 48).

Diversification of civic actors in the 1980s and 1990s

The military takeover in 1980, struck a blow to associational life developed thus far in Turkey. The ensuing junta regime held associational life and their 'unlimited freedom' responsible for the chaos Turkey had slipped into in the late 1970s (Evren, 1991: 275–276). Not only did the junta crush all civic assets by closing over 20,000 associations (Şimşek, 2004: 48), suspending all professional associations and trade unions; and rendering strikes illegal (Ahmad, 2000: 182–185) but it also took legislative and institutional measures to depoliticize groups, especially the youth. The generation born during and soon after this period grew up in an environment where civic activism – when not prohibited – was regarded as either dangerous or futile. This led to a generation which distanced itself from associational life and that was identified with an apolitical attitude until recently (Zihnioğlu, 2017).

Starting from the 1980s, and especially throughout the 1990s, Turkish civil society's outlook changed. During this period, identity and religious politics expanded and this had visible repercussions on civil society. Religious groups attained a larger place in civil society in different forms. First, in continuation of their earlier efforts, religious groups founded numerous, large and small charities, self-help groups and associations for mosque building and renovation. Major aid organizations such as The Foundation for Human Rights and Freedoms and Humanitarian Relief (İHH) and the Deniz Feneri Association were established in the mid-1990s. In addition, religious groups were also organized in economic realms such as with the Independent Industrialists' and Businessmen's Association (MÜSİAD), established in 1990. Finally, and most interestingly, during this period there was the rise of religiously-motivated rights movements and organizations. In the 1990s, veiled students were not allowed to enter classes. In addition, the Higher Education Council made a regulation in 1999 that promoted enrolling on higher education programmes that coincide with the secondary school type the student graduated from. This regulation gave religiously-oriented vocational high school (*İmam Hatip*) graduates a disadvantage, unless they sought entry to theology departments. As the legal appeal process was exhausted, veiled students were further restricted in their career goals. These two issues converged and led to mass protests and rallies against the political center (Kalaycıoğlu, 2002: 263–264). These issues as well as the changing environment, also led to organized major advocacy (and to partial solidarity) groups such as the Women's Rights Against Discrimination Association (AK-DER) and The Association for Human Rights and Solidarity for the Oppressed (MAZLUMDER).

During the same period, identity politics also has become widespread in Turkey. Several Kurdish civil society groups were organized, mainly in Turkey's southeast. Some focused on civil rights abuses (Human Rights Association), while others promoted Kurdish language and culture (Mesopotamia Cultural Center). Considering that Turkey had long denied the existence of Kurds' ethnic identity, the sprouting and even official registration of these organizations was a breakthrough in Turkey's political and social life (Center for American Progress et al., 2017).

Apart from these groups, various other issues, including environmental protection and women's rights, were also politicized in the 1990s. Women were one of the first groups to re-organize after the military takeover in 1980. The new women's movement[1] issued magazines, organized consciousness raising meetings, campaigns and mass demonstrations. The campaign for Turkey to sign the Convention on the Elimination of All Forms of Discrimination against Women (CEDAW) in 1986, and the mass demonstration against a domestic violence case in 1987 were particularly striking. During the 1990s, the women's movement has become more widespread, diversified and has grown stronger. Women's organizations from different ends of the ideological spectrum were founded in this period.

Several reasons are put forward to explain the change in Turkey's civic space during this period. One prominent argument is the changing meaning of modernity since the 1980s, challenging the secular-rational thinking as the exclusive source of modernity. Coupled with this is the rise of Islamic discourse both as a political actor and a foundation for identity formation. This change in the meaning of modernity also manifested itself in a new language of civil society, civil rights and democracy. This led to politically active civil society organizations that called to democratize the secular and state-centric model of Turkish modernity. In addition, the state lost its position as the primary context for politics as civil society and culture became one of the new reference points in political language (Keyman and İçduygu, 2003: 222–226; Sarıbay, 2000: 105).

More generally, Turkey's hosting of the Habitat II Conference in 1996 and the presence of hundreds of civil society organizations from all around the country drew attention to civil society. The Susurluk Scandal in the same year disclosed the concealed relationships between the government, the police and organized crime. The scandal ignited popular rage and led to several demonstrations by large sectors of society against corruption. The Marmara earthquake in 1999 was also important in mobilizing civil society in this period. Civil society organizations quickly mobilized following the disaster and actively participated in the search, rescue and relief efforts. Various other groups joined in with philanthropic activities. Optimists considered the civil society's mobilization as disproving the "cliché about Turkey for decades that civic associations do not work and that people sit back and wait for the state to do everything" (Makovsky, 1999). There was a genuine hope this would turn into a movement to liberalize the state. Others, however, were more critical, and claimed that civil society was not able to sustain the momentum it enjoyed immediately after the disaster and returned to a state of disorganization and disconnection soon after (Kubicek, 2002).

Despite the changing circumstances, the state's openness to civil society during this period was at best ambivalent. First, there was the 'establishment' civil society organizations that remained loyal to the republican project. These groups foresaw the protection of their rights alongside the promotion of Kemalist tenets. Therefore, they were willing to ally with the state rather than with anti-establishment groups (Kaliber and Tocci, 2010: 196–197). For instance, establishment civil society organizations sided with the military at the time of the 1997 military memorandum. Second, there was a vast group of solidarity, self-help, charity and economic associations. These organizations were neither supported nor restrained by the government (Kalaycıoğlu, 2002: 268–269). Third, the state maintained an entirely different stance to politically-oriented 'anti-establishment' groups. It showed no tolerance to ethnic and religious organizations that pursued ethnic, cultural or religious claims, challenged the Republican system or were perceived as threats to the status quo. Such groups were resisted, relegated to the margins and often banned (Kaliber and Tocci, 2010: 197).

The final group is the women's associations, whose relations with the state altered drastically during this period. Initially in the 1980s, women's associations faced the exclusivist attitude of the state. This slowly changed when women's associations began to cooperate with local governments on issues such as shelters. They also established themselves with different legal associations to lobby for improving women's rights. Added to this was international pressures and treaties. These multi-layered efforts led to an evolving of the confrontation between women's associations and the state into a dialogue and eventually cooperation (Kalaycıoğlu, 2002: 262).

A new narrative on Turkish civil society

Europeanization, accession process and Turkish civil society

Turkish civil society entered the new millennium with new actors, issues and windows of opportunity. It also enjoyed a higher profile following the Habitat II conference in İstanbul and thanks to their efforts in the aftermath of the Marmara earthquake. The EU's announcement of Turkey's candidacy in late 1999 has changed the parameters for civil society organizations and provided new opportunity structures. Soon after the candidacy was announced, Turkey embarked on an ambitious reform process, first to start the accession negotiations and later to meet the accession criteria. The three-party coalition government started the reform process. The AKP government, who first came to power in 2002, followed suit. It has prioritized Turkey's relations with the EU, and devoted substantial energy to the reform process in its first term in government. The successive reform packages, among other things, addressed freedom of association and freedom of assembly. Despite persisting drawbacks in implementation, the new codes, regulations and amendments considerably improved the legal and institutional environment for civil society (see Chapter 2 for a detailed discussion). In addition, Turkey's candidacy has opened new venues of funding for civil society. The EU provided financial and technical support so that an empowered civil society promotes fundamental rights, ensures the inclusive development of Turkish democracy and assumes an active role in matters relating to Turkey's accession (see Chapter 6 for a detailed discussion).

Through various activities and multi-pronged efforts, civil society actors in Turkey have championed Turkey's EU membership bid during this period. Several organizations focused on EU-related issues, mobilized their members and, more importantly, the public at large. They carried out intense and consistent publicity campaigns, communication, promotion and lobbying activities. In doing so, they made successful use of their networks, established strong partnerships and broad-based coalitions. Some lobbied at home, while others also lobbied abroad, sometimes in collaboration with other organizations in EU member states.

A well-known example is the Turkish Industry and Business Association (TÜSİAD), which promoted Turkey's EU membership bid at different levels. TÜSİAD promoted the reform process in Turkey. For this, it fostered public debates on various issues pertaining to Turkey's EU's membership aspirations. In 1997, even before the announcement of Turkey's candidacy, it drafted a report titled "Perspectives on Democratization in Turkey." The report, which was drafted by a professor of constitutional law, touched upon sensitive political issues and put forward concrete proposals for reform. The publishing of the report was followed by seminars to foster public debates on issues raised in the report. The report sparked interest, but also stirred controversy and elicited criticism from the military, state elites and some of TÜSİAD's own members (Öniş, 2005: 183). During the early 2000s, TÜSİAD also made controversial statements in support of resolving the Cyprus problem. In addition, TÜSİAD established the EU Harmonization Committee, commissions and working groups as part of its structure to follow Turkey's harmonization efforts vis-à-vis negotiation chapters (Altınay, 2005: 109; Atan, 2004: 107).[2] It lobbied members of Turkish parliament to accelerate the democratic reform process and opened a permanent representative office in Ankara to assist its efforts and its participation in policy-making process.

In addition, TÜSİAD lobbied for support in Brussels and across the EU capitals. TÜSİAD organized meetings at the EU institutions and permanent delegations in Brussels. As a member of the Union of Industrial and Employers' Confederation in Europe, now known as BusinessEurope, TÜSİAD often worked in collaboration with its European counterparts and conveyed its messages to and through representatives of businesses across Europe.

The Economic Development Foundation (İKV) is another prominent organization that devoted substantial energy to further Turkey's relations with the EU during this period. The İKV was established in 1965 through the initiative of the İstanbul Chamber of Commerce and the İstanbul Chamber of Industry to inform Turkish businesses and the Turkish public about European integration and EU–Turkey relations. Accordingly, the İKV held seminars on Turkey's EU accession process in several provinces to raise the Turkish public's awareness. Following the start of accession negotiations, the İKV gave training courses on Regulatory Impact Assessment and studied the effects of horizontal implementation of the acquis on leading Turkish sectors. The İKV was also active at the EU level; it organized seminars to better inform EU experts working on Turkey regarding the latest political, economic and social developments in the country. It also created a discussion platform between members of the European Parliament and representatives of Turkish civil society to give both sides an opportunity to better understand each other (Economic Development Foundation, 2019).

What was more interesting during this period was the formation of major collaborative efforts. These efforts appeared especially in the run up to the Copenhagen European Council in 2002, to mobilize support for Turkey's position and to accelerate the reform process. One of the most prominent collaborative civil society initiatives was the Turkey Platform. The Platform brought together over 250 civil society organizations following the invitation of the Union of Chambers and Commodity Exchanges of Turkey in 2002. The İKV took over the Platform's coordination, and under the İKV's leadership the Platform carried out intense communication and lobbying activities both in Turkey and in the EU. For instance, soon after its establishment, it adopted a declaration: "*Türkiye'nin yeri Avrupa Birliği'dir, kaybedecek zaman yoktur*" [Turkey's place is in the European Union, there is no time to waste]. There were other short-lived and less institutionalized efforts, which brought together several civil society organizations.

Finally, there were broad-based civic initiatives that actively carried out pro-EU campaigns during the 2000s. A well-known example of this is the European Movement 2002. The Movement not only lobbied lawmakers for the adoption of political reforms, but organized publicity campaigns supporting Turkey's accession into the EU. They placed a countdown timer in front of the Turkish Parliament to count down to the Copenhagen European Council on 12 December 2002. The Movement is also known with its publicity campaign in 2006 in support of political reforms in Turkey with the slogan '*Başka yarın yok*' [There is no other tomorrow]. Using the advantage of being a popular movement, it enlisted well-known figures from academia, media, business and the arts, and enjoyed widespread media coverage of their campaigns and activities. This helped them to disseminate and further popularize their messages and activities. The Movement was also active in several EU capitals, including Brussels.

Civil society groups came to the forefront and gained visibility as Turkey's accession gained momentum in the early 2000s. While numerous organizations took part in these activities, one should underline that they were mostly initiated or led by major interest groups. In particular, well-known organizations and initiatives received substantial support from the media. Their activities, campaigns and declarations have frequently appeared in media outlets, sometimes even free of charge (Altınay, 2005: 111). In addition, they were built on the existing momentum of EU–Turkey relations. On the one hand, there was an overall positive atmosphere within the EU towards Turkey, which overshadowed the critical voices. On the other hand, the AKP government had prioritized Turkey's relations with the EU and devoted substantial energy to Turkey's membership aspirations. In this way, Turkey's accession process had captured momentum.

During this period. the AKP government was also more open to civil society's contribution to EU related matters. An important joint initiative during this period was the EU Communication Group, which included different public institutions, leading business and civil society organizations. The Group brought together the Ministry of Foreign Affairs, Secretariat General for the EU Affairs, Directorate General of Press and Information on the one hand, and TOBB, TÜSİAD and İKV on the other, to better inform the EU public in a bid to overcome prejudices against Turkey. During early meetings of the Reform Monitoring Group, the screening process of the negotiations were also open to civil society's participation. Although the civil society's participation was limited and not without problems, it nonetheless provided an avenue for interaction between public officials and civic actors. Those civil society organizations that were willing and able had the opportunity to build their efforts on this existing momentum.

Over the last two decades, several studies have looked into how Turkey's Europeanization has impacted upon civil society and ultimately tried to explain the Europeanization of Turkish civil society. There is an extensive literature on 'Europeanization' and as we have seen in Chapter 1, it is a much-debated concept. Accordingly, what the literature makes of Europeanization of Turkish civil society widely varies and sometimes contradicts one another. Europeanization may stand for, inter alia, support for EU accession process, the adoption of and the references made to European norms, the use of EU funds or participation in EU level networks (Rumelili and Boşnak, 2015: 127). Some understand it as a constellation of processes, others define it as a normative/political context. Keeping in mind the complex interaction between Europeanization in the EU and in Turkey, civil society becomes both an agent for change and also a product of the existing structures (Kaya and Marchetti, 2014: 3). I will not belabor these conceptual intricacies. Rather, I will discuss the changes Turkish civil society has gone through in this period in the light of these studies and changes in the opportunity structure.

A good part of the literature finds the Europeanization of Turkish civil society favorable and focuses on its positive impact. Official figures already show that the number of associations continued its increase during this period (see Figure 4.1), nearly doubling in 20 years.[3] This is probably to be expected, considering that legally and financially there is now a more favorable environment for the establishment and functioning of civil society organizations. More importantly

76 *Revisiting Turkish civil society*

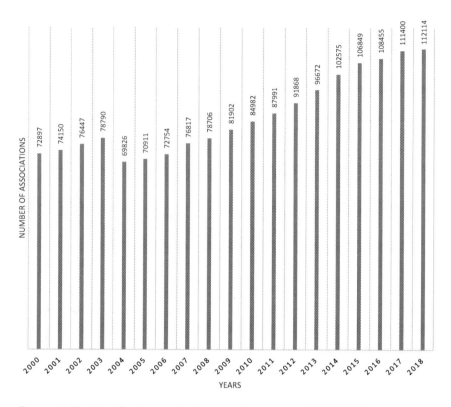

Figure 4.1 Number of active associations according to years (2000–2018).
Source: Ministry of Interior Directorate General of Civil Society Affairs, 2018.

public awareness about civil society has also amplified. This is first because EU civil society support was built on the public's increasing and favorable perception of civil society, following their active involvement in the Habitat II conference and the search and rescue efforts after the Marmara earthquake. Second, EU funds encouraged the visibility of EU-funded projects. Third, several initiatives, such as the European Movement 2002, were mobilized in the early years of Turkey's candidacy in support of its accession to the EU. Their publicity campaigns were often popular and led to a more favorable understanding of civic activism.

On the other hand, several studies found that the change in opportunity structures had a more substantial impact on Turkish civil society. First, these studies share an optimistic view that the EU has changed the context of civil society development in Turkey. EU funds helped civil society organizations to enhance their capacity building and diversify their activities (Ergun, 2010; Grigoriadis, 2009). Some of these studies suggest that EU funds professionalized Turkish civil society organizations and taught them European ways of conducting their activities (Öner, 2012). Accordingly, and in the light of similar debates on European societies, these and other studies argue that Turkey's accession process has contributed to a more democratic pluralist civil society (Göksel and Birden Güneş, 2005; Kirişçi, 2007; Yerasimos 2000).

The literature also reflected on civil society as an agent of this changing opportunity structure. The earlier studies, especially, suggest that civil society organizations became one of the principal sources of pressure for EU-related democratic reforms and contributed to Turkey's democratic transformation (Göksel and Birden Güneş, 2005; Tocci, 2005). They discussed civil society's participation in the accession process and the importance of the role it played by advocating Turkey's membership.

During the earlier years of Turkey's candidacy, the EU became a common reference point in domestic debates (Diez et al., 2005: 2). Civil society actors involved in certain public debates made reference to European norms and policies. The EU became a "legitimating context" to mobilize coalitions and disempower their critics for a wide array of issues stretching from the Cyprus conflict to the Kurdish question (Kaliber, 2016: 60; Rumelili, 2005: 46). Various civic actors working on different issue areas – for example, women's groups, environmentalists, human rights activists – referred to the EU's conditionality to promote policy initiatives. In return, studies suggest that such referencing enhanced the overall legitimacy of civic actors and the issues they advocated for, as the public perceived that these organizations were not only working for their cause but also for Turkey's accession to the EU (Rumelili and Boşnak, 2015: 134).

A final strand of literature on this topic examines Turkish civil society's partnerships and cooperation with public institutions in Turkey or with civic actors in the EU (Birden and Rumelili, 2009; Rumelili, 2005). The EU funds often promoted and sometimes stipulated these partnerships. As a result, civil society organizations applying for EU funds regularly search or partner with their European counterparts. The EU Delegation in Ankara also organized meetings for facilitating the formation of such partnerships (Rumelili and Boşnak, 2015: 134). However, project-based cooperation between groups rarely turn into lasting partnerships. Some of the better-established groups benefit from participating at EU-level networks. For instance, women's organizations' participation at the European Women's Lobby to lobby the government more effectively on domestic issues is a good example of this (Boşnak, 2015).

The EU also promotes public institutions to cooperate with civil society actors in Turkey. This corresponds to the public's image of civil society, which does not necessarily view civil society organizations as needing to be completely detached from the state. The links these organizations develop with public institutions in fact often lead to greater public support for their activities and may provide added legitimacy. This cooperation has been developing in recent years and the extent of cooperation varies across the public institutions. With no legal framework for and no tradition of cooperation between the public sector and civil society, civic organizations are likely to benefit at best from indirect access and participation. Their genuine involvement in policy-making remains an exception.

A critical look at the Europeanization of Turkish civil society

The broader impact of the EU's civil society support in Turkey is not without criticism. Various studies noted the funds' complicated application procedures and competitive nature, as well as the bureaucratic overload of running EU-funded projects. In addition, representativeness, while an important criterion, is not a priority. Despite the emphasis on civil society development, funding criteria rarely prioritize how representative these civil society organizations are. This leads to what Altan-Olcay and İçduygu (2012: 169) called an "oligopolistic" field in Turkish civil society, privileging larger and more professionalized civil society organizations. The bureaucracy of EU funding is also criticized for diverting staff energy to EU-funded projects only, with little or no human resources left for member training (Paker et al., 2013: 771).

Despite efforts to support civil society organizations from less developed regions, at least in the initial years, civil society organizations outside major cities shied away from applying to EU funds due to capacity limitations (Birden and Rumelili, 2009). Others argue that EU funds risk undermining civil society's culture of volunteerism (Ergun, 2010; Kuzmanovic, 2010) and the necessity for generating funds from members is reduced (Paker et al., 2013: 770). EU funds are also criticized for creating a project culture in such a way that civil society organizations lose focus on their core activities (Kuzmanovic, 2010: 436).

Civil society organizations may be approaching EU funds, the reform process and even the Europeanization discourse instrumentally. Different studies found that civil society organizations support Europeanization when they think it serves their cause or interest. Civil society organizations ignore or even make negative references to Europeanization when it does not suit their interest (Kaliber, 2016; Zihnioğlu, 2013).

More interestingly, during this period Turkish civil society's composition did not change much. Between 1999 and 2008, the percentage increase in all types of associations was pretty much even; around 39 to 40 percent (see Figure 4.2). The only exception is associations classified as working on international activities. Their numbers were increased by 42 percent during that decade. As a result, just like in 1999, associations working on religious services, sports and solidarity continued to dominate organized civil society. Considering EU funds are not evenly distributed among the different types shown in Figure 4.2, the funds' influence in the increase in association numbers may be more limited than usually assumed. The even increase is likely to be a result of other windows of opportunities, such as an improving legal environment, which itself is a result of Turkey's accession process. Then again, the opening of civic space during the early years of the accession process is discussed in relation to rather liberal groups. The use of this space by illiberal or uncivil groups in Turkey remains largely unstudied (Kaliber, 2016: 62).

The downturn in EU–Turkey relations since 2007 also influenced the EU's relations with Turkish civil society. Scholars now discuss the de-Europeanization process.[4] De-Europeanization not only means a slowdown or even reversal of

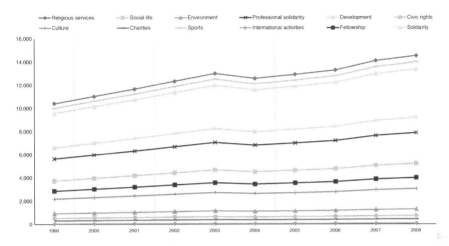

Figure 4.2 The distribution of active associations according to their type (1999–2008).
Source: Department of Associations, 2009.[5]

EU-induced reforms. More importantly, European norms and values cease to inform public debates. In short, the EU is not seen as a normative and political context affecting Turkish politics and policy. This has important repercussions for civil society. According to Kaliber (2016) de-Europeanization of civil society impacted on the civil society organizations vocal on the Kurdish question. On the one hand, the reversals of EU-induced reforms (combined with the end of the peace process in 2015) demobilized civil society. This led to the diminishing role of civil society organizations on the Kurdish question. On the other hand, there is a gradual decline in the incorporation of European institutions, norms and values vis-à-vis the Kurdish question. This has "resulted in the weakening of Europeanization as a normative/political context that can be mobilized by these civil society organizations" (Kaliber, 2016: 60). Over the last decade, civil society organizations avoid using the EU as a reference point or making references to EU policies and institutions. Overall, the extent of EU's legitimization impact has diminished (Rumelili and Boşnak, 2015: 139).

Turkish civil society today

What makes Turkish civil society

It is beyond the scope of this section to depict a thorough picture of Turkish civil society today. Therefore, this section will discuss the prominent features of, and the current trends in, Turkish civil society.

First, the public takes the idea of civil society and views its actors positively. That said, they have a rather particular understanding of who the legitimate actors of civil society are and what they should do. According to an all-round survey on Turkish public perception on civil society (YA-DA, 2014: 9–14), philanthropy (21.6 percent) and social benefit (10 percent) are the two concepts that come to people's minds when they hear 'civil society organization.' Likewise, when asked about the three things civil society organizations in Turkey remind them of, a great majority said aid/philanthropy (62.6 percent). This is followed by social benefit (35.3 percent) and professional solidarity (34.9 percent). Not only do the people in Turkey mainly associate civil society with philanthropy and social services, but they also consider these to be the most positive features of civil society organizations. Accordingly, charities and humanitarian aid organizations are considered legitimate civic actors and they enjoy more public support. People expect civil society organizations to fill the gaps in public welfare services.

In short, people want to see a civil society that complements the state and not contradicts it. Second, in conjunction with this, civil society organizations should neither be political nor act ideologically. An organization *being political*, in other words challenging the policies and practices, is considered to be *doing politics*. And for the public, doing politics is the task of political parties. Politicized organizations are criticized for having political engagements. In the eyes of the public, these organizations abandon the civic space and enter the zone of political parties. For the public, this goes beyond their organizational objectives and accordingly they lose their impartiality and legitimacy.

For public officials in Turkey, being ideological is listed as the main factor influencing civil society organizations' reputation negatively (YA-DA, 2014: 18). This makes the situation especially complicated for advocacy groups that regularly confront public institutions and challenge their policies and practices. Civil society organizations often reflect this sensitivity, too. Even those organizations that work on political issues tend to emphasize they are non-political or try to demonstrate how they act above party politics. Except for some highly politicized groups, most of the organizations "do not go into the political side of things" (CSO 2) and prefer to do their work "without getting involved in politics … because to be able to conduct our business, come through without stumbling we think we should not be engaged anywhere" (CSO 43).

The third point relates more broadly to the public perception of the state and civil society relations. In general, people in Turkey are not totally convinced that civil society organizations need to be completely detached from the state. This is because, in parallel with the first point, for the public, civil society organizations should complement the state. Accordingly, the links they develop with public institutions provide added legitimacy for these organizations and greater public support to their activities. Both as a reflection and a result of this public perception, civil society organizations are also open to cooperation with public institutions. In particular, certain big interest groups benefit from their cooperation with the state, rather than with other organizations. In that sense, and as a rule, civil society organizations consider the state not as an adversary, but an ally against other organizations with which they compete (Kalaycıoğlu, 2002: 257).

On one level, civil society's cooperation with public institutions may be promising for better participation. But this is not without drawbacks and risks. For one thing, there is no legal framework regulating the cooperation between the public sector and civil society. Added to this is the lack of any tradition of such cooperation. While implementation may differ between different public institutions, there is the risk of tokenism where symbolic efforts to be inclusive give an appearance of cooperation. What looks like participation may indeed be limited to information sharing or non-binding counselling. At times, the cooperative attitudes evolve into a corporatist relationship (Kalaycıoğlu, 2002: 259). A final risk on this point relates to the selection of civil society organizations. Organizations across the ideological spectrum may seek to enter into partnerships with public institutions, while those that stand closer to government tend to have easier access. In Turkey's highly polarized society, this bears the risk of intensifying divides within civil society.

Fourth, Turkish culture is determinative in shaping the main features of civil society. Interpersonal trust is one of the key elements of social capital. Various studies reveal that interpersonal trust has consistently been very low in Turkey.[6] A recent survey found that only one person out of 10 believes that most people can be trusted (Çarkoğlu and Aytaç, 2016: 23). In addition, less than half the population believes that civil society organizations can be influential in solving the existing problems (ibid.: 31). All together, these lead to low levels of volunteerism, associationalism and philanthropy.[7] This is reflected in the numbers. The 2014 World Giving Index puts Turkey 128th out of 135 countries. According to the official figures, of the 76.7 million people in Turkey, 10.9 million people are members of associations. While these figures exclude non-member volunteers, people who are members of more than one association are counted multiple times. All in all, less than 15 percent of the population are members of associations (Directorate General of Civil Society Affairs, 2018a). Mass participation does not match the steady increase in the number of civil society organizations. Indeed, only a small part of Turkish society seems to be engaged in organizing and mobilizing.

Different studies show that Turkish culture is also characterized by a lack of social tolerance (Çarkoğlu and Toprak, 2007; see also World Values Survey). This reproduces itself in civil society as organizations of people who think and act alike. As a result, most associations are formed by primordial bonds such as hometown societies, religious affinities and local or regional ties (see Figure 4.3). The caveat here is that such organizations exhibit rather bonding social capital (Putnam, 2000) than bridging social capital (Szreter and Woolcock, 2004). Bonding social capital refers to connections with others who are like themselves, while bridging social capital refers to relationships amongst people who are dissimilar in some demonstrable way.

This becomes particularly significant in the light of Turkey's polarized environment. Turkish politics has long been a polarized activity, one in which all actors are divided into 'us' and 'them.' This polarization in politics reproduces itself in civil society. Civic actors position themselves through polarizing other

82 Revisiting Turkish civil society

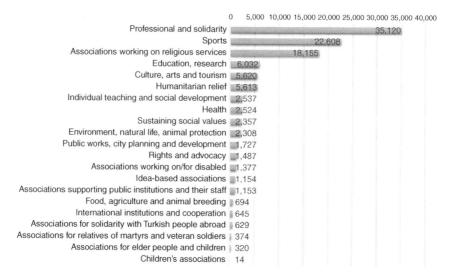

Figure 4.3 Distribution of associations according to their types.
Source: Directorate General of Civil Society Affairs, 2018b.

groups. They do not recognize the need to communicate and cooperate with those not in their camp. The absence of bridging social capital reiterates polarization, while bonding social capital makes this divide more visible. While there may be exceptions to this, such cooperation within Turkish civil society are an exception, rather than a rule.

While social and cultural factors have not been not favorable to the development of rights-based organizations, more recently more and more organizations are taking on less political discourse and activities. Some groups do not completely abandon political activities but complement them with non-contentious ones. For instance, LGBTI groups spend more time on social events, such as showing movies and having discussion sessions. Northern Forests Defense organizes camps and hiking. Such activities are one way of keeping members attached to their organization, as they may be less willing to join protests. At the same time, these activities help them to recruit new volunteers. While both the LGBTI groups and Northern Forests Defense sustain their rights-based or contentious activities, these have shrunk considerably over the past couple of years. Based on figures made available by Turkey's Ministry of Interior, the European Court of Auditors in a recent report noted that the number of members of Turkish associations that advocate rights dropped from 200,096 to 50,598 (European Court of Auditors, 2018: 17). The sharp decrease in the number of members leave no room for doubt on shrinking rights-based activism in Turkey. Some other groups, like human rights activists, continue their work as they have a confrontational relation with the government and have no easy way to switch from non-rights-based activities or discourse. There are also activists organized in non-traditional forms pursuing rights-based activism. These are discussed in more detail in the next section.

More recently, the influx of Syrian immigrants since the outbreak of the war in 2011 has mobilized Turkish civil society. As people arrived en masse, public efforts remained limited. Especially for those who live outside the camps, a civil society response was necessary. Today, Turkey hosts more than 3.5 million Syrians and less than 5 percent sheltered in the camps established by the Turkish government.[8] Local, national and international organizations mushroomed in Turkey's southeast and other major cities where migrants concentrated. Many of these organizations had existed prior to 2011 but some shifted or expanded their focus with the unprecedented influx of Syrians. The crisis also triggered the founding of new organizations. In addition, several informal volunteer groups connected individual volunteers over social media (Mackreath and Sağnıç, 2017: 13).

Despite the increasing intensity of activities for immigrants, such activism seems to reflect Turkish civil society's aforementioned features. Research shows that many of the new organizations founded following the influx of Syrians to Turkey provide material assistance and focus on social services, such as language classes, counselling, information sharing on services, employment and legal aid (ibid.). But there are disputes over whether providing material assistance should be the main focus of these organizations' activities. Some suggest that these organizations should advocate rights and work for the development of an inclusive environment. In addition, lack of cooperation and even competition among civil society organizations based on different world views prevails in this area as well. Finally, the rise of civic volunteers is a promising trend. But these people lack connections to civil society organizations. The low capacity of many of these organizations causes difficulties in incorporating these volunteers into their programmes. It is also worth noting that rising volunteerism in this area is likely to be a response to an immediate humanitarian crisis, rather than reflecting a shifting attitude in society.

New civic activism

Scholars and practitioners agree that profound changes are under way in civil society across the world (see Youngs, 2017). They point to the rise of new forms of civic activism in recent years. These new forms range from large scale protest movements to locally organized community-level forums. There is now a growing debate on the nature, extent and resilience of these groups, as well as their relations with traditional civic actors.

In parallel with these, significant changes are afoot within Turkish civil society. Since earlier this decade, a burgeoning group of activists reinvigorated the civic sphere in Turkey. These groups have become more visible during and after the Gezi protests in 2013. Although activists have dramatically scaled back their protests lately, there is still potential for them to gain ground in the civil society sphere. This new activism is still an evolving phenomenon in Turkey, and it is difficult to draw its exact boundaries. It includes diverse groups with different demands. Still, several commonalities characterize new civic activists in Turkey.

In parallel with the global trend, most new activists prefer to work in loose networks with flexible structures. This is partly because they regard the hierarchical and bureaucratic structures of traditional organizations as millstones and administratively burdensome. They also see a looser structure as a practical way, especially for rights-based groups, to circumvent the government's attempts to control their activities. In addition, they largely feel disconnected from the formal system. While their protests reflect this, they also try to create an inclusive and participatory structure for decision-making.

These activists introduced different ways of organizing. One good example is the local forums established during the Gezi protests. Initially, around five or six forums were established towards the end of the protests at the Gezi Park in İstanbul, to discuss how to proceed with the protests, though the forums continued to meet for a period even after the protests ended. As the size of İstanbul made it difficult to meet in one spot, the protestors were soon scattered around different parks in the city. The forums focused on mostly local issues relating to their own neighborhood. The number of participants eventually shrank, but these forums were an attempt for an elaborative public sphere that tried to make citizen participation possible.

New civic activists tend to focus on local problems. This gives them the advantage of spotting an emerging problem more easily. With their flexible structure, they can also react more quickly. Reaching out to local people and incorporating their concerns adds to their legitimacy. Focusing on local problems does not mean these activists are indifferent to macro issues but rather that they address them through more specific issues. On the contrary, they often link their problems with broader governance issues that in turn resonate with wider public. For example, several local protests against mining operations indicate a reaction to the government's environmental policies that put economic interests ahead of environmental concerns and locals' livelihoods. The protests against the demolishment of the historical Emek Theater became a symbol for reacting against unchecked urban development (Oda TV, 2014). Ultimately, people protest against projects that are forced through without any public debate, which adds to their perception of being disconnected from the system.

Advances in ICT and widespread use of social media are certainly important aspects of this non-traditional form of activism. Active use of social media helps these groups to gain speed in their communication and organizing, especially in increasingly challenging circumstances and with low levels of trust in the mainstream media. Effective use of social media also helps activists to share information about the problem and their activities with a larger public.

One of the major challenges ahead of these loose networks of activists is to consolidate their strong reaction and turn it into a sustained effort. This becomes particularly problematic considering that many of the issues raised by new civic activists are against projects with environmental impacts or urban development plans. Protesting against these plans is difficult enough. New civic activists often must challenge the controversial legal decisions. This requires activists to trigger judicial processes, which can easily extend a legal struggle for years. This is a challenge for the activists, first, because such legal struggles require committed lawyers with legal experience in the given area. While such lawyers may be more readily available in some, often major, cases, this may not be possible for every issue. Second, even with committed lawyers, it is difficult for activists organized around fluid networks to follow such judicial processes.

The second issue is on policy change beyond campaigns. These activists are often criticized for failing to put forward specific policy proposals that relate to their claims. How to connect their claims with governance is a challenge sometimes discussed among the activists themselves. Certainly, one-off protests are rarely enough to influence lawmakers to result in any change. Policy change requires constant lobbying over a long period of time, which is usually difficult for activists operating within a loose structure.

At this point, the new activists' relations with traditional civic actors, such as civil society organizations and chambers, become important. The traditional actors possess the knowledge and expertise to fill the gap and have experience in working with public institutions. In addition, their institutionalized structure allows them to sustain campaigns and follow the judicial process all the way through.

Much focus has been on new civic activism as an alternative to traditional activism by civil society organizations. However, scholars demonstrate (Glasius and Ishkanian, 2015; Zihnioğlu, 2019) that new and traditional civic actors cooperate more often than not in a way that benefits them both. These actors have shown a capacity to sustain long-term cooperation in pursuit of the same cause. That said, new and traditional civic actors are not completely distinct from one another. Many of the activists are former, or even current, members of traditional actors, acting as a bridge between the two.

In discussing this new activism in Turkey, one should not overlook the role of the Turkish youth. In particular, during the Gezi protests, but also in the activism that followed afterwards, the overwhelming presence of young people has not escaped attention. For many, this was unexpected as young people in general have been identified with apathy to activism and considered to have an apolitical attitude. As we mentioned earlier in this chapter, during the years following the 1980 coup, civil society's radius of action has become more restricted. This led to a generation characterized by low levels of civic engagement and distanced from the associational life. Even after the political and associational life relatively normalized in the following decade, young people remained distant to organizational life. Different studies show young people's low level of political engagement.[9] On the other hand, Lüküslü and Yücel (2013) argue that Turkish youth is actually well-aware of and sensitive to social problems but choose not to participate in the political arena. This is because the young believe that the political arena will be inadequate in solving problems and they cannot express

86 Revisiting Turkish civil society

themselves easily in political institutions (political parties, political associations). Indeed, Lüküslü notes that young people act with a "necessary conformism," meaning that they conform to the social rules they do not believe, only because they think they would not succeed in prevailing against them.

In this respect, the Gezi protests have shown the potential of young people and their capacity for activism. Following Lüküslü's argument, the protests and the activism that followed afterwards, not only show that there is a considerable group among the youth, who are very aware of Turkey's political and social problems. But more importantly, these people can also develop a political attitude towards the problem and react in an organized way. The ensuing activism which involved large numbers of young people suggest that the youth may be taking its chances on new and alternative models of civic and political engagement.

Turkish civil society has undergone important changes since the late 1980s, with new issues and actors. It has come to the forefront especially following Turkey's EU candidacy as many came to see civil society as an important platform to trigger a social learning process in Turkey. More recently, important segments of Turkish civil society have been depoliticizing. The reason for this is two-fold. On the one hand, the changing environment in which civic actors operates is less permissive for rights-based, advocacy work. The EU's diminishing leverage over Turkey, and Turkey's political and social polarization impact on this closing civic space. On the other hand, the EU's civil society support has been contributing to civil society's depoliticization. The following chapters discuss in more detail how these two reasons have been shaping a more depoliticized civil society in Turkey.

Notes

1 The history of the women's movement in Turkey goes back to the late Ottoman period. The reason for the reference to post-1980 women's movement as 'new' is to acknowledge the earlier existence of the women's movement in Turkey.
2 See also TÜSİAD Annual Reports for more detailed information on TÜSİAD's activities during this period at https://tusiad.org/tr/faaliyet-raporlari (in Turkish).
3 The official figures the author received from the Department of Associations and published (Zihnioğlu, 2013) were slightly different, and the drop in 2004 was negligible. The earlier figures were 71,832 for 2003 and 69,439 for 2004. The same data showed there were 59,465 active associations in 1998.
4 See South European Society and Politics special issue on de-Europeanization (volume 21, issue 1).
5 The classification of associations belongs to the Department of Associations. Some of the types (for example, Association of Kemalist Thought, Turkish Aeronautical Associations) are clearly not a type, but nationwide CSOs. There is no explanation why the Department of Associations preferred this classification. The author obtained these figures from the Department of Associations in 2009. In 2012, the author asked for updated figures, but the Department could not deliver. Later, the classification of associations changed making it difficult for comparison. Figure 4.2 covers only the major groups listed by the then-Department of Associations in 2009.
6 See, for instance, World Values Survey, European Social Survey and International Social Survey Programme of OECD, World Map of Interpersonal Trust.

7 See World Giving Index, TÜSEV's research on "Philanthropy in Turkey: Citizens, Foundations and Social Justice" and "Civil Society Monitoring" project.
8 As of 18 October 2018 there are 3,587,930 Syrian refugees registered in the scope of temporary protection, 3,416,290 of these live outside the temporary shelter centers. Source: Directorate General of Migration Management www.goc.gov.tr/icerik6/temporary-protection_915_1024_4748_icerik.
9 For an overview of these studies, see Demet Lüküslü, 2008: 290–292.

Bibliography

Ahmad, F. (2000) *The Making of Modern Turkey*. London: Routledge.
Ahmad, F. (2003) *Turkey: The Quest for Identity*. England: Oneworld Publications.
Altan-Olcay, Ö. and İçduygu, A. (2012) Mapping Civil Society in the Middle East: The Cases of Egypt, Lebanon and Turkey, *British Journal of Middle Eastern Studies*, 39(2), pp. 157–179.
Altınay, H. (2005) Does Civil Society Matter?, in M. Lake (ed.), *The EU & Turkey. A Glittering Prize Or a Millstone?* London: The Federal Trust.
Atan, S. (2004) Europeanisation of Turkey Peak Business Organisations and Turkey–EU Relations, in M. Ugur and N. Canefe (eds), *Turkey and European Integration. Accession Prospects and Issues*. London, Routledge.
Birden, R. and Rumelili, B. (2009) Rapprochement at the Grassroots: How Far can Civil Society Engagement Go? in O. Anastasakis, K. Nicolaïdis and K. Öktem (eds), *In the Long Shadow of Europe: Greeks and Turks in the Era of Postnationalism*. Leiden and Boston: Martinus Nijhoff.
Boşnak, B. (2015) *Differential Empowerment of Civil Society in Turkey: Interplay between the EU and Historical Legacies*, PhD thesis, Eberhard Karls Universität Tübingen.
Çarkoğlu, A. and Aytaç, S. E. (2016) *Individual Giving and Philanthropy in Turkey*. Istanbul: Third Sector Foundation of Turkey.
Çarkoğlu, A. and Toprak, B. (2007) Religion, Society and Politics in Changing Turkey, TESEV Research Report, http://research.sabanciuniv.edu/5854/1/2007_08_Religon,_Society_and_Politics_in_a_Changing_Turkey.pdf.
Center for American Progress, Istanbul Policy Center, and Istituto Affari Internazionali. (2017) *Trends in Turkish Civil Society*.
Diez, T., Agnantopoulos, A. and Kaliber, A. (2005) "Introduction" in File: Turkey, Europeanisation and Civil Society, *South European Society and Politics*, 10(1), pp. 1–15.
Directorate General of Civil Society Affairs. (2018a) *The Ratio of Association Members to Turkish Population*. www.dernekler.gov.tr/tr/AnasayfaLinkler/dernek-uye-sayilarinin-turkiye-nufusu.aspx.
Directorate General of Civil Society Affairs. (2018b) *Distribution of Associations According to Their Type*. www.dernekler.gov.tr/tr/AnasayfaLinkler/derneklerin-faaliyet-alanina-gore.aspx.
Economic Development Foundation. (2019) *Projects*. https://oldweb.ikv.org.tr/icerik_en.asp?konu=projeler&arsiv=&baslik=PROJECTS&sayfa=1.
Ergun, A. (2010) Civil Society in Turkey and Local Dimensions of Europeanization, *Journal of European Integration*, 32(5), pp. 507–522.
European Court of Auditors. (2018) *EU Pre-Accession Assistance to Turkey: Only Limited Results So Far*. Special Report No 7. www.eca.europa.eu/Lists/ECADocuments/SR18_07/SR_TURKEY_EN.pdf.

Evren, K. (1991) *Kenan Evren'in Anıları* (Vol. 3). İstanbul: Milliyet Publications.
Glasius, M. and Ishkanian, A. (2015) Surreptitious Symbiosis: Engagement between Activists and NGOs, *Voluntas*, 26, pp. 2620–2644.
Göksel, D. N. and Birden Güneş, R. (2005) The Role of NGOs in the European Integration Process: The Turkish Experience, *South European Society and Politics*, 10(1), pp. 57–72.
Grigoriadis, I. N. (2009) *Trials of Europeanization: Turkish Political Culture and the European Union*. New York: Palgrave Macmillan.
Kalaycıoğlu, E. (2002) State and Civil Society in Turkey: Democracy, Development and Protest, in A. B. Sajoo (ed.), *Civil Society in the Muslim World: Contemporary Perspectives*. New York: I. B. Tauris.
Kaliber, A. (2016) De-Europeanisation of Civil Society and Public Debates in Turkey: The Kurdish Question Revisited, *South European Society and Politics*, 21(1), pp. 59–74.
Kaliber, A. and Tocci, N. (2010) Civil Society and the Transformation of Turkey's Kurdish Question, *Security Dialogue*, 41(2), pp. 191–215.
Kaya, A. and Marchetti, R. (2014) *Europeanization, Framing Competition and Civil Society in the EU and Turkey*, Working Paper No. 6. IAI Instituto Affari Internazionali. www.iai.it/sites/default/files/GTE_WP_06.pdf.
Keyman, E. F. and İçduygu, A. (2003) Globalisation, Civil Society and Citizenship in Turkey: Actors, Boundaries and Discourses, *Citizenship Studies*, 7(2), pp. 219–234.
Kirişçi, K. (2007) The Kurdish Question and Turkey: Future Challenges and Prospects for a Solution, *ISPI Working Paper No. 24*, Milan.
Kubicek, P. (2002) The Earthquake, Civil Society, and Political Change in Turkey: Assessment and Comparison with Eastern Europe, *Political Studies*, 50, pp. 761–778.
Kuzmanovic, D. (2010) Project Culture and Turkish Civil Society, *Turkish Studies*, 11(3), pp. 429–444.
Lüküslü, D. (2008) Günümüz Türkiye Gençliği: Ne Kayıp Bir Kuşak Ne De Ülkenin Aydınlık Geleceği, in N. Yentürk, Y. Kurtaran and G. Nemutlu (eds), *Türkiye'de Gençlik Çalışması ve Politikaları*. İstanbul: Bilgi University Publications.
Lüküslü, D. and Yücel, H. (2013) Sınıf, Kimlik, Kültür ve Siyaset Ekseninde Gençlik ve Gençlik Araştırmaları, in D. Lüküslü and H. Yücel (eds), *Gençlik Halleri: 2000'li Yıllar Türkiye'sinde Genç Olmak*. Ankara: Efil Publishers.
Mackreath, H. and Sağnıç, Ş. G. (2017) *Civil Society and Syrian Refugees in Turkey*. İstanbul: Citizens' Assembly-Turkey.
Makovsky, A. (1999) Turkey Reacts to Quake with New Energy, Old Notions, *Washington Post* (25 August).
Oda TV. (2014) *Bu Kent Emek İster [This City is Demanding/Needs Emek]* (5 April) http://odatv.com/bu-kent-emek-ister-0504141200.html.
Öner, S. (2012) Europeanisation of Civil Society in Turkey during the Accession Process to the European Union, in Ç. Nas and Y. Özer (eds), *Turkey and the European Union: Processes of Europeanisation*. Burlington: Ashgate.
Öniş, Z. (2005) Entrepreneurs, citizenship and the European Union: The Changing Nature of State-Business Relations in Turkey, in F. Keyman and A. İçduygu (eds), *Citizenship in Global World: European Questions and Turkish Experiences*. London: Routledge.
Paker, H., Adaman, F., Kadirbeyoğlu, Z. and Özkaynak, B. (2013) Environmental Organisations in Turkey: Engaging the State and Capital, *Environmental Politics*, 22(5), pp. 760–778.
Putnam, R. (2000) *Bowling Alone: The Collapse and Revival of American Community*. New York: Simon & Schuster.

Rumelili, B. (2005) Civil Society and the Europeanization of Greek–Turkish Cooperation, *South European Society and Politics*, 10(1), pp. 45–56.

Rumelili, B. and Boşnak, B. (2015) Taking stock of the Europeanization of Civil Society in Turkey the Case of NGOs, in A. Tekin and A. Güney (eds), *The Europeanization of Turkey: Polity and Politics*. London: Routledge.

Sarıbay, A. Y. (2000) Türkiye'de Sivil Toplum ve Demokrasi, in A. Y. Sarıbay and E. F. Keyman (eds), *Global Yerel Eksende Türkiye*. İstanbul: Alfa Publications.

Şimşek, S. (2004) The Transformation of Civil Society in Turkey: From Quantity to Quality, *Turkish Studies*, 5(3), pp. 46–74.

Szreter, S. and Woolcock, M. (2004) Health by Association? Social Capital, Social Theory, and the Political Economy of Public Health, *International Journal of Epidemiology*, 33(4), pp. 650–667.

Tocci, N. (2005) Europeanization in Turkey: Trigger or Anchor for Reform? *South European Society and Politics*, 10(1), pp. 73–83.

YA-DA. (2014) *Sivil Toplum Kuruluşlarına Yönelik Algı ve Yaklaşımlar*. İstanbul: YA-DA.

Yerasimos, S. (2000) Civil Society, Europe and Turkey, in S. Yerasimos, G. Seufert and K. Vorhoff (eds), *Civil Society in the Grip of Nationalism*. Istanbul: Orient-Institut.

Youngs, R. (ed.) (2017) *Global Civic Activism in Flux*. Washington: Carnegie Endowment for International Peace.

Zihnioğlu, Ö. (2013) *European Union Civil Society Policy and Turkey: A Bridge Too Far?* Basingstoke: Palgrave Macmillan.

Zihnioğlu, Ö. (2017) Turkey: The Struggles of a New Civil Society, in R. Youngs (ed.), *Global Civic Activism in Flux*. Washington, D.C.: Carnegie Endowment for International Peace.

Zihnioğlu, Ö. (2019) The Prospects of Civic Alliance: New Civic Activists Acting Together with Civil Society Organizations, *Voluntas* 30(2), pp. 289–299.

5 Changing landscape of Turkish civil society

The course of Turkey's overall relations with the EU over the past two decades has affected Turkey's civic space both directly and indirectly. The EU's persistent emphasis, made freedom of association and freedom of assembly a crucial part of the intense reform period in the early 2000s. Along with the rest of the reform process, these improvements, too, slowed down in the latter half of the decade and through the early 2010s, leaving many issues half-finished or untouched. More recently, in parallel with Turkey's deteriorating democracy and the EU's diminishing leverage over Turkey, the environment in which civic actors operates became less permissive for rights-based and advocacy work.

The improving legal framework

Chapter 2 overviewed the intense reforms Turkey has undertaken during the initial years of its candidacy until the mid-2000s. The scope of reforms was extensive and improvements in freedom of association and peaceful assembly had their share.

Turkey has taken the initial steps to enhance constitutional safeguards for civil society organizations in 2001 by amending the relevant sections of the Constitution. Accordingly, the requirement to obtain permits to establish associations was removed, but specific grounds (national security, public order, for the prevention of crime, public morals, public health, or for the protection of the rights and freedoms of others) to restrict this right was added. This was followed by a new Civil Code in 2002, that adopted a reformist outlook, while still retaining some of cumbersome procedures for the establishment and activities of associations. In addition, the new Civil Code denies the official existence of unregistered associations. The 1926 Civil Code found it sufficient to have a framework of rules and to announce the desire to become an association to acquire juridical personality (Article 53). However, the new Code requires a notification of authorities that will then examine the issue.

The ensuing eight 'Harmonization Packages' between February 2002 and July 2004, further widened the space for civil society through several amendments to Associations Law, Foundations Law and Civil Code. The amendments addressed various issues, including inter alia establishment, membership, cooperation, international activities, foreign funding, other financial undertakings and limitations to state interference. The Associations Law was replaced with a new one in 2004 and was supplemented with a new regulation in 2005 that further improved the legal framework. That said, the regulation retained cumbersome procedures for international cooperation, foreign funding as well as the activities and registration of foreign organizations active in Turkey.

In the meantime, under the Ministry of Interior a new Department of Associations was established in 2002. This new Department in charge of associations was entrusted with the authority, which had previously been in the hands of the Directorate General for Security.

Despite the fast pace reforms were undertaken, drawbacks prevailed in practice suggesting that improving the implementation would be more challenging. Pressures against human rights organizations, especially those active in Turkey's southeast such as the Mesopotamia Culture Centre and several branches of Human Rights Association, continued. Some faced investigations, prosecutions, censorship of written materials and the closing of offices. Several LGBTI groups (for example, Kaos GL Gay, Lesbian Cultural Research and Solidarity Association and Lambda İstanbul Solidarity Association) encountered judicial harassment on the basis that their associations were contrary to law and morality. The Jehovah's Witnesses' application to establish an association based explicitly on religious objectives was also challenged in court, but later allowed by the Court of Cassation's acquittal decision.

Legal improvements for foundations were introduced slightly later in 2008. The new law brought about the Bylaw on the foundations established in accordance with Turkish Civil Code, Communications from Directorate General of Foundations and the related sections in the Civil Code under a single framework. The new Law introduced changes for community foundations on property rights, their activities abroad, foreign funding, right to change objective and function. Most importantly, the new Law established the Foundations Council as the highest decision-making body where five of the 15 seats are filled with representatives of foundations. This Council allows for the first time the foundations to be involved in the decision-making process. The new Law was amended in 2011.

During this period, Turkey's civic space has further expanded through improvements to freedom of assembly. First, with constitutional amendments in 2001 some of the restrictive measures on the right to hold meetings and demonstration marches, as well as the prohibition and postponing of this right were removed from the text. That said, the provision to restrict this right based on "national security, public order, for the prevention of crime, public morals, public health, or for the protection of the rights and freedoms of others and by law" was added to the article. Freedom of assembly gradually expanded following several changes to the Law on Public Meetings and Demonstration Marches with consecutive Harmonization Packages. In addition, a new regulation obliged security officers on duty to wear helmets with numbers on them to facilitate their identification and thereby to discourage excessive use of force.

Practical restrictions persisted despite these reforms and ensuing circulars from the Ministry of Interior not to impinge on the freedom of peaceful assembly. Throughout most of this decade arbitrary limitations to the right to peaceful assembly or disproportionate police force continued in major demonstrations on Women's Day, Newroz or Labor Day. Further, disciplinary investigations against officers using excessive force have proven futile. The opening of such cases has often been stonewalled as they require the Governor's authorization.

The half-finished reforms

The fast pace of reform process in the early 2000s was short-lived and came to a halt by mid-decade. Apart from the new Foundations Law in 2008 and the amendments to this law in 2011, there were no new improvements to freedom of association since then. This left several issues pertaining to civil society half-finished or untouched, giving rise to problems particularly in implementation.

The fundamental issue is the absence of a comprehensive legal framework for civil society. There is no definition of civil society or civil society organization in the relevant legislation. This leads to confusion in practice. In addition, there is no overall civil society strategy or policy. While the 64th government's 2016 Action Plan aimed for a Civil Society Law to be completed by the end of 2016 (Turkish Prime Ministry, 2016: 39), this has not yet been realized. Administration of civic space is fragmented with several public institutions involved. The law stipulates civil society organizations to be established only in the forms of associations and foundations. Because registration is mandatory for a legal identity, unregistered or informal associational forms (for example, initiatives, networks) are excluded from the legal framework.[1] Despite their widespread presence, other collective groups are unable to benefit from the rights of a legal identity (for example, accessing public funds, opening bank accounts).

Some of the cumbersome bureaucratic procedures are still in place, although much of the administrative requirements for associations and foundations were eased with earlier reforms. These are mostly related to registration and book-keeping. In 2013, the Ministry of Internal Affairs published a directive on the Law of Associations to ease some of the book-keeping procedures. More important issues are related to inspections and penalties. Inspections are not periodic, and the rules of inspection are not clearly defined. This creates inconsistencies in their frequency, duration and scope. Studies often report unequal treatment of rights-based organizations (Dereci and Ersen, 2017: 20). Failing to comply with these bureaucratic requirements result in fines that are burdensome for many civil society organizations.

A major expectation for improvement in legal and operational framework concerns aid collection. The Law on Collection of Aid sets detailed regulation and restrictive obligations. Civil society organizations must obtain a special permit every time they raise funds in public spaces (for example, online fundraising, SMS campaigns and other public campaigns). The requirements implied by the law is restrictive and becomes an obstacle for organizations to raise funds to achieve their aims and maintain their financial sustainability. The law excludes donations made at the organizations' offices. In addition, associations with public benefit status and foundations with tax exemption status enjoy several tax deductions. However, only a limited number of associations and foundations enjoy this status, given after a highly bureaucratic (and what many organizations consider as political) process by the Council of Ministers.

Amendments to freedom of assembly fell short of easing the restrictive nature of the legislation. The right to hold peaceful assembly and demonstrations without having to obtain any prior authorization is enshrined in the Constitution. However, the exercise of this right may be restricted on specified grounds stated in the Law on Meetings and Demonstrations including "preservation of national security, public order, prevention of crime, protection of public health and public moral or the rights and freedoms of others" (Article 19). As these are not defined clearly in the Law, they are often interpreted in a restrictive and arbitrary manner. In addition, the over-regulating secondary legislation such as directives, mandates or regulations also limits the legal environment. The Law further restricts freedom of assembly by requiring cumbersome notification process in which the organizing committee must hand in to the district Governor's office a comprehensive set of information, along with a declaration 48 hours prior to the assembly.

An equally important problem are the broad concepts involved, such as 'general morality,' 'national security' or 'public order.' Despite the fact that these are prevalent in the legal texts, they lack concrete definitions. This creates inconsistent and arbitrary interpretations by different public institutions.

The downturn in reforms and the shrinking civic space

Turkey's shrinking civic space has become a much-mentioned topic following the Gezi protests in 2013. It is true that the government's repressive measures have gained pace starting from 2013. However, the beginning of the downturn in political reforms, including those relating to civic space, date earlier. While it is difficult to set an exact date for this, in retrospect, signs were visible as early as 2009, and they have gradually deteriorated since then.

The decline of Turkey's democracy and the reasons behind this have been subject to many studies over the past decade. Without delving too much into this broad literature, I will underline the reasons behind Turkey's shrinking civic space.

In essence, there are two major reasons. First is the AKP's drift to a majoritarian conception of democracy during this period (Özbudun, 2014). This rather narrow understanding of democracy holds elections as the only source of legitimacy for a democratic government. In this "ballot box reductionism" (Gürcan and Peker, 2015: 159), securing the majority support is equated with the national will itself, which legitimizes not only their rule, but also their policy choices. Winning elections and representing what they consider to be the majority's interests is interpreted to be abiding by democratic principles. Consequently, democratically elected leaders should not cave into critics and protestors who only represent a vocal minority (Kubicek, 2016). As the AKP and its leader Erdoğan, won election after election since their first electoral contest in 2002, their recourse to a majoritarian understanding of democracy increased. Erdoğan frequently referred to the ballot box when his democratic credentials were challenged by the opposition. Indeed, going further, following the corruption allegations in 2013, Erdoğan asserted that the upcoming local elections in 2014 would serve as a means to judge their guilt or innocence.

The second reason behind Turkey's shrinking civic space is Erdoğan's quest to establish a cultural and social hegemony. With the AKP's uninterrupted rule since 2002, Erdoğan is confident in his and the AKP's political power. But, for Erdoğan, "being in political power is a different thing. Social and cultural power is another thing" (Hürriyet, 2017). Erdoğan concedes that they still have problems in their social and cultural power and is uncertain of their reach in these spheres. Civil society is useful in two respects. On the one hand, civil society organizations help raise and expand the "devoted cadres" that Erdoğan seeks. On the other hand, civil society is a fundamental platform for the AKP to expand its political struggle to a societal level. In consolidated democracies, we can expect civic actors to interact in a variety of ways to contest, change or expand the existing social order. This entails a risk that the AKP will face actors challenging its established and proposed social order. Therefore, it adopts measures limiting the space for some actors, while leaving the space wide open for others.

Several exacerbating factors accompany these two fundamental reasons. Some of these address broader conditions, while others refer to more specific developments. These factors on their own are not the reasons behind Turkey's shrinking space, but they make it more conducive. Without considering these factors, we would be unable to understand and explain what has been shaping and impacting upon Turkish civil society.

The first exacerbating factor is the polarization within Turkish civil society. Neither Turkish politics nor society is a stranger to polarization. The dividing lines may change over the years but the division of political actors between 'us' and 'them' has been a recurrent problem. Polarization is reflected in all aspects of societal life including civil society organizations. That said, polarization in Turkey since the early 2010s has reached levels unknown for decades. As polarization intensified, what little horizontal relations there may had been among different groups of civic actors ended – either gradually or abruptly. The 'others' have become 'outsiders' and not considered part of civil society. As a result, closing of the civic space is disregarded should the state's interventions concern the 'others' only.

The second factor is Turkey's Kurdish problem. This perennial problem has been a major factor behind periodic deteriorations in Turkey's democratic openings. Except for brief periods of openings (most recently in 2009 and between 2013 and 2015), Kurdish organizations have been raided by police and closed down on often vague terrorism charges. Kurdish civil society groups get stuck between the state and the PKK. What little civic activity that may have flourished during the openings and more stable periods in Turkey's Kurdish populated southeastern provinces quickly wanes (Center for American Progress et al., 2017: 16–17).

The third exacerbating factor stems from the loss of momentum in Turkey's accession process. The EU's conditionality and the membership incentive were major factors driving the reform process in the early 2000s. However, loud objections to Turkey's potential EU membership and several new barriers[2] raised since 2005 first introduced uncertainty to accession negotiations and soon after compromised the credibility of the EU's conditionality in the eyes of both the public and officials in Turkey. The EU soon lost its leverage and when the downturn in reforms gained pace the EU's consistent criticisms fell on deaf ears.

The fourth and final exacerbating factor is a broader challenge on civil society across the globe. As it has become widely known in recent years, shrinking civic space has come to be a global 'trend' (Carothers, 2015; Carothers and Brechenmacher, 2014; CIVICUS, 2016). Since it first began around 2004–2005, the problem intensified in depth and scope (Youngs and Echagüe, 2017). Over 100 governments in multiple regions aim at restricting the activities of civic organizations. For this, not only do they adopt restrictive legal measures. But some governments limit the international support, delegitimize and even physically harass these organizations and their members. More recently, international organizations and donors have taken up the issue seriously and devised new instruments to meet the challenge. On the one hand, it is good news for Turkish civil society that many international organizations, including the EU, concern themselves with this problem. On the other hand, though, the fact that this is a growing trend points to deep-seated structural problems and raises concerns about international liberal order – all of which would make it more challenging in Turkey to counter this pushback against civil society.

The term 'shrinking' has two connotations; one concrete, and the other more symbolic. The discussions on shrinking civic space focus mostly on its tangible aspects, such as repressive legal measures, harassments and the like. However, from a broader perspective, the term refers to a sense of a loss of justice among people and subsequently the diminishing of their willingness to engage in civil society organizations. This symbolically squeezes the civic space (Yalçın, 2015: 84–85). Despite the challenges they pose, it is easier to track, protest and even fight against the concrete aspects. Symbolically shrinking civic space gets deep inside the social fabric, with an impact far beyond what legal measures can achieve.

The downturn of reforms in Turkey began towards the end of 2000s. Initially, during the first few years, this backsliding was subtle and was coupled with progress in some areas. One temporary progress was regarding International Workers' Day celebrations. Throughout the 2000s, the unions' efforts to celebrate International Workers' Day in Taksim Square, an iconic place for Turkish workers, have put them in conflict with the state and rallies were marked with police crackdowns. For instance, in 2007, the Governor of İstanbul made a statement that Taksim would be closed to International Workers' Day rallies and thousands of police encircled the square. Following negotiations, a few hundred workers were let in to make a statement at Taksim square, while the police stopped other groups heading to Taksim and detained hundreds. In 2008, even tighter security measures and crackdowns were witnessed. However, the government changed its policy in 2009. In April 2009, 1 May was made an official holiday called Labor and Solidarity Day and around 5000 people rallied at Taksim square in 2009, with some scuffles between police and the demonstrators. The following year, Taksim was officially opened to rallies for the first time after 32 years and thousands streamed into the square. Since 2013, bans have re-emerged on the Workers' Day gatherings there. Behind this short-lived opening might be the government's search for support for the upcoming constitutional referendum in 2010. Whatever the underlying reason, these peaceful rallies served to lighten the mood at least on and around 1 May for a few years.

The Constitutional amendments introduced some minor improvements for labor unions. The amendments repealed the requirement that limits membership in only one labor union or employers' association and the union's liability for material damage during a strike. Most importantly, the amendments repealed the prohibitions on "politically motivated strikes and lockouts, solidarity strikes and lockouts, occupation of work premises, labor go-slows, production decreasing, and other forms of obstruction." The amendments also gave public servants the right to conclude collective agreements. The amendments were welcome as they expanded the freedom of association. Yet, legislation still fell short of EU standards and International Labour Organization Conventions, particularly regarding collective bargaining, dispute settlement and the right to strike for public servants (Akbaş, 2014: 25).

The government's openings were limited and came alongside a crackdown on other issues. In 2009, the government announced a Kurdish Opening (later to be renamed as Democratic Opening). The opening ended abruptly with the return of a small group of outlawed PKK affiliates from Iraq, that became a media show with jubilant crowds and members of Parliament from the pro-Kurdish Democratic Society Party (DTP) meeting the returnees. This sparked outrage and led to the banning of the DTP and an intensification of arrests of Kurdish activists involving alleged members of the Kurdistan Communities Union (*Koma Ciwaken Kurdistan*, KCK). By the summer of 2011, around 3000 people, including politicians, mayors, journalists, writers and academics were arrested, many people questioned the involvement in violence of those who had been arrested. The deteriorating security situation, with over 700 deaths in 2012, made it only worse (Independent Commission, 2014: 17–18). During the years following 2009, several human rights defenders faced prosecution on charges of terrorist propaganda during demonstrations. Rights-based civil organizations working particularly on human rights, LGBTI rights and the Kurdish issue reported facing government interference more frequently than non-rights-based groups. The arrests on charges of terrorist propaganda also included protestors against hydro-electric power plants in Turkey's different provinces (TACSO, 2011: 6).

The government was no more tolerant to other critical actors during the same years. For instance, Doğan Group, a major media outlet with newspapers and television stations that had been harshly critical of the government, was fined approximately US$2.5 billion in September 2009 for tax evasion. This came on top of another more than US$500 million fine in February 2009. The amount owed at the time was nearly as much as the value of the company itself. Many considered these gigantic fines to be political retribution for criticizing the government. Although Erdoğan has distanced himself from the case, he had earlier called on his supporters to boycott Doğan media publications after their critical reporting of his government's performance (Arsu and Tavernise, 2009). This event contributed to a growing self-censorship in Turkey.

By 2013, what may have remained of the government's conciliatory approach has disappeared. Protests against the replacement of the historic Emek Theatre in İstanbul with a shopping and entertainment complex occurred in spring 2013. The Emek Theater initially had been publicly owned and in 1992 was leased to a private developer (Özyurt, 2013). An initial wave of reaction started back in 2006, after the Council of Ministers' decision to open the way for the theatre's demolishment (Emek is Ours Initiative, 2016). What sparked the major protests in the spring of 2013 was that neither the municipality nor the company waited for the courts to conclude on the legal action initiated by Union of Chambers of Turkish Engineers and Architects a couple of years earlier. The municipality granted the construction permit to the company in 2013, and the company started demolishing the theatre soon after with protests ensuing. Riot police used water cannons and tear gas to disperse protestors.

As mentioned above, the government changed its position on International Workers' Day celebrations in Taksim square in 2013. After three years of peaceful demonstrations, the government denied access to Taksim square on account of construction work being carried out.

The ensuing Gezi protests were a major turning point in this period. In late May, a bulldozer was noticed demolishing the Gezi Park's outer walls and was advancing toward uprooting the trees. This was part of the government's long-known urban renewal plan to build a replica of Ottoman-era military barracks with a business mall in Gezi Park. Taksim Solidarity[3] stopped the bulldozer that day and a group of activists initiated a sit-in protest to protect one of the few green areas left at the heart of the city. The use of excessive force against the protestors, including first tear gas, water cannons and later setting fire to protestors' tents, drew more protestors to the park. In just a matter of a few days, the protests jumped to other major cities and continued to spread across the country with growing numbers of protestors. The protests soon snowballed into a nationwide display of discontent. According to Tuğal, at the beginning the majority of protestors consisted of professionals who were hurt, not by exploitation and impoverishment in absolute economic terms, but by the impoverishment of their social life (2013: 166). According to the Interior Ministry, 2.5 million people attended the protests in 79 of Turkey's 81 provinces, while some estimate the number of protestors to be around 3.5 million (Amnesty International, 2014).

The Gezi protests were marked not only by unprecedented number of protestors, but also by the use of excessive force by riot police to disperse and repress the protestors. The government announced that in the first 20 days of the protests 130,000 tear gas capsules were used and that it planned to purchase more as 150,000 capsules were bought for 2013 (Milliyet, 2013). Later in August, it was reported that the government placed an order for 400,000 new tear gas capsules and 60 new water cannon vehicles (T24, 2013). There were 12 casualties[4] and the Turkish Medical Association (2013) reported over 8000 wounded as a result of an excessive use of force by security forces to disperse and repress the protestors. Hundreds of complaints were filed against the police, while only five court cases were opened (Amnesty International, 2013: 6–7). Prime Minister Erdoğan defied the protestors and condemned them as vandals and looters. In a reflection of his majoritarian approach, he questioned the legitimacy of the protests and pointed to upcoming local elections to face off the demonstrations (Hürriyet Daily News, 2013). Erdoğan was particularly uncomfortable with some of opposition parties' support of the protests. He considered their support as resorting to an undemocratic approach, due to their inability to defeat the AKP in elections – the only legitimate way for democratic opposition.

The major wave of arrests during and after the demonstrations helps define the scope of the government's measures to repress these protests. In the first year of Gezi protests, over 5500 people were on trial in nearly a 100 different cases. Most cases involved resisting a public officer, damaging public property and opposition to the Law on Meetings and Demonstrations. Yet a few others were on more serious terrorism charges that could lead to decades long prison sentences (Amnesty International, 2014). Different charges were pressed against five members of Taksim Solidarity, from which all were acquitted in April 2015. Although clashes escalated, especially in the latter half of the protests, protestors hold provocateurs responsible for throwing petrol bombs at police vehicles (Guardian, 2013b). That said, the government was no more tolerant to entirely peaceful demonstrations. Some protestors who quietly joined what is referred to as the "standing man" were also detained (Amnesty International, 2013: 6).

An important challenge for civic actors has been to get sufficient media coverage in Turkey's polarized Turkish media. Although this problem has long existed, it intensified in 2013. Some TV channels remained mute in the early days of the protests. The Supreme Board of Radio and Television (RTÜK) fined several TV stations that transmitted live coverage of the Gezi protests on the basis of incitement to violence. The Turkish Journalists' Union (2013) reported at least 59 journalists were fired or forced to resign due to their coverage of the Gezi protests. In addition, internet and social media have come under pressure. In February 2014, a new internet law allowed the telecommunications authority to block websites without first obtaining a court order, which must be obtained within 24 hours. The law also required all internet providers to store data on users' activity for up to two years and to provide the authorities with the data upon request.

The government made several attempts to either control or ban some social media platforms, although access to social media cannot be blocked as in mainstream broadcasting. Turkey's active social media community even then knew how to circumvent the court-ordered internet bans, therefore rendering them ineffective. What the government and its supporters embarked on more robustly was demonizing Twitter as a source of information. During the Gezi protests, then-Prime Minister Erdoğan labelled social media as "the worst menace to society" (Guardian, 2013a). Government officials, some on Twitter themselves, argued Twitter was not safe, and framed it as a tool threatening national priorities and family values. As Tüfekçi rightly points out, it is more likely that the goal had not been to keep all Twitter users in Turkey to buy these arguments, but to keep its own activist base off Twitter (2017: 242–243).

What these issues bring about is a growing sense of fear that attending a peaceful demonstration may entail different risks. In return, this led many people to shy away from demonstrations and to only offer their support on social media. As a result, activist groups gradually shrank, the protests downsized and their impact waned.

The Gezi protests showed once again the cumbersome procedures enshrined in the Law on Meetings and Demonstrations. The Law entitles the right to hold meetings and demonstrations without permission, although the 48-hour notification requirement, the cumbersome procedure and most importantly, the restrictive interpretation of legislation are considered to be equally limiting. The changes introduced to the Law in 2014 did not meet expectations. In response to criticism, the Ministry of Interior put up a promising circular that could have eradicated excessive use of police force. According to the new circular, the police would give a warning before using tear gas, wait for a sufficient amount of time for protestors to leave and use water cannons before tear gas. However, the circular has been mostly overlooked in practice.

During the initial years following the Gezi protests, major protests continued to bring large crowds on to the streets. Thousands joined the protests in major provinces after the Soma coal mine disaster in March 2014, which claimed 301 miners' lives. The government's plan to destruct a forest in Cerattepe to open a mine have triggered on and off demonstrations in the region and in major provinces from mid-2015 until early 2016. In other cases, for instance the banning of the thirteenth LGBTI Pride Parade in İstanbul in June 2015, showed how civil society activity had clearly narrowed in scope. In addition, on numerous occasions, when protestors were critical of public policies, they faced an excessive use of force.

In the meantime, the legal environment for civic engagement further deteriorated. In October 2014, massive protests erupted across Turkey against the government's decision not to intervene in the self-proclaimed Islamic State's siege of Kobane, a pre-dominantly Kurdish-populated Syrian city on the border with Turkey. Curfews were imposed in several south-eastern provinces with large Kurdish populations for the first time in over two decades and Turkish troops were deployed to suppress the riots. Violent protests prompted the government to draft new internal security arrangements. Despite the opposition parties' objections and widespread public criticisms, the Turkish parliament passed the Law Amending the Law on Powers and Duties of the Police in March 2015. Commonly referred to as the Internal Security Reform Package, the new law considerably strengthens the powers of the police during demonstrations, extends its authority to detain anyone without a prosecutor's order and tightens restrictions on meetings and demonstrations.

The peace process launched by then-Prime Minister Erdoğan in 2013 had been a much promising development in this period. Despite the several achievements of this process, the ceasefire broke down in July 2015. The ensuing low-grade civil war in south-eastern provinces was accompanied by widespread civilian displacements. Kurdish civil society groups were once again squeezed between the state and the PKK, which led to the diminishing of whatever civil society activity that might have flourished since 2013 in the region (Center for American Progress et al., 2017: 17). The aggravated security situation continued to worsen well into 2016, with rising deadly terrorist attacks. In addition, polarization increased with a political deadlock following the June 2015 elections. All in all, the conditions were not conducive to provide an enabling environment for civic engagement.

Not long after, on 15 July 2016, Turkey was shaken by an attempted coup. The AKP government thwarted the putsch through mobilizing large crowds to take to the streets and stand up to the coup forces. Despite the unhappiness with Erdoğan's rule among the opposition, there was widespread agreement that military overthrow is not the right solution (Sloat, 2018: 3). The next day, cross-party politicians issued a joint condemnation of the plot at an emergency session of parliament. Less than a week after, Turkish parliament, with an overwhelming majority, approved a state of emergency to investigate and punish in a more efficient way those responsible. A state of emergency was extended at three-month intervals for two years and ended in July 2018.

Needless to say, the government has the right and responsibility to pursue criminal proceedings against people involved in this violent attempt and bring all those responsible to justice. While the government holds self-exiled Muslim cleric Gülen responsible for the coup attempt, the ensuing crackdown has soon extended beyond his community. Erdoğan himself called the coup attempt "a gift from God" as it would help cleanse the military, although many interpreted that as a golden opportunity to purge his opponents from every sphere of life and to silence any opposing views. A state of emergency gave the Council of Ministers the power to issue statutory decrees that carry the force of law.

In addition, a state of emergency has given the Council of Ministers the right to issue regulations suspending or restricting fundamental freedoms, in particular freedom of peaceful assembly. Widespread use of this authority has severely restricted the scope of civil society activities across the country. For instance, early in October, Ankara governorate banned Ashura Day gatherings in the city based on intelligence of terror attacks. The governorate later limited the ban to open venues after wide condemnation by Turkey's Alawite community and the opposition. In mid-October, all public gatherings and demonstrations were outlawed in Ankara until the end of November due to a terror alert over potential attacks. And soon after that, the governorate has imposed an indefinite ban on all events by LGBTI groups to protect health and morality, as well the rights and freedoms of others.

The large number of arrests, closure of civil society organizations, bans and restrictions on public gatherings and assemblies significantly narrowed civic space. In particular, changing boundaries of what is politically permissible in terms of civil society activities put immense pressure on civil society. Indeed, human rights activists claim that the state can open a court case against something they did two to three years ago (Özçetin and Özer, 2015: 12). This has come about over vague legal provisions and what many activists complained of as arbitrary implementations. The constitutional amendments approved in April 2017 granted the president sweeping new powers. In addition, a presidential decree in July 2018 expanded the president's authority over civil society organizations through the State Supervisory Board (Republic of Turkey Official Gazette, 2018). The decree empowers the Board with a new authority to issue dismissals as a precautionary measure and also conduct administrative investigations, in addition to its previous task for monitoring and supervision. Uncertainty and fear have become the defining characteristics of Turkish civil society since the coup attempt (Center for American Progress et al., 2017: 15).

Apart from control and repression, cooptation and autonomy of civic groups are among the major concerns. Indeed, the government has no intention of demonizing civil society in its entirety. Time and again, President Erdoğan meets civil society representatives and states that his party sees civil society as "a corner stone of our national unity." That said, Erdoğan clearly articulated that "civil society is not opposed to state, on the contrary it complements it." In 2017, when the Islamist human rights organization Mazlum-Der published its controversial report that challenged official statements on the Kurdish conflict, it received a fierce reaction from President Erdoğan. Soon after, under the rule of a court-appointed trustee, the organization's management transferred to a new leadership, 16 of its branches (mostly those from the east and southeast) were closed and thousands lost their membership.

This understanding is also reflected in public institutions. Surveys indicate that it is easier for service-based civil society organizations to interact and establish partnerships with public institutions than rights-based ones. That said, this advantage has its limits. In cases when such organizations share any perceived problems with the public policy, relations with the public institutions are likely to be damaged and even end (Akay, 2016: 36).

Despite the absence of an enabling environment, there is still hope for rights-based activism in Turkey. First, several professional organizations, such as the Turkish Bar Association, Turkish Medical Association and various constituents of the Union of Chambers of Turkish Engineers and Architects, as well as the union itself have been active on a range of issues. Despite the fact that they carry a state-mandated membership, making them vulnerable to state interference, they are outspoken and do not shy away from protesting public authorities.

Second, several other informal rights-based groups can still draw crowds together. For instance, a series of 'No' campaigns were organized by civic groups ahead of the constitutional referendum in April 2017. More interestingly, a group of civic activists established what was commonly referred to as the 'No Assemblies' (in Turkish *Hayır Meclisleri*). These assemblies were local initiatives that supported the 'No' campaigns at the grassroots level in nearly 30 districts in İstanbul and elsewhere (Bianet, 2017; The No Assemblies, 2017). Mass protests sprouted in reaction to fraud allegations stemming from the Supreme Election Board's decision to count nearly 1.5 million unstamped ballots as valid. Thousands took to the streets in major cities to protest against the results. As the protests faded, several activists were detained, and the Council of State rejected the main opposition's appeal against the Supreme Election Board's decision on unstamped ballots. A month after, on the day President Erdoğan was re-elected as the head of the AKP, a separation that was lifted with the referendum, the No Assemblies organized a march under the slogan "You Are Not Legitimate" (BirGün, 2017).

Some of these groups continue their contentious activities to the present day. For instance, they campaigned against power plants in Turkey's north-western Thrace region (Northern Forests Defense, 2019). They even held a demonstration in front of the German Consulate in İstanbul to protest the plans to cut down a large part of the Hambach forest in Germany for lignite mining operations (Tarcan, 2018). In 2019, a network of environmentalist initiatives and organizations held a collaborative campaign against a bill that allowed coal-fired thermal power plants to continue their operations without flue gas filters until 2021. Their efforts resulted in success, and the Members of Parliament have withdrawn the bill (Ünker, 2019).

However, there is a considerable decrease in the number of people actively taking part in these campaigns. Most demonstrations often end with a small group of protestors. As a result, most activist groups dedicate much of their time and energy into organizing community events and social gatherings. For instance, environmentalist groups regularly organize trekking tours through some of the few forests around İstanbul. In 2018, some environmental groups also jointly organized a camp. Northern Forests Defense recently started movie screenings and also gatherings with other activist groups, once a week. With such activities, civic activists can provide a venue for people to come together for issues for which they are concerned, remind their supporters of their cause and also attract new supporters. In doing so, they may keep a flame of contention alive. The recent trajectory of civic activist groups suggest rights-based activism still has potential in Turkey, although expectations should be cautious (Zihnioğlu, 2017).

Notes

1 The law also recognizes platforms, but they are not acknowledged as legal entities.
2 These include inter alia, the launching of the EU's forgotten criterion of absorption capacity, references to issues that are not directly related to the Copenhagen Criteria (for example, peaceful settlement of disputes with Armenia), blocking of several chapters following the deadlock in Cyprus problem.
3 Taksim Solidarity is a platform comprised of 128 associations, foundation, unions, chambers and political parties.
4 Berkin Elvan, who been injured during the protests, was in coma for 269 days and died on 11 March 2014.

Bibliography

Akay, H. (2016) *10 Years with the European Union: Financial Assistance, Civil Society and Participation*. İstanbul: Turkey Europe Foundation.
Akbaş, K. (2014) Nonprofit Law in Turkey, *Working Papers of the Johns Hopkins Comparative Nonprofit Sector Project, No. 51*. Baltimore, MD: Johns Hopkins University Center for Civil Society Studies.
Amnesty International. (2013) *Gezi Parki Eylemleri. Türkiye'de Toplanma Özgürlüğü Hakkı Şiddet Kullanilarak Engelleniyor*. United Kingdom: Amnesty International.
Amnesty International. (2014) *Adding Injustice to Injury. One Year After the Gezi Park Protests*. United Kingdom: Amnesty International.
Arsu, Ş. and Tavernise, S. (2009) Turkish Media Group Is Fined $2.5 Billion, *New York Times* (9 September) www.nytimes.com/2009/09/10/world/europe/10istanbul.html.
Bianet. (2017) "Hayır" Meclisleri Kuruluyor [The "No" Assemblies Are Established], (17 February) https://m.bianet.org/bianet/siyaset/183749-hayir-meclisleri-kuruluyor.
BirGün. (2017) Meşru Değilsiniz Eylemine Polis Saldırdı [Police Attacked the You Are Not Legitimate Demonstration], (21 May) www.birgun.net/haber-detay/mesru-degilsiniz-eylemine-polis-saldirdi-160578.html.
Carothers, T. (2015) *The Closing Space Challenge: How Are Funders Responding?* Washington D.C.: Carnegie Endowment for International Peace.
Carothers, T. and Brechenmacher, S. (2014) *Closing Space: Democracy and Human Rights Support under Fire*. Washington D.C.: Carnegie Endowment for International Peace.
Center for American Progress, Istanbul Policy Center, and Istituto Affari Internazionali. (2017) *Trends in Turkish Civil Society*.
CIVICUS. (2016) *State of Civil Society Report 2016* www.civicus.org/images/documents/SOCS2016/summaries/SoCS-full-review.pdf.
Dereci, S. and Ersen, T. B. (2017) *Monitoring Matrix on Enabling Environment for Civil Society Development. Turkey Country Report*. Istanbul: Third Sector Foundation of Turkey.
Emek is Ours Initiative. (2016) *Press release* (5 January) http://emeksinemasi.blogspot.com.
Guardian. (2013a) "Social Media and Opposition to Blame for Protests," says Turkish PM, (3 June) www.theguardian.com/world/2013/jun/02/turkish-protesters-control-istanbul-square.
Guardian. (2013b) Turkey Violence Intensifies as Police Try to Clear Taksim Square – as it Happened, (11 June) www.theguardian.com/world/2013/jun/11/turkey-police-move-into-taksim-square.

104 Changing landscape of Turkish civil society

Gürcan, E. C. and Peker, E. (2015) *Challenging Neoliberalism at Turkey's Gezi Park*, USA: Palgrave Macmillan.

Hürriyet. (2017) Cumhurbaşkanı Erdoğan: "Sosyal ve kültürel iktidarımız konusunda sıkıntılarımız var" (28 May) www.hurriyet.com.tr/gundem/cumhurbaskani-erdogan-sosyal-ve-kulturel-iktidarimiz-konusunda-sikintilarimiz-var-40472482.

Hürriyet Daily News. (2013) "Patience has its limits," Turkish PM Erdoğan Tells Taksim Gezi Park Demonstrators, (9 June) www.hurriyetdailynews.com/patience-has-its-limits-turkish-pm-erdogan-tells-taksim-gezi-park-demonstrators-48516.

Independent Commission on Turkey. (2004) *Turkey in Europe: More than a Promise*, Report of the Independent Commission on Turkey, British Council and Open Society Institute. www.emmabonino.it/campagne/turchia/english.pdf.

Independent Commission on Turkey. (2014) *Turkey in Europe: The Imperative for Change*, Third Report of the Independent Commission on Turkey.

Kubicek, P. (2016) Majoritarian Democracy in Turkey: Causes and Consequences, in C. Erişen and P. Kubicek (eds), *Democratic Consolidation in Turkey. Micro and Macro Challenges*. London: Routledge.

Milliyet. (2013) Devletin gazı 20 günde bitti [The State Ran out of Gas in 20 Days], (19 June) http://gundem.milliyet.com.tr/devletingazi-20-gunde-bitti/gundem/detay/1724846/default.htm.

Northern Forests Defense, (2019) KOS'tan Çerkezköy'de Termik Santral Kapanış Töreni [Thermal Power Plant Closing Ceremony in Çerkezköy by KOS], (20 February) https://kuzeyormanlari.org/2019/01/20/kostan-cerkezkoyde-termik-santral-kapanis-toreni.

Özbudun, E. (2014) AKP at the Crossroads: Erdoğan's Majoritarian Drift, *South European Society and Politics*, 19(2), pp. 155–167.

Özçetin, B. and Özer, M. (2015) The Current Policy Environment for Civil Society in Turkey, *Working Papers of the Johns Hopkins Comparative Nonprofit Sector Project*, No. 53. Baltimore: Johns Hopkins University Center for Civil Society Studies.

Özyurt, O. (2013) 10 soruda Emek Sineması [Emek Theater in 10 Questions], *Sabah* (13 April) www.sabah.com.tr/cumartesi/2013/04/13/10-soruda-emek-sinemasi.

Republic of Turkey Official Gazette. (2018) *Presidential Decree on State Supervisory Board, no 5*. www.resmigazete.gov.tr/eskiler/2018/07/20180715-2.pdf.

Sloat, A. (2018) *The West's Turkey Conundrum*. Brookings Institute. www.brookings.edu/wp-content/uploads/2018/02/fp_20180212_west_turkey_conundrum.pdf.

T24. (2013) Polise 400 Bin Biber Gazı, 60 Yeni TOMA Geliyor [400,000 Tear Gas, 60 New Water Cannon Vehicle to Police Are Coming], (13 August) http://t24.com.tr/haber/polise-400-bin-biber-gazi-60-yeni-toma-geliyor/2367284.

TACSO. (2011) *Turkey Needs Assessment Report*. İstanbul.

Tarcan, P. (2018) Kuzey Ormanları Savunması'ndan Almanya'daki Hambach Direnişine Destek [Support to Hambach Resistance in Germany by Northern Forests Defense], (24 September) https://m.bianet.org/bianet/ekoloji/201092-kuzey-ormanlari-savunmasi-ndan-almanya-daki-hambach-direnisine-destek.

The No Assemblies. (2017) http://tercihhayir.org/hakkimizda.html.

Tüfekçi, Z. (2017) *Twitter and Tear Gas: The Power and Fragility of Networked Protest*. New Haven: Yale University Press.

Tuğal, C. (2013) Resistance Everywhere: The Gezi Revolt in Global Perspective, *New Perspectives in Turkey*, 49, pp. 147–162.

Turkish Journalists' Union. (2013) 59 Gezi'de 59 Medya Çalışanı İşinden Oldu [59 Media Employee Lost Their Job at Gezi] (26 July) https://tgs.org.tr/baskilar-gazetecileri-yildirmayacak.

Turkish Medical Association. (2013) Göstericilerin Sağlık Durumları (Demonstrators' Health Conditions) as of 15.07.2013. www.ttb.org.tr/haberarsiv_goster.php?Guid= 67155968-9232-11e7-b66d-1540034f819c&1534-D83A_1933715A=ace096e71236bff a5ace19598ca52a7bdded6e7f.

Turkish Prime Ministry. (2016) www.basbakanlik.gov.tr/docs/KurumsalHaberler/64. hukumet-eylem-plani-kitap.pdf.

Ünker, P. (2019) Baskı Sonuç Verdi: Filtresiz Termik Santrallere İzin Çıkmadı [Pressure Yielded Results: No Permission Granted to Thermal Power Plants without Flue Gas Filters], (15 February) www.dw.com/tr/bask%C4%B1-sonu%C3%A7-verdi-filtresiz-termik-santrallere-izin-%C3%A7%C4%B1kmad%C4%B1/a-47528161.

Yalçın, S. (2015) Civil Society in Turkey's Shrinking Political Space, *Turkish Policy Quarterly*, 13(4), pp. 81–90.

Youngs, R. and Echagüe, A. (2017) *Shrinking Space for Civil Society: The EU Response*. Belgium: European Parliament.

Zihnioğlu, Ö. (2017) *Resuming Civic Activism in Turkey*. Washington D.C: Carnegie Endowment for International Peace. http://carnegieendowment.org/2017/12/13/resuming-civic-activism-in-turkey-pub-74987.

6 EU civil society support in Turkey

The previous chapter showed that the recent changes in Turkey's political and legal environment and the EU's diminishing leverage in influencing this environment are important reasons behind Turkish civil society's depoliticization. The following two chapters look at the EU's civil society support in detail and investigate how this support influences Turkish civil society, in particular, vis-à-vis the depoliticization of actors.

Civil society support is one of the key instruments of EU foreign policy. The EU engages with various civic actors not only in its immediate neighborhood, but also in distant geographies, stretching from Latin America to Africa and into Asia. Supporting civil society is now a well-developed instrument with diversified objectives and priorities. On the one hand, the EU expects its civil society support to foster pluralism, democratic accountability and participatory democracy as part of the EU's democracy promotion efforts. On the other hand, the EU also regards civil society organizations as important development actors, service providers and even as actors with an essential role in peace and security agenda. In addition to these, the EU attributes important roles to civil society actors in candidate countries. Civil society organizations are expected to help bring a deeper understanding of not only the reforms, but more generally, the opportunities and challenges of the accession process. Accordingly, the EU embraces different funding modalities and approaches for different bilateral, regional and thematic cooperation.[1]

In a similar manner, the EU's civil society support in Turkey also serve multiple objectives. More broadly, civil society support is part of the EU's democracy promotion efforts in Turkey. By supporting the development of Turkish civil society, the EU aims to contribute to improving democratic principles and fundamental rights. That said, the EU also supports civil society with the aim of facilitating Turkey's overall harmonization to the EU, in particular the political transition.

The EU adopts a very broad definition of a civil society organization. It considers all non-state, not-for-profit, non-partisan and non-violent structures, through which people organize to pursue their shared objectives and ideals as civil society organizations. Civil society organizations could be membership-based, cause-based and service-oriented organizations. This definition includes:

community-based organizations, non-governmental organizations, faith-based organizations, foundations, research institutions, gender and LGBT organizations, cooperatives, professional and business associations, and the not-for-profit media. Trade unions and employers' organizations, the so-called social partners, constitute a specific category of civil society organizations.

(European Commission, 2012: 3)

Understanding EU funds in Turkey

Civil society support becomes particularly important for most enlargement countries, given the state of their political systems and its development before and during their candidacy. Accordingly, one of the major aims behind the EU's support to civil society in candidate countries is to ensure that democratic principles and fundamental rights are upheld (Zihnioğlu, 2015). The EU's successive Enlargement Strategies have a strong focus on improving democracy and governance, rule of law and fundamental rights in candidate countries. This is all the more true in Turkey's case. Both the broader documents setting a framework for financial assistance, as well as more specific ones focusing on civil society,[2] emphasize the importance of an empowered and well-functioning civil society for promoting fundamental rights, fostering pluralism and ensuring the inclusive development of Turkish democracy. To that end, the EU underlines that support should be directed to fighting against discrimination in society and protecting the rights of vulnerable groups (for example, women, children, LGBTI, people with disabilities) (European Commission, 2014a: 19).

In parallel with this, the EU aims at supporting the development of civil society through more active democratic participation in policy and decision-making processes, thereby enhancing the participatory democracy (European Commission, 2014a: 18). Civil society organizations are considered as a vehicle to articulate citizens' needs and concerns. This could deepen participatory democracy, however, only if there are adequate structures and mechanisms for civil society organizations to cooperate with public institutions (European Commission, 2013: 2). Therefore, the EU pays due attention not only to strengthening the dialogue between civil society organizations and the public institutions at local, regional and national levels. More importantly, the EU seeks to establish in Turkey the venues of systematic consultation with and the involvement of civil society organizations in policy development and governance at different levels of the public sector (European Commission, 2014a: 13, 18). Civil society organizations' active participation in policy processes is expected to become a key to effective policies and to overcoming the social and economic challenges and leading to enhanced social cohesion.

Turkey has achieved certain progress in including civil society in decision-making processes. For instance, the Ministry of the Interior consulted civil society organizations when preparing the law on the collection of aid (European Commission, 2014b). However, these initiatives remain as ad hoc consultations. There are no permanent and structured participatory mechanisms for civil society organizations. On the other hand, ensuring civil society organizations' involvement in policy and decision-making is a big challenge in Turkey. TACSO's (Technical Assistance for Civil Society Organizations) Needs Assessment Report (2014: 29) points to these organizations' lack of awareness, especially in rural areas and small towns, in their potential to provide input and influence social policies. The same report finds that the major reason for the lack of efficient dialogue and cooperation is the unwillingness on the side of the public officials both at central level (82.5 percent) and at local level (70 percent), as well as a low level of awareness regarding the role of civil society in democracies.

The second major aim behind the EU's support of Turkish civil society is to facilitate the accession process. This is a result of the EU's experience following the eastern enlargement. Indeed, the EU's first considerable civil society support during the accession process would have been with central and eastern European countries. The 1990s witnessed an emerging discourse on participatory democracy in the EU. In addition, civic actors in some of the central and eastern European countries made a promising start during the 1989 revolutions (Schimmelfennig et al., 2003: 498). However, the EU's accession strategy aimed at completing the accession in the shortest possible time. This entailed a fast-tract reform process and required working with an executive team who can "get things done," at the expense of involving different national actors and society at large. With EU officials already experiencing an NGO-fatigue, the civil society organizations were eventually excluded from the accession process (Grabbe, 2001: 1017–1029).

The EU soon realized the limits of its accession strategy and the need for including the society if democratization efforts were to have lasting results. Without the society's understanding and support of democratic principles, the transfer of legal codes is bound to remain on paper (Keyman and İçduygu, 2003). This put the spotlight on civil society organizations. They could act as a layer between the state and society, not only fostering pluralism and participatory democracy, but also to stimulate dialogue and cooperation on EU accession (European Commission, 2014a: 12). The EU, in return, expected that this would deepen citizens' understanding of the reforms their country needs to complete during the accession process (European Commission, 2013: 1).

One other challenge the EU had to confront following the eastern enlargement was the insufficient level of information and preparedness of citizens of both member states and candidate countries about one another and about the enlargement itself. The search for ways to establish a strong and sustained dialogue between the respective societies, as well as with the EU institutions to provide better mutual knowledge and understanding so as to ensure a stronger awareness of the opportunities and challenges of the accession process (European Commission, 2005) has also drawn attention to civil society organizations.

Soon after the eastern enlargement, the European Commission announced its Communication on Civil Society Dialogue (2005). With this Dialogue, civil society organizations in candidate countries were now given the task to prepare their citizens for enlargement, both by ensuring better knowledge and understanding of the EU within their country and also by informing public opinion on the opportunities and challenges of enlargement. Civil Society Dialogue has extended the pre-existing financial means available for civil society organizations in the candidate countries. It also introduced a new dimension to EU civil society support by not only aiming for the development of a vibrant civil society in candidate countries, but also providing for civil society organizations' active involvement in the accession process.

If the problems ensuing from the eastern enlargement were part of the reasons that led to the Civil Society Dialogue, another part was Turkey's imminent accession negotiations. The poor public opinion in Turkey and in EU countries of one another necessitated establishing a political and cultural dialogue. This dialogue has been a major focus of the EU's civil society support to Turkey, especially after the European Council's decision in 2004 to open accession negotiations. Since then the EU has reiterated the importance it attaches to Civil Society Dialogue.[3] The details of programmes run in relation to this Civil Society Dialogue are discussed in the following section.

Civil society can be effective in promoting the fundamental principles and participatory democracy, as well as in assisting the accession, only if there is an enabling environment for its establishment and activities. The EU regularly emphasizes the need for a legal, judicial, administrative and financial environment for exercising freedoms of expression, association and assembly for the accession countries (Delegation of the European Union to Turkey, 2017a; European Commission, 2013: 2). Lately, in the face of a growing clampdown on civil society worldwide, this issue ceased to be a matter of enlargement policy only. The EU developed a range of tools, mechanisms and strategies, while different EU actors expressed their commitment to address the now widely accepted shrinking space problem. Turkey is particularly a concern given its deteriorating conditions for civil society, as discussed in detail in Chapter 5. As such, improvement of the environment for civil society is emphasized recurrently in the documents drawing the framework of the EU's financial assistance to Turkey (European Commission, 2011, 2014a). In addition, though, the EU has various mechanisms and more specific programmes that prioritize Turkey's closing civic space. These are discussed in the following section.

Civil society organizations' effectiveness and productiveness also depend on their capacity. However, the EU is rightfully aware that civil society organizations in Turkey, in particular, the smaller and rights-based organizations, have significant weaknesses with regard to their internal management, fund-raising, membership and advocacy (European Commission, 2014a: 18). Accordingly, one of the expected results of the pre-accession funding to Turkey is to develop the knowledge and skills required for improving institutional capacities, such as advocacy, administrative and fundraising skills of civil society organizations, as well as their outreach, representativeness and networking (Delegation of the European Union to Turkey, 2017b; European Commission, 2014a: 18).

The EU uses a combination of political support and financial assistance to achieve its aims. As for its political support, the EU encourages Turkey to make more conducive legislation for civil society and promotes the involvement of civic actors at different levels of the pre-accession process (European Commission, 2014a: 4). Financial assistance includes a range of funding instruments that responds mostly to civil society organizations as defined above. More recently, the EU also has new funding instruments for active citizens and groups with no legal identity. The following section draws a more detailed picture of these financial instruments, their scope and how they function.

The functioning of EU funding mechanism

From the Ankara Association Agreement in 1963 until the entering into force of the Customs Union in 1996, financial cooperation between the EU and Turkey were carried out with financial protocols. Following the Decision no 1/95 of the EC-Turkey Association Council, Turkey started benefiting from the EU budget and funds for economic and financial cooperation for Euro-Mediterranean Partnership (MEDA). Civil society organizations in Turkey, too, became beneficiaries of the MEDA programme. Therefore, the EU's financial support to Turkish civil society predates Turkey's candidacy to the EU. However, the EU, following its acceptance of Turkey's candidacy in 1999, has restructured its financial support mechanism to Turkey. Under this new framework, financial support to civil society has increased dramatically. According to the new structure, there are three venues for the EU's financial support to Turkey: (1) Pre-Accession Financial Assistance, (2) EU programmes, and (3) credits from the European Investment Bank. Turkish civil society can benefit from the first two of these instruments. However, civil society organizations are not the sole beneficiary of these funds. In pre-accession financial assistance, public institutions relevant to each period's priorities have benefited greatly from these funds. These funds have also been used for supporting Turkey's participation to the European Union Programmes and Agencies (Ministry for EU Affairs, 2014: 8; Ministry for EU Affairs, 2016). While funds allocated to civil society usually adds up to a limited portion of these financial instruments, these funds nonetheless make up an unprecedented amount of foreign funding for Turkish civil society. By now, the EU funds are one of the largest foreign funding that Turkish civil society receives. Due to the EU programmes multifaceted structure, it is difficult to cover all the funding channels and this book mainly focuses on those coming through the Pre-Accession Financial Assistance. In addition, these funds are better known among civil society organizations in Turkey and therefore many associate 'the idea of EU funds' with those that come through the Pre-Accession Financial Assistance.

Turkey started receiving funds from Pre-Accession Financial Assistance in 2002, and the first period lasted until 2006. The aim of this Assistance was to support efforts, activities and projects that would facilitate Turkey's accession process and its harmonization to the EU's acquis. Political reforms became the priority during this funding phase. To that end, Pre-Accession Financial Assistance distributed a sum of €1.3 billion grants to 164 projects.

In the meantime, the European Commission announced the aforementioned Civil Society Dialogue in 2005, to better engage civil society organizations to the accession process by way of supporting a cultural dialogue between the organizations in member states and candidate countries relating to future enlargements (European Commission, 2005). In relation to this, the Commission launched the Civil Society Dialogue Programme in 2008. Since then, this Programme has financed 429 projects in Turkey, bringing together civil society organizations from Turkey and the EU around common topics, to exchange knowledge and experience. Three consequent phases saw €42.5 million distributed under Turkey's pre-accession assistance. The Programme is running its fourth phase presently (Civil Society Dialogue).

Together with its 2007–2013 budget, the EU's financial assistance mechanism for the candidate and potential candidate countries were consolidated under a single framework; called the Instrument for Pre-Accession (IPA). Of its total budget of more than €10 billion for nine countries[4] participating in the IPA, €4.8 billion were allocated to Turkey (Ministry for EU Affairs, 2016). In addition to capacity-building projects towards Turkey's harmonization with and implementation of the EU's acquis, the IPA also supported projects aimed at economic and social development. The main components of the IPA have been Transition Assistance and Institution Building, Cross Border Cooperation, Regional Development, Human Resources Development and Rural Development (Ministry for EU Affairs, 2016).

While the EU adopts a rather broad definition of civil society that includes chambers, cooperatives and others; associations and foundations are usually considered as the two main actors of Turkish civil society. From 2002 until the end of 2014, associations and foundations have carried out 972 projects and received close to €90 million of grants under the above-mentioned pre-accession financial assistance (Ministry for EU Affairs, 2014: 53). With the new phase of IPA II discussed below, as of July 2017, the total number of completed projects supported under subsequent pre-accession financial assistance increased to 1015 and the total amount of grants awarded to these projects is over €90 million (Central Finance and Contracts Unit). According to one public officer, some of the funds that previously had been allocated for civil society have been directed to other areas when there was a need. Therefore, funds provided to civil society in different instances have dropped below the amount initially allocated.

In both phases, the pre-accession assistance provided funds for civil society organizations for projects that supported the above-mentioned priorities. In a way, support to civil society became instrumental in Turkey's overall harmonization with the EU (Zihnioğlu, 2019: 5). The focus in the first wave of pre-accession assistance (2002–2006) was achieving political reforms. This is because the EU had recently announced Turkey as a candidate country in 1999 and Turkey, in return, embarked on a series of political reforms to start accession negotiations. The designing of the second phase (2007–2013) coincided with the opening of accession negotiations in 2005. As a result, the focus of pre-accession assistance shifted to economic and social improvements. In the final wave of pre-accession assistance (2014–2020), the focus is on economic and social cohesion. In this way, funds were channeled to the projects that addressed the requirements for harmonization under each chapter. This is not to suggest that programmes on political reforms were completely abandoned in the second and third waves. Indeed, there were several major projects, such as on judiciary's functioning and effectiveness or courts' management systems during the latter phases. These projects continued alongside solid waste management projects and a programme to implement the EU's INSPIRE and Environmental Responsibility Directives.

Funds allocated to civil society partly followed this course. Initial programmes opened for civil society organizations mainly focused on political reforms. This focused expanded with the IPA starting from 2007. The new calls included a diverse set of programmes that also address issues such as regional development, cross-border cooperation, registered employment and harmonization with the EU acquis. This change is more an expansion of areas, than a shift in focus for funds to civil society. The majority of programmes opened to civil society continued to address political reforms; covering issues including the improvement of human rights and democracy, civil society's empowerment and, more broadly, the political criteria.

The Civil Society Dialogue Programme treats civil society as equally instrumental. In addition, we can see a similar change with the Dialogue programmes. In its first phase (2008–2009), the Dialogue programme supported projects that contributed broadly to the dialogue between different actors in Turkey and in EU member states. In later phases (second, third and fourth) there were explicit emphases on areas within the scope of the EU's acquis and on policies such as agriculture, fisheries, environment and the like.

In short, funding under pre-accession assistance has mainly been directed to projects facilitating Turkey's accession either through harmonization or enhancing the dialogue. Despite good examples, such as the establishment of Civil Society Support Team (later becoming the Civil Society Development Center) that carry out activities to support civil society's development, funds allocated to that end under the IPA have been very limited.

According to the Financial Regulation, grants are direct financial contributions from the EU's budget to finance "(a) an action intended to help achieve a Union policy objective; (b) the functioning of a body which pursues an aim of general Union interest or has an objective forming part of, and supporting, a Union policy ('operating grants')" (European Commission, 2014c: 228). It is important to note that under the IPA funds in Turkey, the EU does not provide the latter group of operating grants. Rather, the EU provides activity-focused funding to carry out certain, pre-determined activities. While the budget for EU-funded projects may cover the employment costs of paid-staff, the rationale for such staff is to better help implement the planned activities and not for the organization's institutional development.

The IPA II, a follow-up of the IPA, that started in 2014 and will run through 2020, initially had a planned total budget of €4.5 billion. In parallel with its predecessor, IPA II aims at developing capacity for Turkey's harmonization with the EU's acquis and for its economic and social cohesion. To provide a more efficient use of the funds, the Commission's strategic choice for implementing IPA II is a sector approach. The aim of the sector approach is to complement the government's efforts in pre-selected sectors. In return, it is expected that this will increase synergies and national ownership over public policy and decisions on resource allocations in the given sector. In the sector approach, funding decisions are based on achieving national sector policy objectives and results that are relevant for accession (European Commission, 2016; HTSPE Limited, 2014).

In IPA II, nine priority sectors, as well as the lead institutions and implementing units for each of these sectors have been identified. While areas such as environment, transportation and energy are among the priority sectors, what grabs the attention is the specification of civil society as a sub-sector under the democracy and governance sector. In principle, civil society can receive support under all sectors. However, the civil society sub-sector is the main venue to organize efforts and channel support for civil society's development.

Accordingly, a Sector Planning Document has been prepared for civil society. The Sector Planning Document is a guiding document discussing the relevant sector's approach assessment, detailing the priority areas, planned actions and programmes and their budget under the given period. This document is noteworthy as there had not been any coherent policy or strategy for civil society in Turkey. Equally important is that the Ministry for EU Affairs, which was later subsumed under the Ministry of Foreign Affairs as the Directorate for EU Affairs, has been consulting civil society organizations through dialogue with Civil Society Meetings to incorporate their needs, expectations and concerns to future programmes. However, such 'dialogues' with civil society organizations are not unknown to Turkish civil society organizations. During the early years of accession negotiations, the then Chief Negotiator invited certain civil society organizations to draft a sample Negotiation Position Paper and then organized meetings at the Secretariat General for EU Affairs – the predecessor of the Ministry for EU Affairs. However, these meetings would take place once the position paper was completed and therefore would not involve any discussion. This was followed by several meetings with broad participation of civil society organizations in 2009 and 2010. Both cases lacked genuine discussion and the impact of civil society organizations' input remained unclear. Therefore, the current dialogues, if they are not going to be yet another showpiece, should show more clearly how civil society organizations are part of this policy-making process.

The Sector Planning Document for civil society identifies four priority areas: (1) Improving legislative environment for active citizenship; (2) Strengthening cooperation between public sector and civil society organizations; (3) Strengthening the capacities of and networking between organized active citizens/civil society organizations; (4) Connecting people for mutual understanding between citizens in Turkey and the EU. In pursuing its aims, the Sector Planning Document emphasizes the need for positive discrimination policies for rights-based organizations. Accordingly, several programmes have been running since 2014. The planned budget for civil society sub-sector for the 2014–2020 period is approximately €180 million (Ministry for EU Affairs, 2014: 14).

Considering the ever-closing civic space in Turkey, prioritizing the improvement of legislative environment is important. One of the major related projects aims to improve the institutional capacity of the Department of Associations,[5] eliminate the legal and administrative practices restricting the activities of civil society organizations and lessen the bureaucratic procedures and controls over them (European Commission, 2015: 10). However, the Sector Planning Document has a rather narrow focus on the legislative environment and only mentions the problems pertaining to Law on Collection of Aid and the lack of broad legal framework governing the civil society and public sector dialogue. The broader challenge of closing civic space does not appear in this document. Absent the political will, the improvement of the legislative environment and its implementation is not likely to go far.

One suggestion put forward by the European Court of Auditors is to use project conditionality (2009: points 30–34). Similar to conditionality at a political level, in project conditionality, the Commission sets and uses conditions prior to contracting or paying the assistance. And if these conditions are not met, the Commission can take corrective measures including the cancelling of the project or reducing its scope and funding. So far, the Commission has made only limited use of conditionality at project level.

Following the European Court of Auditor's critical report in 2009 on the management of pre-accession assistance to Turkey, the EU Delegation in Ankara took the initiative to improve its civil society support. Based on consultations with 730 civil society organizations in 2010 and 2011, the Delegation launched the *Sivil Düşün* (Think Civil) programme in 2012. While funded under the IPA II, *Sivil Düşün* differs in many respects from other IPA-funded programmes. The novelty of *Sivil Düşün* lies behind the new understanding of civil society it introduced. *Sivil Düşün* supports not only civil society organizations as defined above, but also other civic actors, including civic initiatives, platforms, networks and even individual activists. With its explicit focus on rights-based activism, the programme supports civic activism and active citizenship (*Sivil Düşün*, 2017). On the whole, *Sivil Düşün* gives activity funding similar to other IPA programmes. However, the Networks and Platforms Programme of *Sivil Düşün* allows networks and platforms to cover their operational costs (personal interview, Ayça Bican). As such, this programme can be seen as the preliminary effort of a new practice of the EU's support to Turkish civil society.

The European Commission has the overall responsibility for the management of the IPA, while until recently it had entrusted Turkish authorities with the responsibility of managing the major part of this (European Court of Auditors, 2018: points 7, 8). This is known as the "indirect management" mode of EU budgetary management. This decentralized approach is similar to the shared management of most EU funds by the Commission and the EU member states (for example, the European Regional Development Fund).

In Turkey, this decentralized approach required Turkish authorities to undertake the overall management of the IPA funds (planning, implementation, monitoring and audit) under EU and national rules. For this, the National IPA

Coordinator was responsible for the general coordination of the IPA between the different Turkish stakeholders. Initially, the undersecretary of the Ministry for EU Affairs was the National IPA Coordinator in Turkey. However, after the Ministry for EU Affairs was subsumed under the Ministry of Foreign Affairs as a Directorate, the Deputy Minister of Foreign Affairs and Director for EU Affairs resumed these tasks. All work relating to the IPA has been carried out by the Ministry on behalf of the Coordinator. In addition, Central Finance and Contracts (CFCU) was established in 2003 under the Treasury. CFCU has been responsible for the tendering, contracting, payments, accounting and financial reporting of IPA projects under the supervision of a National Authorising Officer (NAO). This was followed in 2012, by the establishment of Human Resources Development Programme Authority to carry out similar functions for programmes and projects in the areas of education, employment and social policy (Ministry for EU Affairs, 2014: 17–18).

The Commission recently decided to change this decentralized approach based on the "changing operating environment for the [civil society organizations] following the coup attempt of 15 July 2016" (European Commission, 2017). As a result, the Commission decided to take over the management of €16 million allocated for civil society projects, which it had originally planned to be managed by the Turkish authorities. The funds will now be under the direct management of the Commission/ EU Delegation. Only a few programmes, such as those opened under the Civil Society Dialogue, remain under the management of the Turkish authorities.

Centralizing the management of the IPA projects might help overcome some of the current problems in implementation. As the Court of Auditors' recent report (2018: points 46, 48) on the EU's pre-accession assistance to Turkey underlines, one major problem with the IPA is the significant delays in project programming and implementation. Indeed, the report itself is focused on IPA I (2007–2012) only due to widespread implementation delays with the IPA II (2014–2020). The auditors found, inter alia, weak administrative capacity, including excessive staff turnover at the CFCU as the main reasons behind the delay. Therefore, one might expect the centralization to bring increased capacity for managing the IPA funds and thereby overcoming some of the mentioned problems. However, direct management of civil society funds may have its own problems. While the EU Delegation in Ankara is one of the largest EU Delegations, it may not have the sufficient manpower to undertake this extra workload. This may have adverse effects over the smooth and effective functioning of programmes.

The IPA support in Turkey is complemented by the European Instrument for Democracy and Human Rights (EIDHR). The EIDHR is a specific tool of the EU to support and promote participatory and representative democracy, human rights and fundamental freedoms in third countries. It was launched in 1994 and further developed in 2006. To achieve these ends, the EIDHR pays attention to reinforcing civil society's role in the system and therefore provides support to relevant civil society organizations and activists. The grants are open to other actors such as intergovernmental organizations, not-for-profit public sector institutions, parliamentary bodies and people with no legal identity. Since 2014, the emphasis on the role of civil society has increased with a specific reference to its cooperation with local authorities and relevant state institutions. The EIDHR in Turkey has mostly supported projects focusing on human rights and fundamental freedoms, including freedom of expression, securing justice, cultural diversity, minority rights, gender equality, LGBTI, Roma citizens and the youth. So far, the EIDHR has allocated approximately €17 million for over 100 projects in Turkey (Delegation of the European Union to Turkey, 2017a; European Commission, 2017).

The Technical Assistance for Civil Society Organizations (TACSO) project was also important for strengthening the capacity of organized active citizens in Turkey. The TACSO project has run between 2009 and 2017 with the aim of supporting capacity development of civil society in Turkey and in the Western Balkans. TACSO in Turkey acted more like a gap filling, flexible and facilitating project than a key project meeting Turkey's needs. Capacity, according to the TACSO Turkey office, means the specific knowledge and skills necessary for each organization to achieve its objectives. Therefore, capacity development support carried out by TACSO Turkey ranged from leadership education to Roma organizations, to needs assessment to newly-founded organizations in southeast Turkey who do not even know where to start. Other activities supporting capacity development include various training on elements such as internal communication, strategic planning and fund raising. In addition to capacity development, the TACSO project also aimed at improving the civic space, which requires addressing issues such as self-regulation, transparency and ethical norms. However, this pillar of the TACSO project did not work well in Turkey since, according to the TACSO Turkey office, there had never been a good time to bring these issues forward with regard to Turkish civil society (personal interview, Ayça Bican).

EU civil society support, which has gained more currency following Turkey's EU candidacy, today has a multi-layered and complex structure. There are various venues of support and the amount of funding has substantially increased over the past two decades. The EU aims at developing a strong civil society in Turkey, not only to improve Turkey's democracy and fundamental rights, but also to facilitate Turkey's accession process to the EU. The following chapter investigates the impact of this increasing support on Turkish civil society.

Notes

1 See European Commission's Communications (2002, 2012) for further details on the EU's broader support to civil society as part of its external relations.
2 See Instrument for Pre-Accession Assistance Multi-Annual Indicative Planning Document 2011–2013, section 3.1.2, Instrument for Pre-Accession Assistance (IPA II) Indicative Strategy Paper for Turkey (2014–2020), Part IV, Section 1 for the broader aims of EU financial support and Sector Planning Document on civil society.
3 See for instance Instrument for Pre-Accession Assistance Multi-Annual Indicative Planning Document 2011–2013, section 3.1.1, Instrument for Pre-Accession Assistance (IPA

II) Indicative Strategy Paper for Turkey (2014–2020), Part IV, Section 1, Sector Planning Document on civil society p. 2.
4 Albania, Bosnia Herzegovina, Croatia (until 2013), Iceland (since 2011), Kosovo, Macedonia, Montenegro, Serbia, Turkey.
5 Department of Associations was been transformed into the Directorate General of Civil Society Affairs in 2018.

Bibliography

Central Finance and Contracts Unit. *Grants Database*. www.cfcu.gov.tr/.
Civil Society Dialogue. http://civilsocietydialogue.org/us/.
Delegation of the European Union to Turkey. (2017a). *The European Instrument for Democracy and Human Rights*. www.avrupa.info.tr/tr/demokrasi-ve-insan-haklari-icin-avrupa-araci-63.
Delegation of the European Union to Turkey. (2017b). *EU Support to Civil Society*. www.avrupa.info.tr/en/eu-support-civil-society-36.
European Commission. (n.d.) *What is EIDHR?* https://ec.europa.eu/europeaid/how/finance/eidhr_en.htm_en.
European Commission (2002). *Communication from the Commission to the Council, the European Parliament and the Economic and Social Committee Participation of Non-State Actors in EC Development Policy*. COM(2002) 598 final. Brussels: European Commission.
European Commission. (2005) *Communication from the Commission to the Council, the European Parliament, the European Economic and Social Committee and the Committee of the Regions, Civil Society Dialogue between the EU and Candidate Countries*. Brussels: European Commission.
European Commission. (2011) *Commission Implementing Decision of 28.6.2011 Adopting a Multi-Annual Indicative Planning Document (MIPD) 2011–2013 for Turkey*. C(2011) 4490 final. Brussels: European Commission.
European Commission. (2012) *Communication from the Commission to the European Parliament, the Council, the European Economic and Social Committee and the Committee of the Regions, The Roots of Democracy and Sustainable Development: Europe's Engagement with Civil Society in External Relations*, 12.9.2012, COM(2012) 492 final. Brussels: European Commission.
European Commission. (2013) *Guidelines for EU Support to Civil Society in Enlargement Countries, 2014–2020*. Brussels: European Commission.
European Commission. (2014a) *Instrument for Pre-Accession Assistance (IPA II) Indicative Strategy Paper for Turkey (2014–2020)*. Brussels: European Commission.
European Commission. (2014b) *Progress Report for Turkey*. Brussels: European Commission.
European Commission. (2014c) *Financial Regulation Applicable to the General Budget of The Union and Its Rules of Application*. Brussels: European Commission.
European Commission. (2015) *Instrument for Pre-Accession Assistance (IPA II) 2014–2020 Turkey Civil Society Action Document 2015*. Brussels: European Commission.
European Commission. (2016) *Evaluation of Sector Approach under IPA II Assistance, Roadmap, Directorate General for Neighbourhood and Enlargement negotiations*. Brussels: European Commission.

European Commission. (2017) *Commission Implementing Decision of 30 November 2017 Amending Commission Implementing Decision C(2016) 4889 final of 20 July 2016 Adopting a Civil Society Facility and Media Programme for the Years 2016–2017 under IPA II*. Brussels: European Commission.

European Court of Auditors. (2009) *The European Commission's Management of Pre-Accession Assistance to Turkey*. Special Report (No. 16–2009). Luxembourg: European Court of Auditors.

European Court of Auditors. (2018) *EU Pre-accession Assistance to Turkey: Only Limited Results So Far*. Special Report 07. Luxembourg: European Court of Auditors.

Grabbe, H. (2001) How Does Europeanization Affect CEE Governance? Conditionality, Diffusion and Diversity, *Journal of European Public Policy*, 8(6), pp. 1013–1031.

HTSPE Limited. (2014) The European Union's IPA Program for Western Balkans and Turkey Mapping of Sector Strategies, *Final Report* (28 February 2014) https://ec.europa.eu/neighbourhood-enlargement/sites/near/files/pdf/financial_assistance/phare/evaluation/2014/20140714-mapping-of-sector-strategies-final-report.pdf.

Keyman, E. F. and İçduygu, A. (2003) Globalisation, Civil Society and Citizenship in Turkey: Actors, Boundaries and Discourses, *Citizenship Studies*, 7(2), pp. 219–234.

Ministry for EU Affairs. (2014) *Avrupa Birliği Hibe Programları Kapsamında Sivil Toplum Kuruluşlarına Sağlanan Destekler*. Ankara.

Ministry of Foreign Affairs. (2016) *Turkey–EU Financial Cooperation*. www.ab.gov.tr/5_en.html.

Personal interview, Ayça Bican, 26 January 2017.

Personal interview, Hale Akay, 18 August 2016.

Schimmelfennig, F., Engert, S. and Knobel, H. (2003) Costs, Commitment and Compliance: The Impact of EU Democratic Conditionality on Latvia, Slovakia and Turkey, *Journal of Common Market Studies*, 41(3), pp. 495–518.

Sivil Düşün. (2017) http://sivildusun.net/english/.

Technical Assistance for Civil Society Organizations (TACSO). (2014) *TACSO Civil Society Needs Assessment Report TACSO 2 Turkey*.

Zihnioğlu, Ö. (2015) NeoKorporatizmden Birleştirici Demokrasiye: Sivil Toplumun Avrupa Birliği'ndeki Uzun İnce Yolu, *Uluslararası İlişkiler*, 12(45), pp. 5–21.

Zihnioğlu, Ö. (2019) European Union Civil Society Support and the Depoliticisation of Turkish Civil Society, *Third World Quarterly*, 40(3), pp. 503–520.

7 The impact of EU funds over Turkish civil society

Supporting civil society as part of democracy promotion has long been a common practice. Especially since the "associational revolution" (Salamon, 1994) of the early 1990s, support from not only the EU, but in general from the West to civil society organizations in developing democracies has grown rapidly. Since then, various studies examined the role of civic actors in strengthening democratic development. These studies were soon followed by more critical literature. Various cases ranging from feminist groups in Latin America (Alvarez, 1999) and in India (Roy, 2015) to LGBTI groups (Paternotte, 2016) and anti-mining movements in India (Kapoor, 2013) found donor and recipient relations to be far more complex and Western support to civil society to be problematical. These studies argue that with Western support, grassroots organizations and movements that confront the state are being replaced by professional and institutionalized NGOs that run projects to help implement state policies. In a nutshell, we see the NGO-ization of civil society (Alvarez, 1999).

NGO-ization does not simply mean the proliferation of NGOs. It refers to a process that affects the structure, agenda, discourse and accountability of civil society organizations. What underlies the NGO-ization literature is a critique of neo-liberal policies and how they relate to civil society. The structural adjustment to economic liberalization required the newly emerging Third World economies to retreat from key areas in public services. As the state stepped down its traditional role, NGOs stepped in to deliver, and not only demand, development (Gupta, 2014; Roy, 2014, 2015: 102). During this period, the Western institutions began funding NGOs for their work in these areas. This is because NGOs could meet the immediate needs of those hurt by the withdrawal of the state from service provision (Biekart, 1999) and therefore become a strategic tool to ease in neoliberal changes (Howell and Pearce, 2001; Kihika, 2009; Mercer, 2002). Foreign funding has been channeled to those projects that were 'compatible' with public policies, had visible outcomes in the short-term and to those organizations that were deemed 'reliable' (Alvarez, 1999: 198). In other words, organizations with projects promoting neoliberal policies and corresponding state reforms in the most efficient and visible manner are supported. This has not only paved the way for NGOs to take place of grassroots organizations. More importantly and at the same time, these organizations spirited away the political character and contentious nature of grassroots movements. This is because what has been expected from NGOs is for them to implement projects focusing on technical issues and in less contentious areas (Alvarez, 1999; Armstrong and Prashad, 2005; Choudry, 2010; Jad, 2004; Kamat, 2004). Therefore, one of the main criticisms against foreign funding is that it leads to a *demobilization* of civic actors or, more broadly, to a depoliticization of civil society.

In a similar vein, accession negotiations are a process of adjustment to the EU's legislation, standards and norms. As we discussed in the previous chapter, the EU's support in Turkey has instrumentalized civil society organizations in this process. Reliable civic organizations are funded to deliver projects with visible outcomes that are compatible with EU policies. With EU funds, civil society organizations deliver, not demand. No doubt that Turkey's domestic political setting plays a crucial role for a less contentious civil society. But EU funds, too, contributed to the depoliticization of Turkish civil society due to its structure being more conducive for rather non- or less contentious projects and activities.

Methods of analysis

The questions raised in this chapter require a multi-pronged research design. To do that, first, I looked at Turkish civil society's participation in EU programmes in a more general way. I scanned public sector projects in which public institutions cooperated with civil society organizations and I examined the programmes opened specifically for civil society and the projects conducted. I traced a trend in the activities that civil society organizations carried out with their EU-funded projects.

There are two major difficulties in assessing the impact of these programmes. First, following the EU's broad definition of a civil society organization, a diverse group of actors may be eligible for benefiting from civil society programmes. These actors include, but are not limited to, NGOs, unions, cooperatives, universities, municipalities and SMEs. It would be beyond the scope of this book to study the impact of EU funds on all these actors. In addition, these actors have different roles in society and a wholesale analysis is both difficult and misleading. Therefore, I focused only on associations, which are more commonly known as civil society actors in Turkey.

Second, there is no comprehensive and aggregate database on the details of the projects. Evaluation reports are also limited in scope. All these make it very difficult to monitor the implementation and post-implementation results of these projects. For civil society programmes, I resorted to the grants database at the CFCU's website. This database provides a list of the programmes opened, and the projects funded. The list includes details such as the name of the lead organization, duration and the budget of the project. Based on this information I checked the organizations' websites for further details on the activities. However, the information on the organizations' websites are often limited and intended for advertisement rather than informative purposes. When possible,

I complemented this data with interviews and other research. The information on public sector programmes draws on earlier research and websites on different projects. Put together, an overall tendency can be seen within the activities of EU-funded projects.

To better understand the impact of EU funds, I held face-to-face interviews with 45 civil society organizations in Turkey (See Appendix 1 for the full list). I selected the organizations through elements of purposive sampling and snowball sampling based on the grant database at the CFCU's website. The sample shows variety in terms of the organizations' working area, size and geographical location. This reflects the composition of Turkish civil society in line with the questions raised in this chapter. I interviewed organizations working in areas prioritized by the EU and those others that are less related to EU funding priorities. In addition, some of the organizations work on politicized issues, while others work on less contentious ones. The sample includes organizations working at the local or national level. Some of the organizations working at the local level are branches of nationwide organizations. I interviewed organizations from eight cities from different regions in Turkey: Ankara, Antalya, Iğdır, İstanbul, İzmir, Kayseri, Samsun and Van. The geographical distribution also reflects variation in the concentration of civil society organizations and in the use of EU funds. The sample also included a control group of organizations that have not received EU funding.

The interviews were half-structured with several questions on the organizational structure, functioning, activities (with and without the EU funds), and relations with members, volunteers and the society at large. The interviews were recorded and were supplemented by my notes taken during the interviews. I also reviewed the organizations' websites and publications to collect any other information possible.

EU funds for civil society organizations

Civil society organizations in Turkey benefit in two ways from the EU's pre-accession funds. First, and more related with the purpose of this book, they benefit from the programmes exclusively opened for civil society. Second and indirectly, they participate in some of the projects carried out by the public sector. As for the former, civil society organizations' principal access to EU funding is through programmes opened for civil society under pre-accession assistance. This section looks at these programmes in detail and discusses if and how EU funds impacted on civil society organizations in Turkey.

Over the past more than a decade, the EU supported civil society programmes addressing a large variety of issues. A major group of these programmes aim at the protection of vulnerable groups and improvement of their rights. These focus on women, youth, children and disabled people. Despite their nature, rights-based or advocacy activities constitute a limited part of their activities. Most commonly, projects under these programmes carry out awareness-raising activities. This goes also for programmes on consumer rights and the environment. In principle, raising awareness on the rights of vulnerable groups is a crucial part of advocacy work. Rights-based activism not only challenges the legal framework, but usually societal norms as well. Therefore, successful rights-based activism requires a change in understanding of policy-makers and the public at large. However, EU-funded projects tend to last around 10 to 18 months (some even shorter). This is a very limited implementation time to bring any real change in the perceptions or behavior of certain actors. In addition, due to a lack of financial sustainability, most organizations cannot continue their project using their own funds. Therefore, awareness-raising activities under EU-funded projects cannot bring the expected impact (Akay, 2016: 39).

Access to education and vocational training are also common among these projects, in particular, under those programmes focusing on women, children and disabled people. It is difficult to deny the value of vocational training, especially for vulnerable groups. However, such training activities have several drawbacks. First, most training is for precarious and poorly paid jobs, such as childcare, sales, handicraft (for women) or for skills like using computers or elocution (disabled people). This training may help social integration, improve employability and provide the beneficiaries with certain income, but it is unlikely to bring self-sufficiency or empowerment. Some of these also have training for entrepreneurialism, but such training will be at a dead end unless accompanied by micro credits – which the EU funds do not provide. In addition, only a limited number of people benefit from this training. Therefore, these projects do not improve the rights of the groups in question, but at best, potentially improve the lives of participants. This poses a serious drawback in view of the purposes of these programmes.

Service-based activities feature an important number of projects. For instance, the programmes on fighting violence against women abound with providing shelters, counselling and medical support, while establishing purpose-made centers and parks are widespread in projects for disabled people.

Only a small number of projects planned advocacy activities to defend rights and improve legislation. Few other projects carried out monitoring, networking, capacity building of civic actors and advocacy groups for similar purposes. These are most prevalent in human rights programmes. That said, some of them have over-ambitious aims like the mainstreaming of children's rights or adoption of certain agricultural techniques. Important as they may be, such big aims are not realistic considering the limited implementation time of EU-funded projects.

The prevalence of service-based activities over rights-based ones is a result of both the EU programmes' structure and the organizations' preferences. First, most service-based activities for these programmes can easily be outsourced. Activities such as vocational and skills training, counselling and medical support must be provided by certain experts. One cannot expect those experts or their expertise to be readily available at these organizations. Civil society organizations, for these projects, mainly serve as coordinators. Purpose-made centers, parks and shelters are usually needs that civil society organizations working on that area have long known, but could not establish due to a lack of financial means. Civil society organizations opt for these as EU-funded projects support the establishment of such places, while they remain at their disposal for future activities.

However, rights-based activism like advocacy is not easily outsourced. Such activities tend to rely on the organizations' own capacities. This supposes certain expertise. In addition, successful rights-based activism may require systematically challenging public institutions, criticizing their practices and policies. At some point, this is likely to lead to confrontation with relevant public institutions or policy-makers. Most civil society organizations take being political as doing politics. And because this entails confronting or criticizing public (also read government) policies, being political automatically places these organizations next to opposition parties. Therefore, except for highly politicized groups, most civil society organizations prefer to do their work "without getting involved in politics ... because to be able to conduct our business, come through without stumbling we think we should not be engaged anywhere" (CSO 43). They were less willing to challenge public officials during the post-July 15 state of emergency and, even after the state of emergency was lifted, for a project that would run for around a year and would probably not go on due to a lack of resources.

Second, the EU attaches importance to outputs and visibility of the projects it funds. Outputs of the aforementioned activities can easily and clearly be presented. For instance, the organization can concretely speak about how many people will take part in educational activities and training, and for how many hours; or how many people can benefit from centers and shelters. Even awareness-raising activities can be considered in this context. The numbers of people attending awareness-raising meetings, printed and distributed materials all provide data with which civil society organizations can prove the *success* of their project. In addition, these activities are likely to improve the visibility of the projects and EU funds.

Rights-based activism aims at bringing change in legal and institutional structures, practices, behaviors and ultimately understanding. On the one hand, achieving concrete results for rights-based activism (for example, a change of legislation) is possible over the long-term. On the other hand, rights-based activism itself is a process. Especially for vulnerable groups, achieving certain rights is only a step forward. For instance, even when women's rights may be formally established, gender equality is an issue requiring a constant struggle. The short implementation span of EU-funded projects, as well as their focus on outputs and visibility, make these programmes ill-suited for rights-based activism.

In addition, political engagement often requires a rapid reaction to unexpected problems. Breach of rights or controversial legislative debates must be tackled, challenged or confronted without wasting time. However, the time that elapses from a call for applications through to evaluation, until signing the grant contract, stretches over months. This prevents civil society organizations making use of EU funds to run campaigns or react against conjectural problems.

Third, civil society organizations easily bend their mandates and goals for EU-funded projects. For instance, an organization working on empowerment of women in economic life may run projects on violence against women. This is not a problem for applications so long as their statutes give them the mandate – and when it does not, the statutes are adopted. The problem is the compartmentalization of civil society organizations due to their size and capacity, which then leads to specialization only in narrowly defined areas. When these organizations choose to do something outside of their confined space, they unavoidably tilt towards service-based activities that do not require expertise. In this way, even when the EU opens programmes to enhance in general the rights of vulnerable groups, it ends up supporting service-based projects, that at best improves the lives of a few among many and potentially contribute to raising awareness of an issue during the lifetime of the project.

The EU's financial support to civil society organizations in Turkey under the IPA is not confined to vulnerable groups, rights-based or contentious issues. Part of these funds are allocated for *dialogue* programmes. These programmes follow on the Commission's Civil Society Dialogue and, broadly speaking, they aim at developing a mutual understanding between people in Turkey and in the EU, and thereby overcome prejudices. They also seek to improve Turkish society's knowledge on the EU and the accession process. Accordingly, from broad topics, such as culture, to more specific ones, like rural youth activism, the EU funds projects promising dialogue and exchange as well as a transfer of knowledge and best practices.

The Dialogue programmes, while implicitly seeking civil society's empowerment, have only limited impact over civic actors. The main focus of these programmes and the activities performed is to prepare Turkish society for accession. Civil society organizations have become the instruments for that. One can imagine the dialogues and networks established for these projects would contribute to their development and improve their capacities. However, studies show that with the projects ending, these relations slowly break down due to a lack of foreign language and human resources (Zihnioğlu, 2013: 65–66). While these projects may help small-scale organizations build self-confidence and contribute to their visibility, they add little to their capacities.

Another problem that the Dialogue programmes reveal but one that pertains to all programmes under the civil society title, is the EU's adoption of civil society in its broadest sense. These programmes are usually open to all non-governmental entities. As a result, for certain programmes, the principal beneficiaries are not civil society organizations, while in a few others no civil society organization benefits from the grants under a civil society programme. For instance, Civil Society Dialogue I had a programme on universities in which only one civil society organization received a grant, apart from the universities. However, only municipalities, chambers of commerce and industry[1] and cooperatives received funding under Agriculture and Fisheries Programme in Civil Society Dialogue II. There is no doubt municipalities, chambers and universities can play a crucial role in establishing mutual dialogue and helping to overcome prejudice. However, treating these entities as civil society organizations gives rise to a questioning of not only the EU's definition of a civil society, but also the very funds themselves.

In addition, there is another group of programmes not specifically opened for civil society but from which civil society organizations can directly benefit. These are the various programmes addressing Turkey's human resources, such as improving employment capacity and schooling rate. Civil society organizations have participated considerably in these programmes. As it was with previous programmes, here too, activities mostly focused on providing certain services, introducing the accession process and a sharing of knowledge and experience on different issues.

In a nutshell, the EU funds allocated both exclusively and indirectly to civil society aim at facilitating the adoption of or harmonization to the EU's legislation, standards and values. The projects supported cover most commonly service-based activities with concrete and visible outputs. 'Raising awareness' is another catch-word for an EU-funded project. While important in and of itself, the efficacy of such activities is limited and of a short duration. The few advocacy activities carried out in these projects are so over-ambitious that it is difficult to see them bringing about any meaningful result. In addition, political engagement sometimes requires organizations to act more quickly than the EU funding mechanism allows civil society organizations. The lengthy process from call for applications until the starting of a project renders such engagement impossible. Lastly, with no legislation framing the relations between public institutions and civil society organizations, relations face the risk of remaining ad hoc, arbitrary and inauthentic. In return, civil society organizations willing to engage or sustain relations with public institutions unavoidably abstain from contentious activities and discourse in Turkey's polarized political and social setting.

An important and controversial issue relating to EU funds is their broader impact over Turkish civil society. During the early years of EU civil society funding there were widespread concerns that these funds would create a project culture or a project fetishism, where civil society organizations become increasingly dependent on externally funded projects for their activities at the risk of straying from their stated mission. Another much-debated issue is whether these funds create professionalization. What further impact do the structure of EU funds have over the beneficiary organizations and, more broadly, Turkish civil society at large? This is a multidimensional issue that requires a deeper look at different aspects. To address these questions, I looked at the in-depth interviews I conducted with civil society organizations in Turkey.

First, as we have discussed, EU funds are better suited for service-based activities. To better understand what this means for civil society organizations, I first looked at the organizations that applied to these funds. The sample of interviewed organizations include politicized, non-politicized and hybrid organizations. I looked at the organizations' discourse and activities to decide on this status. I classified those organizations that are actively engaged in contentious and rights-based activities or have such a discourse as politicized. When they lacked such discourse and activities, I classified them as non-politicized. The hybrid organizations carry the characteristics of both groups.

Of the 34 interviewed civil society organizations, 17 are hybrid, 16 are non-politicized and one is politicized. The low number of politicized organizations in the sample reflects the fact that rights-based organizations tend to avoid state-based financial aid, including that coming from the EU. The hybrid organizations that carry out both service-based and rights-based activities are the most interesting. Outside of EU programmes, hybrid organizations have a good track record of rights-based activities or advocacy work. Several of these organizations lobby lawmakers to enact new codes, revise the existing ones[2] or to improve their rights, while others organize meetings with relevant public institutions[3] or make press releases.[4] In addition, they have also petitioned lawmakers,[5] followed and made new policies in the area of human rights,[6] established a platform for a new constitution and democracy,[7] carried out monitoring activities,[8] gave reactions to issues causing public resentment[9] and even staged protests.[10]

It is most interesting that these organizations undertake different types of activities with their EU-funded projects. As part of their EU-funded projects, these organizations mostly gave vocational, skills, handcrafts and literacy training.[11] Some organized informative meetings or seminars.[12] These projects also included organization of cultural activities,[13] preparing brochures,[14] translating EU acquis,[15] press screenings[16] and making surveys.[17] For instance, the Handicapped People's Association of Turkey has long been lobbying policy-makers and lawmakers to change the laws on handicapped people regarding their education and employment. However, their EU-funded project focused on vocational and skills training to handicapped people and did not address their ongoing advocacy work. Kayseri Caucasian Association has been lobbying to include Circassian language courses in school curricula, while their EU-funded project focused on Circassian handicrafts only.

One can expect civil society organizations to undertake both service and rights-based activities and alternate between the two as they see fit. But it is still interesting that the organizations that have frequently carried out rights-based activities or advocacy work prefer to apply EU funds to projects that involve mostly service-based activities. This is likely to be due to the structure of EU programmes. These programmes provide relatively short-term grants for intense activity-based projects with measurable outputs and preferably with high visibility. Civil society organizations themselves are also aware of this. As one interviewee stated, "[the EU] wants to stay at a level that is activity-based, no problem for both sides in the short-term and both high visibility and easy to follow" (CSO 4). In addition, some of the service-based activities such as training or counselling can easily be outsourced. This helps civil society organizations circumvent the lack of experience due to the aforementioned problem of compartmentalization, in other words: a narrowly defined working areas and focus.

Even the clearly politicized civil society organization among the interviewees (CSO 35) shifted its focus from advocacy work to service-based activities with a project funded under a programme for women's empowerment and women NGOs. They made surveys and held meetings to identify the needs of women following a big earthquake in their province. In addition, they provided the women with psychological support.

The abundance of service-based activities also leads to confusion among some organizations. Some of the interviewees were not sure:

> whether [a politicized activity] would have had a positive reaction.... For instance, you know there is Kayseri's folkloric dances, you know there is such an activity, something related to that. We thought why should they give us [the grant] when there were such activities.
>
> (CSO 25)

It is also important to remember that most organizations need external funding to sustain themselves. What many organizations need "is actually a little general support.... After some point [EU funds] turn into a pragmatic thing" (CSO 4).

The prevalence of non-politicized organizations running EU-funded projects is also striking. This is understandable for the Dialogue programmes that primarily aim at fostering cultural links and better understanding between the societies in Turkey and in the EU. However, these organizations frequently benefit from other programmes that one might expect to see rights-based activities taking part in, such as those programmes promoting civic empowerment, civic participation and combating violence against women. These groups replicate their non-contentious activities with their projects under these programmes. For instance, one organization held meetings and prepared reports for a programme opened for combating violence against women (CSO 2). Another organization (CSO 15) organized meetings with local people to change the perception on mentally disabled people for a programme on strengthening civil society, using EU funds.

These may not be directly depoliticizing the beneficiary organizations. However, creating incentives that are more conducive to service-based activities on political issues, where rights-based activism is possible, affects the course these organizations follow. In turn, this widens the depoliticized civic space in Turkey.

An equally curious question is whether EU funds have caused professionalization of Turkish civil society. The official data indicates an increasing professionalization of Turkish civil society over the past decade (see Figure 7.1). The figures coincide with ever-increasing funding coming from the EU to civic actors in Turkey. However, one should be careful not to draw easy parallels between the two. A detailed look into the civil society organizations that carried out EU-funded projects tells us why.

Of the 33 interviewed civil society organizations that benefited from EU funds, eight were professionalized, meaning their activities are consistently designed and implemented by functionally specialized and paid staff and not their volunteers or members. Seven of these organizations were established as professional organizations from the start. In other words, these organizations were established in consideration of financial resources for paid staff. Interestingly, all seven organizations

128 *The impact of EU funds over Turkish civil society*

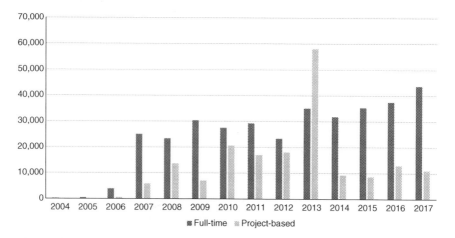

Figure 7.1 Number of paid-staff in associations in Turkey (2004–2017).
Source: Ministry of Interior Directorate General of Civil Society Affairs, 2018.

were sectorial or interest groups, where volunteerism is in general limited. The other organization, the Culture Routes Society, relies heavily on the efforts of a single person (founder and chair) who is actively trying to institutionalize the organization to make it sustainable. It is the chair and the paid staff that plan and implement activities. While the organization is actively seeking alternative resources to run the organization with professional staff, the rationale behind this professionalization is not EU funds. The interviewed organizations that have not benefited from EU funds but were professionalized were also established with financial resources and an institutional structure from the beginning. In short, there is no apparent causal relation between running EU-funded projects and transferring the workload to professional staff.

Two other organizations that benefited from EU funds, The Women Entrepreneurs Association of Turkey (KAGİDER) and Leader Creative Participants Association, are both partially professionalized. Both organizations run several projects. The professional staff are responsible for some of these projects, while members also take the lead or actively engage in other projects. The number of paid staff in KAGİDER has been increasing over the years, but this is not replacing the volunteer work of the members, who continue to assume responsibility for some of the projects. The majority of the interviewed organizations that have carried out EU-funded projects were not professionalized.

The interesting question then is why EU funds have not led to professionalization. There are two major reasons for this. First, in two thirds of the interviewed organizations, the key positions of the projects (for example, project coordinator, expert) were assumed by existing members or volunteers. These people tend to be board members or active members or volunteers of the organization, who usually, also prepared the application. The organizations use EU funds as financial incentives for their active members and volunteers. In most cases, working for their organization's EU-funded project is not considered an employment per se. Some of the interviewees who had said they did not employ anyone for their EU-funded project later acknowledged having employed their members or volunteers. This is because 'employment' connotes the recruitment of outsider professionals. For instance, one interviewee noted that they "did not employ anyone in the project with insurance.[18] ... Of course, there is project coordination. We carried that out officially" (CSO 23).

In addition, many interviewees consider it natural that those who draft the projects should also work towards its implementation. This is because it is considered that they know the project better than anyone else. The project also becomes a part of their tasks in the organization. An interviewee who coordinated several EU-funded projects for her organization noted that she was employed:

> because I had that skill. To run the project, to report it, in other words to master in the project, to know your subject well.... I was doing it because I had that skill. Otherwise, there are a lot of members in the association. They did not assume that task because they lacked that skill.
>
> (CSO 34)

These employed people often continue their volunteer work once the project ends. As a result, while EU-funded projects may be employing people who may otherwise volunteer, this does not necessarily affect the volunteerism for that organization.

A limited number of interviewed organizations employed outsider professionals to run their EU-funded projects. These professionals left the organization after the completion of the project because the organizations cannot maintain the financial means EU funds provide, and therefore cannot offer any continuing salaries for these staff. In addition, these professionals gain expertise in running EU-funded projects and as they do "they become sought-after employees ... they can get a job somewhere else before they leave [the organization]" (CSO 18). The exception to this is the KAGİDER, which found other financial resources to keep their staff. In two other cases, civil society organizations implemented their EU-funded projects with the professional assistance of a consultancy company. This relation also terminated after the completion of the project.

The outsider professionals employed for implementing EU-funded projects, or more broadly EU-funded projects themselves, do not seem to have had much impact on the professionalization of the beneficiary organizations. Some of the interviewees noted that implementing EU-funded projects improved their capacity in identifying and solving problems, and in general systematizing their work (for instance, CSO 14, CSO 23, CSO 43). EU-funded projects disciplined them in a way that they "at least learn to act in a more orderly way, namely to learn to set goals. At least, plan how to reach these goals" (CSO 34). While this may suggest a level of institutionalization, it does not amount to a professionalization of the organizations where volunteers are replaced with professional staff in designing and implementing activities. There are several reasons why the impact is limited.

First, EU civil society support under the IPA has been activity-oriented, meaning that funds were provided for civil society organizations to undertake certain activities to achieve pre-determined objectives. While the employment costs of paid staff are often accepted, the rationale for such staff is for the better management and implementation of the project rather than institutional development. Second, most projects last around 10 to 18 months, while some projects may be even shorter. In addition, a project is not re-funded, which makes winning a new grant and keeping the professional staff more challenging. Therefore, the time that the professional staff spends with the civil society organizations remains very limited. A project's lifetime is often very limited to change the institutional habits and structure of the civil society organization. In addition, EU-funded projects are activity-intense and often come with a demanding timetable. Implementing an EU-funded project "financially, activity wise, implementation, with methodology is a difficult thing.... Goes so fast. In fact, you can face various unpredictable situations" (CSO 4). Therefore, while EU-funded projects may bring some "managerialism" (Choudry and Kapoor, 2013), it is unlikely to lead to a lasting impact on the organizational structure.

The second reason why EU funds have not led to professionalization relates to the overall civic culture in Turkey. Due to low levels of volunteerism in Turkey, civil society organizations are often run by few people. This creates quasi-professionals, which may lead to a hierarchical structure, where a few people have a strong hold over the organization. In return, however, this prevents outsider professionals exerting a strong impact over the organization.

It is also important not to draw easy conclusions based on the figures of professional staff. Following the leap between 2004 and 2007, the increase in the number of full-time paid staff has slowed down. In addition, in view of the over 110,000 associations, the number of paid staff is still quite limited. This suggests that professionalization may be in response to certain crises. One example may be the rapid rise in humanitarian groups following the Syrian war and the resulting migration crisis providing a clear need for professional staff to manage the aid and address humanitarian issues.

Several non-degree and graduate programmes on civil society management confirm the interest in working for the civil society sector. That said, this is a demanding career path with limited opportunities in Turkey. Most civil society professionals

> have a very strong bond to the issue, [otherwise] it is not possible to sustain it for a long time. Therefore, [the professionals] must have already had a political bond with that issue and therefore they must have come from such a street movement.
>
> (Personal interview, Hale Akay)

Therefore, it is not accurate to see the professional staff as complete outsiders to the organization's cause.

One of the major concerns in the early years of EU civil society support was that this support would create a project fetishism among the civil society organizations. One dimension of this is the civil society organizations that are established explicitly to make use of the EU funds, the so-called 'brief-case' or 'signboard' organizations. It is true that such organizations were established and still exist, although some of these organizations closed down after their first or second project. While it is difficult to quantify these organizations, it is erroneous to think that such organizations at any time dominated Turkish civil society.

However, while the earlier criticism that EU funds create a project culture may be partly true, the causal relation between the two is rather complicated. Project culture often connotes a project-based organizational culture. However, this understanding overlooks at the medium of the individuals and their choices. For instance, the Van Lake Folklore, Tourism, Sports Club Association has carried out five consecutive EU-funded projects, written and implemented mostly by a single member of the association. When that member has decided to focus her attention to another cause, the association ceased to apply for EU grants, although they still carry out numerous activities that do not require any funding.

All in all, the real charm of EU funds is less tangible. EU funds allow the receiving organization to run more and larger activities than they could do on their own. This increases their visibility. This is particularly true in smaller towns. In addition, to better quantify the results of the project, civil society organizations try to reach as many beneficiaries as possible (especially for their training activities, seminars and meetings). As a result, they may achieve better access to the groups that they claim to represent. For instance, with their EU-funded projects, the Van Women's Association and the Association for Raising Consumer Awareness gave seminars to thousands in their respective areas, while the Handicapped People's Association of Turkey provided vocational education to hundreds. Reaching out to more people does not make the organizations more representative. However, their legitimacy in the eyes of their members, base and society increases and this results in greater recognition. "This association can do any job now, it has the capacity, it goes with a plan and project and has education support, has staff ... [The EU-funded project] had a great effect" (CSO 22). This reinforces their self-confidence. With high visibility and greater recognition, they are even able to attract new volunteers to their cause. For instance, in some cases, "during the project, we had volunteers ... a new group of volunteers emerged with experience in this area" (CSO 1). The impact need not be limited to the project's lifetime.

> When a new member goes to [a civil society organization] or when [a civil society organization] wants to recruit a new member, when it says 'I ran this project, I understand this job, I have an office, I have computers, I have conference halls, I do seminars' people are influenced.
>
> (Personal interview, Kunut Açan)

Participation of civil society organizations in public sector projects

Civil society organizations can benefit from EU funds through also participating in public sector projects. Albeit indirectly, such participation may have an impact on civil society organizations and are relevant to arguments especially on civil society's depoliticization. At this point we should take a pause to clarify why civil society organizations' participation in public sector projects relates to arguments on their depoliticization. A political civic organization is one that exhibits rights-based activism with discourse and activities that challenge the policies and practices in their area. Neither participation in policy or decision-making in public policies makes an organization more (or less) political, nor does being political entail a lack of dialogue with public institutions. That said, this section examines what type of civil society organizations participate in EU-funded public sector projects and at which levels. It shows rights-based organizations' limited participation to and benefit from these projects despite major programmes on the rights of vulnerable groups. In that sense, EU funds have provided only little incentive for the development of rights-based activism and a more political civil society in Turkey.

Public sector projects make up the bulk of the EU's pre-accession assistance. They cover a wide array of issues addressing political reforms, economic and social harmonization or more broadly, improvement of Turkey's governance in the run up to the accession.[19] Public institutions are the coordinators and principal beneficiaries of these programmes. While it is not mandatory, civil society organizations, too, participate in some of these projects at different levels. Some of the earlier projects are good examples of civic participation. For instance, the Ministry of Interior's project on shelters for battered women in 2005 included some of the well-known rights-based women's organizations such as Mor Çatı Women's Shelter Foundation and the KAMER Foundation in the drafting and implementation of the project. Likewise, for its project for promoting gender equality, the Directorate General on Status of Women consulted women's organizations and later established a Steering Committee including these organizations.

Public institutions' cooperation with civil society organizations for projects on political issues is not without criticism. The European Court of Auditor's (2009) initial scanning of some of these projects acknowledge the important outputs they produced. However, these outputs have generally not resulted in expected outcomes. One major reason behind this is public institutions' ongoing lack of trust towards civil society organizations, their tendency to dominate the project and therefore allowing for only a limited space for civil society organizations' participation (Akay, 2016: 60). In relation to this, critics emphasize public institutions' expectations from participating organizations to highlight the pros of each case and abstain from critical comments. This is problematic considering that each public sector project is developed in response to a certain problem or a drawback. This is particularly difficult for rights-based organizations, which tend to be more political. As a result, this is likely to lead rights-based groups to be alienated from public sector projects.

On the other hand, a careful look at public sector projects reveals several fundamental drawbacks of civic participation. Apart from the aforementioned and a few other examples, public institutions cooperate with civil society organizations mostly for service-based activities. These activities usually include helping various vulnerable groups' access to basic or social services. For instance, for its project on the implementation of local administration reforms, the Ministry of Interior had foreseen social services being provided by civil society organizations. For the Ministry of Youth and Sports' project on the improvement of the living standards of youth and children, civil society organizations were given the task of preparing educational materials and providing training.

Several activists note that the relations between public institutions and civil society organizations have been deteriorating after a brief improvement between 2005 and 2010. There are suspicions that public institutions prevent in a politically correct way, the participation of critical organizations or more generally, those organizations whose political orientation is not in tandem with the government. Indeed, the overly general language used in project documents on the participation of civil society organizations makes this possible. Further, as earlier studies (Akay, 2016: 46–48) find that only around 6 percent of the public sector projects aim at high levels of participation of civil society organizations both in the drafting and implementation of their projects. The most common methods for participation are information sharing, counselling and an invitation to take part in a project's activities. However, most projects do not clearly define the purpose of civil society organizations' participation. Therefore, it is difficult to assess the impact of the organizations' participation. Only in rare occasions do civil society organizations take part for joint project development or in the decision-making on projects. While information sharing is completely one-sided, counselling might be considered participatory only if there is a meaningful discussion between civil society organizations and public institutions. However, if civil society organizations do not know whether public institutions consider the points they raise and if not, the reasons behind them, then their participation becomes superficial. Therefore, what seems like a dialogue becomes an instrument to cover up controversial issues. Civil society organizations are then not participating but being instrumentalized.

The impact of EU funds were also limited in this area. Although the EU considers external audit and civil society organizations important, the European Court of Auditor's assessment found that the IPA dealt insufficiently with Turkey's capacity to engage with civil society actors (2018: point 26). The report emphasizes that the amount allocated for this remained low due to the limited absorption capacity of the Turkish authorities.

It is important not to overgeneralize the public sector's attitude towards civil society. There are certainly significant differences between different public institutions. Interviewees note the positive approach of some of the ministries that have been actively participating in Turkey's accession process. Officials in these ministries have eventually developed a certain understanding of working with civil society organizations. However, in the absence of a legislation framing the public sector's relations with civil society organizations, these positive examples may be dependent on individuals and not become sustainable. However, relevant public officials are also critical of civil society organizations. They point to the fact that civil society organizations cannot carry out advocacy adequately, especially at the Parliament level due to their lack of in-depth knowledge of the legislative process (Akay, 2016: 40–41). Therefore, without first addressing these more fundamental problems, civil society organizations' participation in public sector projects will be incomplete.

Many of the public sector projects addressed Turkey's different problems and triggered, if not resulted in, change. Despite the big sums invested, the state of certain problem areas such as the rule of law, human rights and vulnerable groups is daunting. It is legitimate to wonder why progress is so limited despite the flow of funds for now well over a decade. No doubt that the political environment has been a decisive factor, but we also need to be more critical of EU-funded projects, their design and implementation and the participatory mechanisms they have for civil society. Due to the reasons explained above, civil society's participation in public sector projects is problematic although these funds enabled for unprecedented mechanisms between public institutions and civil society organizations. What characterizes this as a problem is the very nature of political activism. Essentially, public institutions try to establish a way of working relations devoid of conflict. However, conflict is not only unavoidable, but also expected in relations with rights-based organizations for rights-based work. One way to overcome this and the ensuing lack of trust is to institutionalize relations. This would prevent arbitrary practices of individuals, turn ad hoc ties into sustainable relations and thereby deepen mutual trust. Institutionalization of relations is necessary, especially in times of political uncertainty.

Notes

1 Because chambers of commerce and industry are established by law and membership is obligatory, their status as a civil society organization is frequently challenged.
2 CSO 17, CSO 18, CSO 19, CSO 25, CSO 28, CSO 37, CSO 39, CSO 43.
3 CSO 13, CSO 20.
4 CSO 39, CSO 40.
5 CSO 3.
6 CSO 4.
7 CSO 14.
8 CSO 40.
9 CSO 43.
10 CSO 11.
11 CSO 13, CSO 14, CSO 18, CSO 20, CSO 28, CSO 37, CSO 39, CSO 43.
12 CSO 4, CSO 11, CSO 13, CSO 17, CSO 19, CSO 43.
13 CSO 25, CSO 40.
14 CSO 13, CSO 43.
15 CSO 3.
16 CSO 4.

17 CSO 40.
18 The interviewee refers to social security and means officially employed.
19 This section draws on the information available on the grant database at Central Finance and Contracts Unit, public institutions' web sites for relevant projects as well as earlier research on the EU's pre-accession financial assistance.

Bibliography

Akay, H. (2016) *10 Years with the European Union: Financial Assistance, Civil Society and Participation*. İstanbul: Turkey Europe Foundation.

Alvarez, S. E. (1999) Advocating Feminism: The Latin American Feminist NGO "Boom," *International Feminist Journal of Politics*, 1(2), pp. 181–209.

Armstrong, E. and Prashad, V. (2005) Exiles from a Future Land: Moving Beyond Coalitional Politics, *Antipode*, 37(1), pp. 181–185.

Biekart, K. (1999) *The Politics of Civil Society Building: European Private Aid Agencies and Democratic Transitions in Central America*. Utrecht: International Books.

Choudry, A. (2010) Global Justice? Contesting NGO-ization: Knowledge Politics and Containment in Antiglobalization Networks, in A. Choudry and D. Kapoor (eds), *Learning from the Ground Up Global Perspectives on Social Movements and Knowledge Production*. New York: Palgrave Macmillan.

Choudry, A. and Kapoor, D. (2013) Introduction: NGOization: Complicity, Contradictions and Prospects, in A. Choudry and D. Kapoor (eds), *NGOization Complicity, Contradictions and Prospects*. USA: Zed Books.

European Court of Auditors. (2009) *The European Commission's Management of Pre-Accession Assistance to Turkey*. Special Report (No. 16–2009). Luxembourg: European Court of Auditors.

European Court of Auditors. (2018) *EU Pre-accession Assistance to Turkey: Only Limited Results So Far*. Special Report 07. Luxembourg: European Court of Auditors.

Gupta, S. (2014) From Demanding to Delivering Development, *Journal of South Asian Development*, 9(2), pp. 121–145.

Howell, J. and Pearce, J. (2001) *Civil Society and Development: A Critical Exploration*. Boulder: Lynne Rienner Publishers, Inc.

Jad, I. (2004) The NGO-isation of Arab Women's Movements, *Institute of Development Studies Bulletin*, 35(4), pp. 34–42.

Kamat, S. (2004) The Privatization of Public Interest: Theorizing NGO Discourse in a Neoliberal Era, *Review of International Political Economy*, 11(1), pp. 155–176.

Kapoor, D. (2013) Social Action and NGOization in Context of Development Dispossession in Rural India: Explorations into the Un-civility of Civil Society, in A. Choudry and D. Kapoor (eds), *NGOization Complicity, Contradictions and Prospects*. USA: Zed Books.

Kihika, M. (2009) Development or Underdevelopment: The Case of Non-Governmental Organizations in Neoliberal Sub-Saharan Africa, *Journal of Alternative Perspectives in the Social Sciences*, 1(3), pp. 783–795.

Mercer, C. (2002) NGOs, Civil Society, and Democratization: A Critical Review of the Literature, *Progress in Development Studies*, 2(1), pp. 5–22.

Paternotte, D. (2016) The NGOization of LGBT activism: ILGA-Europe and the Treaty of Amsterdam, *Social Movement Studies*, 15(4), pp. 388–402.

Personal interview, Hale Akay, 18 August 2016.

Personal interview, Sevgi Kunut Açan, 5 January 2017.

Roy, A. (2014) The NGO-ization of Resistance, *Massalijin News* (4 September) http://massalijn.nl/new/the-ngo-ization-of-resistance/.

Roy, S. (2015) The Indian Women's Movement: Within and Beyond NGOization, *Journal of South Asian Development*, 10(1), pp. 96–117.

Salamon, L. (1994) The Rise of the Nonprofit Sector, *Foreign Affairs*, 73, pp. 109–122.

Zihnioğlu, Ö. (2013) *European Union Civil Society Policy and Turkey: A Bridge Too Far?* Basingstoke: Palgrave Macmillan.

Conclusion

With the shrinking of civic space since 2013, rights-based civic groups in Turkey have come under increasing pressure. During this period, some of the formally established groups were closed, and they are consistently delegitimized by the government. Others try to sustain their work either by keeping a low profile or shifting their focus towards non-contentious activities. In addition, research suggests that the EU's financial support to Turkish civil society has been more amenable to services-based activities and not incentivizing rights-based activities as much. In return, this largest source of external funding facilitated civil society organizations to become service-providers rather than claimants and contributed to Turkish civil society's depoliticization.

This is not to suggest that rights-based activism has ended in Turkey. Some of the established civil society organizations continue their work despite the unfavorable conditions. More recently, new activist groups working through loose networks and structures emerged. Some of these groups adopted a politicized discourse and engaged in rights-based activism. However, the size and scope of their activities gradually waned due to widespread fear and uncertainty among activists. As they find it increasingly difficult to make themselves heard through the mainstream media, they are confined to social media. This narrows the visibility and limits the impact of their activities. As their numbers shrink and their activities are isolated, they are becoming marginalized. Given that civil society has been considered one of the main pillars of Turkey's accession process to the EU, the current state of Turkish civil society in relation to EU–Turkey relations requires further attention. Turkish civil society's gradual depoliticization has wider implications on Turkey's relations with the EU.

Depoliticization of civil society and democracy

First, depoliticization of Turkish civil society has aggravated Turkey's already faltering democracy. Even before the democratic downturn, rights-based activism, advocacy and contentious work was limited among Turkish civil society organizations at large. Civil society's depoliticization has further diminished the interest in rights-based activism. This is not helping Turkey's deteriorating democracy as what is needed are civil society groups that can demand and advocate rights, constructively engage in public debates and, if need be, challenge public policies and their implementation. This is particularly necessary for disadvantaged groups such as those representing LGBTI, Alevi and Roma communities, where civil society organizations have been central in efforts to further their rights. Although such organizations are limited in numbers, some of them have won important achievements in the 2000s. For instance, Alevi organizations, most notably the Cem Foundation's years-long legal struggle both at the national level and before the European Court of Human Rights secured certain achievements to Alevis in Turkey. It is as a result of these efforts that the decision to revise the curriculum on compulsory religious courses at secondary schools and to legally recognize Alevi's Cem Houses as official places of worship were implemented. As Turkish civic space depoliticizes such organizations increasingly shy away from their earlier advocacy work.

Civil society organizations are important venues for learning active citizenship and democratic participation (Çakmaklı, 2017). In principle, non-political work, such as those carried out by charities, self-help groups and others enable citizens to get involved in their societies. However, it is through working with politicized civic actors that citizens can learn to advocate their and others' rights, engage more constructively in public debates, challenging public policies and their implementation. It is through civic action with politicized organizations that citizens can better learn the roles and responsibilities of democratic participation and enrich their countries' democracy. The depoliticization of civil society in general closes this door for Turkish citizens to learn active citizenship and democratic participation.

In parallel with this, de-legitimization and the subsequent marginalization of rights-based activism have adversely affected certain working areas crucial for democracy. Foremost among these is human rights. Human rights activists have come under increasing pressure and several activists are behind bars. However, other groups, such as environmentalists and identity-based activism, have also come under sustained attacks. The LGBTI Pride Parade, which had peacefully taken place in İstanbul for over a decade was banned in June 2015. Since then, LGBTI groups and individuals have organized the Pride Parade despite the ban and the parade has taken place with police intervention. While such groups were not completely silenced, working in these areas has increasingly come to be regarded as 'dangerous.' These activists are well aware of the consequences of rights-based activism. They often acknowledge in advance that their activism will put them under the spotlight; their protests may entail clashes with the police and even prosecution. This has led many activists working in these areas in particular to shy away. Rights-based groups have gradually shrunk and the most highly-politicized groups are left with a handful of the 'usual suspects.' As a result, the scope of rights-based activism in these areas has been considerably narrowed.

The need for rights-based civic groups is particularly urgent for Turkish democracy given the country's high-level of political and social polarization. As polarization intensifies, discrimination faced by disadvantaged groups is heard less by others in the society at large. Civil society groups are important actors with a potential to not only defend the rights and make known the discrimination faced by these disadvantaged groups, but also shape the society's broader understanding and discourse regarding their rights. For instance, in earlier years, the efforts of the Human Rights Association and the Human Rights Foundation have made significant contribution to transforming the discourse around the Kurdish conflict. Some of the issues raised by these organizations are still sensitive to large parts of Turkish society. These organizations' efforts may not be enough to resolve the problem. However, they may help reinforce society's confidence in its ability to live peacefully together. This is particularly noteworthy considering that grievances still run deep on both sides. In addition, some of the work carried out for disadvantaged groups, such as demands for rule of law, educational reform or women's participation, concern wider sectors of society. Progress made in these areas will bring tangible benefits for all Turkish citizens (Center for American Progress et al., 2017: 26–27).

The cessation of multiple democratic openings including the Kurdish, Alevi and the Roma in the past couple of years, along with the growing exclusionist discourse has fueled further polarization among Turkey's citizens. Added to this is the AKP's recent alliance with the right-wing MHP, which suggests that the government's polarizing approach is likely to continue at least in the coming years. Taken together, initiatives coming from civil society organizations become all the more important in reducing tension, reviving social cohesion and maintaining political dialogue. This is not to suggest that civil society organizations on their own can put Turkish democracy back on track. As we discussed in Chapter 4, participation in civil society organizations is limited. Outside the major cities and urban centers, their influence is side-lined by the government. Addressing Turkey's political problems requires understanding and support of high-level political actors (ibid.: 5–6). However, rights-based civic groups are still important actors in bringing forward and drawing attention to issues that may otherwise go unnoticed. Their depoliticization means another blow not only to disadvantaged communities but also to democratization efforts in Turkey.

One may argue that political advocacy work has enjoyed certain influence given the context provided by the EU and the accession process. It is true that the EU has long provided a legitimizing context and assurance for rights-based groups and their activities. These groups have frequently referred to the EU's political criteria for accession to further their cause and have found open support in reports, statements and other communications of different EU institutions. As the accession process remained on track, rights-based groups in Turkey and the EU were natural allies. This enhanced their overall legitimacy, strengthened their hands, facilitated and reinforced their work. With Turkey's accession process de facto on halt for some time now, the EU's legitimizing context for rights-based groups has also waned. However, this is not to suggest a dead end for these groups. There is still room for them to act, perhaps more strategically in furthering their cause. In the absence of the EU's enabling context, rights-based groups could turn to other international actors that fit their cause to provide a normative and legitimizing basis for their activities. More commonly this could be the United Nations, the Council of Europe or other international institutions and treaties that Turkey is member of or party to. For instance, the United Nation's Convention on the Elimination of All Forms of Discrimination against Women (CEDAW) and the Council of Europe's İstanbul Declaration provide such framing for women's groups. While rights-based groups will still have challenges absent high-level political support, reframing their cause and activities with international actors other than the EU will provide them with additional leverage. For this reason, political advocacy work is still relevant in Turkey. Rights-based groups can reframe their activities and references and retain their legitimacy in society even when the government challenges that.

Depoliticization of civil society and Turkey's transformation

Another major impact of civil society's depoliticization is in their role in transnational social learning through international long-term collaborations and partnerships. Despite the ongoing EU financial support and encouragement for collaborations between civil society organizations from Turkey and EU member states, depoliticization is likely to significantly reduce such partnerships. In return, this has potential adverse effects on Turkey's overall transformation.

As we have discussed in Chapters 6 and 7, the overall nature of and the criteria for the EU's civil society support in Turkey has not promoted politicized groups or activities. Most programmes have been more amenable to service-based activities. Only some specific programmes, which are designed for political groups promote rights-based activities, advocacy or contentious work. These programmes are limited in number and scope. This, in a way, appears to limit the long-term interaction among civil society organizations in Turkey and in the EU. In other words, the EU is not able to encourage Turkish civic organizations' sustainable communication with their counterparts in the EU countries that the social learning process requires. This is mainly because, for politicized organizations focusing on rights-based activism, the subject of their work (for example, human rights, women's empowerment or LGBTI rights) echo in different parts of the world. In their search for alliances, these organizations tend to establish a more regular dialogue with their counterparts in Europe and elsewhere than non-political groups. They are often members of European or international umbrella organizations or are part of a network. They can follow and learn about the ideas, debates, and practices abroad more easily. In this way, rights-based groups are more open to European norms and becoming "norm entrepreneurs." The recent centralization of EU funds to Turkish civil society has not only changed the structure of the funding mechanism, but it is likely to entail new funding priorities. This may lead to more programmes with a focus on rights-based activism. However, time will tell their impact on Turkish civil society.

It is true that the EU's civil society support in Turkey incentivize civil society organizations to collaborate with other organizations from EU member states and other candidate countries. As part of its enlargement policy and support to

Turkish civil society, the EU puts a great emphasis on civil society dialogue that will bring closer the societies in Turkey and in Europe. Accordingly, civil society organizations' partnership has even become a requirement for some of the programmes, especially those opened under the Civil Society Dialogue. These projects brought together civil society organizations in Turkey and across the EU under different topics, such as culture or youth activism. Above all, these projects often served as a platform whereby these organizations and their target groups had a dialogue, exchange and transfer of knowledge. This is important as both sides get the opportunity to better understand each other and overcome prejudices against one another. However, these interactions are often short-lived and tend to be limited due to the duration of EU-funded projects. Earlier research suggests that while organizations that previously had not known one another may enter into partnerships for EU-funded projects, such project-focused partnerships turn out to be unsustainable (Zihnioğlu, 2013: 66).

Here, the problem is the depoliticization of civic groups that have previously been politically active. These formerly politicized groups are likely to turn in on themselves as they pursue more service-based activities and less rights-based activism. They will eventually move away from European and international umbrella organizations and networks. Their overall connection to and relations with their counterparts in EU member states and other candidate countries will gradually diminish. The role of these organizations as norm carriers will dissipate as they depoliticize. This will seriously disrupt the social learning process. In return, these organizations will be even less likely to be able to affect and change the cost-benefit assessment of the Turkish government to push for more reforms that are democratic.

This is all the more important due to the current state of Turkey's accession process to the EU. The joy and excitement surrounding the start of accession negotiations in 2005 soon dwindled away as Turkey has hit new bumps in the road. Ongoing problems with Cyprus along with the Additional Protocol crisis in 2005 soon after resulted in the suspension of accession negotiations in several chapters. In addition, the emphasis on the open-ended nature of accession negotiations, references to issues not directly related to the Copenhagen Criteria, and that have high symbolic value for many in Turkey (for example, peaceful settlement of disputes with Armenia), and German and French leaders' persistent calls for an ambiguous privileged partnership in place of full membership have led to souring of relations. More importantly, the credibility of the EU's conditionality mechanism began to be questioned by the Turkish political elite and the public at large.

Turkey also lost its assertiveness on its membership bid. The once promising reform process of the early 2000s had lost its pace by the middle of the decade and came to a halt soon after. With new regions gaining prominence on the foreign policy agenda, relations with the EU lost priority for the AKP government. Accession process lost steam both in Turkey and in the EU. Despite the occasional opening of the negotiations on new chapters, the accession process has been de facto on halt for some time.

Conclusion

The current state of the accession process with Turkey is a big conundrum for the EU. On the one hand, despite strong public opposition to Turkey's membership across the EU, the European Parliament's calls to freeze the accession process are largely left unanswered in EU capitals. In a way, most EU member states want to maintain the accession process as it is, without advancing it due to motivations ranging from strategic concerns to economic interests (Aydıntaşbaş, 2018: 2). In addition, the freezing of negotiations is not a preferred option by the Commission and the member states in general. If negotiations are frozen, Turkey's accession prospect may disappear for an indefinite period of time. This is because the restarting of membership talks requires a unanimous decision of member states. And it is unlikely for countries with a clear opposition to Turkey's membership, such as Cyprus or Austria, to approve the restart of the talks in the future.

On the other hand, one should not expect the accession process to be back on track any time soon. A political settlement to the Cyprus problem, a major obstacle to progress in the accession process, looks unlikely in the near term. The rise of populist right-wing political parties and movements, the growing Turcoskepticism in the public opinion across the EU is coupled with anti-Western discourse in Turkish political elite and anti-Westernism of the Turkish public. These recent developments caution us against holding any expectation towards the accession process. Indeed, the accession process has lost its defining strength, and many are in search of a new form to describe Turkey's relations with the EU.

As Chapter 3 has shown, EU–Turkey relations have been evolving into bilateral transactional ties in response to the accession conundrum. Transactionalism has been the buzzword among the scholars, researchers and think tanks working on EU–Turkey relations. Several papers elaborated the potentials, feasibility and practicality of a transactional approach, while downplaying the accession process. Transactional relations are interest-based relations, which neither presuppose nor incentivize shared values. Transaction-based relations are not new and even some of the member states have a transactional approach to EU membership. For instance, countries of first arrival want to share the burden of migrants, while populists in central European countries refuse to take in any. In a similar vein, central European countries want to continue receiving EU funds, while the populist in net-contributor countries prefer to reduce these funds and their contribution (Grabbe and Lehne, 2018).

Turkey prefers transactional ties, first, because it replaces the hierarchical tone of accession negotiations with an inherent discourse of equals. Turkey has long seen the West as a reference point and accepted the obvious hierarchy this created in its relations with the West. This is because Turkey saw the world as Western-centric. The West had been seen also as the destination and Turkey wanted to attain the economic and security benefits that this hierarchical relationship provided (Dalay, 2018). However, this has changed in recent decades under the AKP leadership. For the current political elite in Turkey, relations with the EU are still important, although no longer a priority. Accordingly, Turkey has been demanding change in its relationship with the EU to one between equals. Second, there is a growing sense of incompatibility in Turkish leadership between the accession criteria and the country's interests. In particular, the recent transformation of the Turkish political system to strong presidency in full control of domestic affairs and the EU's Copenhagen Criteria go counter at times. In addition, in Turkish politics, particularly in recent years, national sovereignty claims priority and renders any pooling of sovereign power, and therefore the EU membership, less attractive (Janning, 2018).

The EU member states are also happy to have a give and take relation with Turkey. The migration deal is a very good example of this. The transactional approach to Turkey is even more evident in their bilateral ties to Turkey. For example, French President Macron commented in the Greek Kathimerini newspaper in September 2017 that:

> Turkey has indeed strayed away from the European Union in recent months and worryingly overstepped the mark in ways that cannot be ignored. But I want to avoid a split because it's a vital partner in many crises we all face, notably the immigration challenge and the terrorist threat.
>
> (Irish, 2017)

In addition, a few billions of euro worth investment agreements were signed during Erdoğan's visit in January 2018 to Paris. After the Brexit vote, Prime Minister May visited Ankara to find ways to increase trade with Turkey (Aydıntaşbaş, 2018: 6). Evidently, it is easier for the political leadership in these countries to make a case for these ties than for Turkey's accession. In addition, identifying common interests and working together towards achieving them might be a good starting point for re-building trust between Turkey and the EU.

There are, however, inherent risks in transactional relations. First, while transactional relations may provide an opportunity to deepen the bilateral ties on issues such as trade, foreign policy or counter-terrorism, a transactional approach actually reduces the relations to certain areas of mutual interest. No matter how hollow the accession process is, it is still the only major rules-based framework between Turkey and the EU. Even if the accession process may not be working as expected, a purely transactional approach would bring about the breakdown of the broader rules-based relationship. Without another rules-based alternative, the normative pillar of EU–Turkey relations would be lacking. This is undesirable because Turkey has been pursuing EU membership not only for economic gains, but also to improve its political and legal standards and achieve an advanced level of democracy. In addition, it is not possible to reignite the accession process through transactional relations. For instance, the various high-level dialogue meetings between Turkey and the EU on areas of joint interest failed to revitalize the accession process.

Finally, transactional relations in principle entail a parity among the partners, which runs counter to the functioning of the conditionality mechanism. The more the EU approaches Turkey in a transactional manner, the more damage it gives to its own conditionality mechanism. For instance, even when the political elite in Turkey enter into rationalist cost-benefit assessments, they do that through bargaining on issues where there is mutual interest, and not as depicted by the external incentives model. While some of the issues, such as visa liberalization, have their own conditionality, this cannot replace the normative conditionality of the accession process.

As the EU conditionality weakened, the EU's leverage and appeal as a normative reference point in Turkey has diminished (Müftüler-Baç, 2016; Saatçioğlu, 2016). In particular since the downturn in EU–Turkey relations around 2007, EU policies and institutions have ceased to be reference points for Turkish policymakers, opinion leaders, journalists and the general public. Scholars have discussed how Turkey's major political parties no longer framed the accession as a process that contributes to the advancement of Turkish democracy and fundamental rights (Balkır and Eylemer, 2016). More importantly, European norms, values and practices do not inform public debates or shape policy-making any more. This has direct impact on EU-induced reforms. The eventual waning of the normative power the EU had over Turkey has aggravated first the slowing down and later the reversal of democratic reform process.

The EU has not completely lost its normative appeal in Turkey. A recent study demonstrates the continuing acknowledgement of the EU as a normative power across a certain segment of Turkish society despite the negative state of EU–Turkey relations (Aydın-Düzgit, 2018: 624–625). The study shows that the local context of the current polarization concerning the state of democracy in the country seems to be the key factor shaping the public's perception of the EU as a normative power. Those who identify with the opposition and feel more constrained by the measures taken by the government in fundamental rights and freedom are more inclined to attribute a more positive role to the EU than those who are content with the current state of Turkish democracy.

It is precisely due to the current context that a vibrant civil society and, within that, rights-based activism becomes important. Even though some EU member states may prefer the evolving of the relations towards bilateral ties, this does not mean that the EU disregards the state of Turkish democracy. After all, even as a partner the EU would want to deal with a country with functioning democratic institutions. However, the EU's conditionality mechanism is unfunctional and the EU has lost its transformative power over Turkey. At this point, the civil society dimension and the EU's support for civic actors come as a complementary instrument to cover up the drawback of the conditionality mechanism. Absent high-level political will, civic groups cannot reverse Turkish democracy's current regression. Change through elite socialization is also a dim prospect. Therefore, the civil society's impact over the elites would be limited at best. However, civic groups can have communication in "EU-sponsored networks" (Bauer et al., 2007) which could trigger transnational social learning. This may strengthen these groups, and also contribute to their advocacy, networking skills and mobilization in Turkey. Civil society organizations in Turkey may not be strong enough or have enough penetration within society to act as norm entrepreneurs that contribute to changing norms in Turkey. That said, rights-based groups can serve as conduits for the EU to engage with those segments of Turkish society that still refer to the EU with normative power discourse. In the absence of leverage, civic actors can provide linkage. The EU must support a politically active civil society to retain what remains of its normative power in Turkey. It is these rights-based groups that can and will advocate European and international norms even where the EU falls short of providing that normative context for democratic transition.

Purely transactional ties without the membership perspective is more exposed to conflicts and eventually become less predictable. This is particularly so when there are so many factors influencing relations, as it is in the case of EU–Turkey relations. This makes the civil society one of the key dimensions of EU–Turkey relations. Civil society is important as it may provide a sustainable avenue of dialogue and interaction at times when official communication channels are not effective.

There is a fine line here between supporting rights-based activism, advocacy and contentious work on the one hand and opposition groups on the other. While having a dialogue with and supporting rights-based groups is important, what may look like an open support to opposition groups may be an instrument of further polarization in Turkey. This may fuel anti-EU feeling among the already skeptical pro-government groups and serve as a new axis for polarization in Turkish society. That said, this is tricky because the line between the two is often blurred. Participation in rights-based groups and opposition groups frequently overlaps. There is no easy way to square this circle. The programmes should be carefully framed to address the rights and advocacy work without encouraging oppositional or exclusionary discourse and activities.

EU membership may not be a realistic prospect for Turkey in the short- or even medium-term. While both Turkey and the EU may find it convenient to maintain relations as they are, there is an apparent need for a new framework to reinstate the EU's democratic anchor in Turkey. Civil society may not be the panacea here, but it is still an important pillar and actor of EU–Turkey relations.

Bibliography

Aydın-Düzgit, S. (2018) Legitimizing Europe in Contested Settings: Europe as a Normative Power in Turkey?, *Journal of Common Market Studies*, 56(3), pp. 612–627.

Aydıntaşbaş, A. (2018) The Discreet Charm of Hypocrisy: An EU–Turkey Power Audit, *European Council on Foreign Relations*. March 2018. www.ecfr.eu/page/-/EU_TURKEY_POWER_AUDIT.pdf.

Balkır, C. and Eylemer, S. (2016), Shifting Logics: The Discourses of Turkish Political Elites on EU Accession, *South European Society and Politics*, 21(1), pp. 29–43.

Bauer, M., Knill, C. and Pitschell, D. (2007) Differential Europeanization in Eastern Europe: The Impact of Diverse EU Regulatory Governance Patterns, *Journal of European Integration*, 29(4), pp. 405–424.

Çakmaklı, D. (2017) Rights and Obligations in Civil Society Organizations: Learning Active Citizenship in Turkey, *Southeast European and Black Sea Studies*, 17(1), pp. 113–127.

Center for American Progress, Istanbul Policy Center, and Istituto Affari Internazionali. (2017) *Trends in Turkish Civil Society*.

Dalay, G. (2018) Turkey–EU Relations: Dysfunctional Framework, Status Anxiety, *Brookings Institution* (15 February) www.brookings.edu/opinions/turkey-eu-relations-dysfunctional-framework-status-anxiety/.

Grabbe, H. and Lehne, S. (2018) Could an Illiberal Europe Work?, *Carnegie Europe* (11 October) https://carnegieeurope.eu/2018/10/11/could-illiberal-europe-work-pub-77463.

Irish, J. (2017) France's Macron Urges Continued EU Ties with Turkey, *Reuters* (7 September) www.reuters.com/article/us-france-turkey/frances-macron-urges-continued-eu-ties-with-turkey-idUSKCN1BI0SQ.

Janning, J. (2018) Transactional by Default: EU–Turkey Relations in Search of a New Rationale, *Turkish Policy Quarterly*, 17(1), pp. 57–65.

Müftüler-Baç, M. (2016) The Pandora's Box: Democratisation and Rule of Law in Turkey, *Asia Europe Journal*, 14(1), pp. 61–77.

Saatçioğlu, B. (2016) De-Europeanisation in Turkey: The Case of the Rule of Law, *South European Society and Politics*, 21(1), pp. 133–146.

Zihnioğlu, Ö. (2013) *European Union Civil Society Policy and Turkey: A Bridge Too Far?* New York: Palgrave Macmillan.

Appendix

Appendix 1 List of interviewed civil society organizations

	Name of the organization	Location	Working area
CSO 1	ODER Autism Association	İzmir	disabled groups
CSO 2	Association for Leader Creative Participants	İzmir	women's rights
CSO 3	Friends of Cultural Heritage	İstanbul	culture
CSO 4	Black Pink Triangle Association	İzmir	LGBTI
CSO 5	Association of Kilyos Protection of Natural Habitat and Improve Environment Culture	İstanbul	culture/ environment
CSO 6	Tuzla EU and Youth Platform Association	İstanbul	youth
CSO 7	Young Volunteers Association	Ankara	youth
CSO 8	Junior Chamber International Turkey	İstanbul	youth
CSO 9	Association of Friends and Relatives of Detainees and Convicted Prisoners	İstanbul	human rights
CSO 10	The Women Entrepreneurs Association of Turkey	İstanbul	women's rights
CSO 11	Black Sea New Horizons Association	Samsun	disadvantaged groups
CSO 12	Bafra Education and Solidarity Association	Samsun	education
CSO 13	Black Sea Industrialists' and Businessmen Association	Samsun	professional/ sectorial
CSO 14	Dost Education Culture and Social Solidarity Association	Samsun	education/ solidarity
CSO 15	Ondokuz Mayıs Mentally Disabled Children Education Research Association	Samsun	disabled groups
CSO 16	Roof Industrialists' and Businessmen Association	İstanbul	professional/ sectorial
CSO 17	Association for Raising Consumer Awareness	İstanbul	consumer rights
CSO 18	Handicapped People's Association of Turkey	İstanbul	disabled groups

continued

148   *Appendix*

	Name of the organization	Location	Working area
CSO 19	Consumer Protection Association	İstanbul	consumer rights
CSO 20	Turkish Construction Steel Association	İstanbul	professional/sectorial
CSO 21	Information Sector Association	İstanbul	professional/sectorial
CSO 22	Anatolian Handicapped People's Association	Kayseri	disabled groups
CSO 23	Kayseri Volunteer Educationists' Association	Kayseri	education
CSO 24	Kayseri Communication Professionals Consultants Businessmen Association	Kayseri	culture
CSO 25	Kayseri Caucasian Association	Kayseri	minority rights/solidarity
CSO 26	Industrial Kitchen Laundry Complementary Food and Drink Equipment Industrialists and Businessmen Association	İstanbul	professional/sectorial
CSO 27	Sustaining and Supporting Iğdır-Azerbaijan Language History and Culture Unity	Iğdır	culture
CSO 28	Turkish Women's Union Iğdır Branch	Iğdır	women's rights
CSO 29	Iğdır Qualified Instructors' Association	Iğdır	professional/solidarity
CSO 30	International Association to Fight Against False Armenian Claims	Iğdır	foreign policy
CSO 31	Iğdır Caucasian Circassion Association	Iğdır	culture
CSO 32	Turkish Society of Cardiology	İstanbul	professional/sectorial
CSO 33	Informatics Association of Turkey	İstanbul	professional/sectorial
CSO 34	Van Lake Folklore, Tourism, Sports Club Association	Van	culture/sports
CSO 35	Van Women's Association	Van	women's rights
CSO 36	Van Physically Handicapped Sports Club Association	Van	disabled groups
CSO 37	Van Industrialists and Businessmen Association	Van	professional/sectorial
CSO 38	Family Counsels Association	Antalya	professional/sectorial
CSO 39	İmece Women's Solidarity Association	Antalya	women's rights
CSO 40	Active Disabled Youth and Sports Club Association	Antalya	disabled groups
CSO 41	Culture Routes Society	Antalya	culture
CSO 42	System and Generation Association	Ankara	youth
CSO 43	Women and Youth Platform Association	Ankara	women's rights/youth
CSO 44	Republican Women's Association	Ankara	women's rights
CSO 45	Blind People's Culture and Unity Association	Ankara	disabled groups

Index

accession process 32; accession negotiations 33–4, 44; and the AKP *see* AKP: and the accession process; and civil society 73–7, 139–40 (*see also* Europeanization: of civil society); and the coalition government 30; deadlock 141–1; and the economic crises 30–1; energy 57; Harmonization Packages 2, 29, 90–1; public support in Turkey 37; skepticism of the EU leaders 32–5; US support 28
Additional Protocol 26
Agenda 2000 27
AKP (Justice and Development Party) 31, 93–4; and the accession process 31, 36–8, 75, 141; closure case 37
Ankara Association Agreement 25–6, 49–50; preparatory stage 26; transitional stage 26
Aphrodite gas field 59
Association for Human Rights and Solidarity for the Oppressed (MAZLUMDER) 71, 101

Brexit 62–3, 65

Cardiff European Council 28
Central Finance and Contracts Unit 115
civic activism 83–6; and civil society organizations 85; and ICT 84, 99
Civil Code 90
Civil Society Development Center 112
Civil Society Dialogue 108–12
Civil Society Support Team *see* Civil Society Development Center
Clinton administration *see* accession process: US support
closing civic space *see* shrinking civic space

Comprehensive Economic and Trade Agreement, The 65n1
conditionality 2, 3, 144; *see also* external incentives model: and EU conditionality
constitutional amendments 96, 101
constructivist institutionalism *see* sociological institutionalism
Copenhagen European Council 29–30
coup attempt 41, 100
crisis with Germany 42–3
crisis with the Netherlands 43
Cyprus conflict: Additional Protocol crisis 34; and the Annan Plan 29; Hydrocarbon reserves 58–9

Democratic Opening *see* Kurdish Opening
Doğan Group 97

eastern enlargement 35–6
economic and trade relations *see* EU-Turkey Customs Union
Economic Development Foundation (İKV) 74–5
elections: in Turkey 39; for the European Parliament 39
Energy Community 57–8
energy cooperation 56–9; High Level Energy Dialogue 58; institutional cooperation 58
Energy Union 58
epistemic communities 14, 16
external incentives model 9; domestic actors 11–2; and EU conditionality 9–11; in EU-Turkey relations 13
Erdoğan, R.T. 31, 33, 36–43, 55, 94, 97–102, 143
EU civil society support 106–9; definition of a civil society organization 106–7; and financial assistance 110–12, 121

150 *Index*

EU civil society support *continued*
(*see also* EU-funded projects); and its management 114–5; literature 16; and its management 114–5; objectives 106–9, 113–4; in Turkey 106, 145
EU Communication Group 75
EU debt crisis *see* Eurozone crisis
EU-funded projects 121–31; activities 121–2; collaborations 140–1; depoliticization 106, 125–7, 141; dialogue programmes 124; professionalization 127–30; project culture 125, 131; in public sector 132–4
EU funds *see* EU civil society support: financial assistance
EU-Turkey Customs Union 4, 50–3; impact 51–2; modernization 40, 52; public opinion 50–1
Euro-Mediterranean Partnership 110
European Instrument for Democracy and Human Rights 115–16
European Movement 2002 74
European Network of Transmission System Operators for Electricity (ENTSO-E) 58
Europeanization: of civil society 75–9; de-Europeanization 4; definition 7, 8; *see also* accession process: and civil society
Eurozone crisis 62

Facility for Refugees in Turkey 54
Fidesz 3, 64
freedom of assembly 91–3

Gezi Protests 83–6, 97–9; reactions from the EU 38

Habitat II Conference 71
historical institutionalism 8
Human Resources Development Programme Authority 115
Hungary 3, 64–5

Independent Industrialists' and Businessmen's Association (MÜSİAD) 70
Instrument for Pre-accession Assistance *see* pre-accession assistance
Internal Security Reform Package *see* Law Amending the Law on Powers and Duties of the Police
International Workers' Day 95–7

Justice and Development Party *see* AKP

Kurdish Opening 96, 100

Lamassoure report 29
Law Amending the Law on Powers and Duties of the Police 99–100
Law and Justice Party (PiS) 3, 64
Law on Collection of Aid 92–3
Law on Meetings and Demonstrations 93, 99
lesson-drawing model 16
LGBTI Pride Parade 99, 138
Luxembourg European Council (1997) 27

Macron, E. 43, 63, 65, 143
Marmara earthquake 71–2
Merkel, A. 1, 34–5, 40–2, 54, 59
migration crisis 5, 41, 53–6, 63–4; EU-Turkey statement 40–1, 54–5; Joint Action Plan 40, 54; reasons 53–4; Turkish civil society 55–6, 83
military takeover 1980 70, 85

National IPA Coordinator 114–15
Negotiating Framework 32
New EU Strategy 39
new institutionalism 8
NGO-ization 119–20
norm entrepreuneurs 14, 140
Northern Forests Defence 102

Orban, V. 3, 64

Parliamentary Assembly of the Council of Europe 43
Poland 3, 64–5
polarization 139
policy entrepreneurs 10
policy window 10
Positive Agenda 38
pre-accession assistance 110–3; and civil society *see* EU civil society support; European Court of Auditors' report 60, 114–5; reduction 1, 43, 59–62
privileged partnership 34–5; *see also* accession process: skepticism of the EU leaders
project conditionality 114
protests 84; Cerattepe protests 99; Emek Theatre protests 97; Gezi protests; No Assemblies 102; *see also* civic activism
putsch *see* coup attempt

rationalist institutionalism 8–13
Readmission Agreement 38–9
regional nationalism 63
right-wing populist parties 64–5

Sarkozy, N. 34–5
Secretariat General for EU Affairs 28, 44n5, 113
Sector Planning Document 113
shrinking civic space: definition 95; reasons 93–5; in the world 95
Sivil Düşün 114
social learning model 13–5; and civil society 16, 69, 140–1, 144–5
sociological institutionalism 8, 13–16
Southern Gas Corridor 57
state of emergency 41, 100–1
strong state tradition 69
Susurluk scandal 71

Technical Assistance for Civil Society Organizations 116
Trans-Anatolian Natural Gas Pipeline Project (TANAP) 57
Trans-European Networks for Energy (TEN-E) Strategy 57
transactionalism: definition 4, 142; in EU-Turkey relations 2, 39–41, 44, 49, 142–5
Transatlantic Trade and Investment Partnership 51

transnational social learning *see* social learning
Turkish civil society: associationalism 62, 69–70; associations 75–6; depoliticization 137–41 (*see also* EU-funded projects: depoliticization); disadvantaged groups 138; and EU funds 77–8 (*see also* EU-funded projects); foundations 91; Islamic organizations 70–1; legal framework 90–3, 101; and polarization 81–2, 94; professionalization 127–8 (*see also* EU-funded projects: professionalization); public awareness 76; and public institutions 81, 101, 107–8, 132–4; public opinion 79–80; rights-based activism 82–3, 96, 101–2, 109, 137–9; and Turkish culture 81; women's organizations 71–2
Turkish Electricity Transmission Company (TEIAS) 58
Turkish Industry and Business Association (TÜSİAD) 73, 75

Venice Commission 43
veto players 11–12
visa liberalization dialogue 38–9
volunteerism 130

youth 85–6